The New Father

A Dad's Guide to the toddler Years

"I'll teach you about trucks, William, and you teach me about life."

The New Father

A Dad's Guide to the toddler Years

Armin A. Brott

Abbeville Press · Publishers
New York · London · Paris

For Talya and Tirzah,
who remind me every day about what's really important in life;
and my sweetest Evie,
who makes the colors more intense.

EDITOR: Jacqueline Decter
DESIGNER: Celia Fuller
PRODUCTION EDITOR: Owen Dugan
PRODUCTION MANAGER: Elizabeth Gaynor

First edition
10 9 8 7 6 5 4 3 2

Cover photograph by Milton Heiberg.
For cartoon credits, see page 223.

Library of Congress Cataloging-in-Publication Data
Brott, Armin A.
    A dad's guide to the toddler years / Armin A. Brott. — 1st ed.
        p.   cm. — (The new father)
    Includes bibliographical references and index.
    ISBN 0-7892-0396-0 (pb). — ISBN 0-7892-0480-0 (hc)
    1. Toddlers.   2. Toddlers—Care.   3. Father and child.   I. Title.   II. Series.
HQ774.5.B757   1998
649'.122—dc21   96-32876

Contents

Acknowledgments 7

Introduction 9

12–15 MONTHS
Getting Off on the Right
(or Left) Foot 14

15–18 MONTHS
Keeping Communication
Open 35

18–21 MONTHS
Still Wild (or Mild) after
All These Months 56

21–24 MONTHS
What Are Daddies Made Of? . . 80

24–27 MONTHS
Off to School 98

27–30 MONTHS
Time for a Financial
Tune-up 121

30–33 MONTHS
Hey, Who's in
Charge Here? 146

33–36 MONTHS
Learning to
Let Go 169

Selected Bibliography 203

Resources 210

Index 218

Acknowledgments

Many of the people who helped with the previous books in this series were, remarkably, willing to put up with me again. This book wouldn't have been possible without them.

Andrea Adam helped edit the first draft; Sharon Braz reviewed the section on big-time communication breakdowns between partners; Gene and June Brott, my parents, also read the early versions, baby-sat, and were a constant source of emotional and financial support; Jim Cameron and all the folks at the Center for Human Development freely shared their research and their wisdom about temperament; Phil and Carolyn Cowan, who have studied fathers and families for decades, met with me and helped hone my ideas; Jackie Decter guided the whole thing through from start to finish and made it all coherent; Celia Fuller bought the shirts and did the design; Ken Guilmartin and Edwin Gordon spent a huge amount of time with me discussing the importance of teaching music to children; Amy Handy copyedited the manuscript and, as usual, made a ton of insightful comments; Jim Levine put it all together; Eric Mindich suggested beefing up the financial sections; Jeff Porter, accountant and financial planner extraordinaire, reviewed the sections on financial and tax planning and home buying and made them far more accurate and accessible; Dawn Swanson, the children's librarian at the Berkeley Public Library, helped me select and arrange the children's books; Eric Tyson reviewed, commented on, and added to the sections on estate planning and college savings.

"I was just telling them that there used to be a show called 'Father Knows Best.'"

Introduction

What image comes to mind when you hear the word *toddler*? Probably that of a small child, not nearly as helpless as an infant, walking, falling, walking again. A child brimming with confidence and eager to learn.

Much of the same could be said about the fathers of toddlers as well. You've learned a huge amount over the year or so since your child was born and you're really getting the hang of this parenting thing. But as confident as you are, something still happens every day that reminds you that there's still plenty more to learn.

Over the next two years your child will go from crawling to standing to walking to running, and from one- and two-syllable words to telling you that you don't know anything about anything. Parenting columnist Lawrence Kutner likens toddlerhood to a musical fugue in which "the themes of intellectual, physical, emotional, and social development intertwine." But the focus of this book isn't really on that. Sure, we'll spend some time discussing your child's growth and identifying developmental milestones. If you want an exhaustive study of child development, however, you need look no further than your local library or bookstore.

The New Father: A Dad's Guide to the Toddler Years is primarily about you and *your* musical fugue, about how *fathers* develop and grow over time. And that's something you can't find anywhere else.

In writing this book I talked extensively with dozens of leading experts and studied the research and writings of many more. I also drew from my own experiences as the father of two, as well as from the interviews I've done with hundreds of fathers about their experiences and feelings. It is my hope that giving you access to all this wisdom and experience will leave you far better prepared to meet the challenges of being—and staying—an active, involved father.

The big question, of course, is, Why bother to be involved? Three simple reasons: it's good for your kids, it's good for you, and it's good for your relationship with your partner.

"The evidence is quite robust that kids who have contact with a father have an advantage over kids without that kind of contact," says Norma Radin, who has conducted research on fathers for more than twenty years. And these benefits are evident very early in life. In one study, Radin found that children who were raised by actively involved fathers scored higher on verbal ability tests than children raised in more traditional families by less-involved fathers. In another study, toddlers whose fathers took a special interest in child care were consistently rated two to six months ahead of schedule on tests of development, problem-solving skills, and even social skills. And there's also a strong connection between kids' math skills and the amount of contact they have with their fathers.

Working fathers also benefit greatly from being involved with their kids. Too many men worry that there's no real way to balance their work and family lives, and that taking an active role at home would be committing career suicide. But the truth is that men who put child rearing high up on their list of priorities are on average more successful in their careers at midlife than men who focus only on their work. Fatherhood also seems to "promote men's abilities to understand themselves as adults and to sympathetically care for other adults," says fatherhood researcher John Snarey. Men who take an active role at home are—by the time their children are grown—better managers, community leaders, and mentors. Overall, they're more concerned with the generation coming up than with themselves.

And finally, being an active, involved father has a positive impact on men's relationships with their partners. Division-of-labor issues are right up there with money as the top marital stressor. Not surprisingly, the more support your partner gets from you, the happier she'll be in her marriage and the better she'll perform as a parent. And that will make her a happier woman, which will make you happier as well and will make your relationship last longer.

How This Book Is Organized

Because babies (and their fathers) develop so quickly, the previous book in this series, *The New Father: A Dad's Guide to the First Year*, was organized month by month, a format that enabled us to capture the rapid changes that you and your baby were undergoing. But as your baby ages and as you gain in experience, neither of you is developing quite as quickly and a month-by-month approach would have been too cumbersome. Instead, while we're still going through your baby's and your development in chronological order, we've divided things up into three-month blocks. Each of these quarterly chapters is further divided into the following four sections:

What's Going On with the Baby

In this section we take a brief yet extremely important look at how your toddler is developing physically, intellectually, verbally, and emotionally/socially. In many ways your toddler's growth parallels your own growth as a father. And much of what you'll be experiencing over the next few years will be closely related to your child's development. So knowing the basics of child development will not only help you understand your child, but will give you a better, deeper understanding of yourself.

As you no doubt already know, children develop on very different schedules and the range of "normal" development is quite broad. Dividing the book into three-month sections should take care of most—but probably not all—of the variations, so you might want to keep an extra bookmark in chapters immediately preceding and following the one you're reading. If your baby seems to be two chapters (six months or so) ahead of her age, call Oprah. If she's two chapters behind, however, check with your pediatrician.

What You're Going Through

With no real social support and almost no one to talk to about parenting feelings and concerns, far too many fathers end up thinking not only that they're absolutely alone in what they're experiencing but that they're abnormal as well. Chances are, however, that with very few exceptions what you're going through at any particular moment of your fatherhood is fairly similar to what millions of fathers before you have felt and millions more after you will. Just as babies develop along a more or less predictable path, so do fathers. And in this section of each chapter, we'll examine what fathers typically go through at that particular time, so you'll be able to monitor your own physical and emotional development. We'll talk about the emotional ups and downs, the joys, the frustrations, the anger, the confusion, the incredible pride, and the confidence that fatherhood brings to all of us.

You and Your Baby

Besides being very important, this section is undoubtedly the most fun. It gives you all the tools you'll need to get to know your child better and to create the deepest, closest possible relationship with her—even if all you have is only half an hour a day. We'll deal with activities as diverse as playing games, reading, music, making art, cooking, potty training, computers, discipline, handling your child's fears, and overcoming gender stereotypes.

Family Matters

Although the focus of this book is mostly on you and your toddler, you're still very much part of a family, which includes your partner and any other children you might have. For that reason, we've included a separate section to discuss all the things that can have a major impact on everyone in your house. We'll talk about finances, family planning, nutrition, looking for preschools, finding dentists, dealing with tantrums, how your child's temperament affects the whole family, improving communication with your partner, sex, and much more.

A Note on Terminology

He and She

As the father of two daughters, I find it annoying to read a piece of parenting advice that constantly refers to the child in question as "he." And I'm sure parents of boys feel the same way when the situation is reversed. So in an attempt to annoy everyone equally, I simply alternate between "he" and "she" as often as possible. There are, of course, some sections in the book that apply only to boys or to girls, and in those cases the appropriate pronoun is used. Otherwise, the terms are completely interchangeable, and hopefully there's an equal number of both.

You're Not in This Thing Alone, You Know . . .

Whether the mother of your child is your wife, your lover, your girlfriend, your live-in companion, your ex, or your fiancée, she plays an important role in your child's and your life—you wouldn't be a father without her. To keep from making any kind of statement about the importance (or lack of importance, depending on how you feel) of marriage, I've decided to keep referring to the mother of your child as your "partner," as I did in *The New Father: A Dad's Guide to the First Year.*

What's All This *TNF I* Stuff?

This book, like child and father development, is part of an ongoing process that began with *The Expectant Father: Facts, Tips, and Advice for Dads-to-Be* and continued with *The New Father: A Dad's Guide to the First Year.* And like most ongoing processes, previously mastered skills become the basis for learning new ones. Simply put, this means that while all the information in this book is completely new, some of the topics have been touched on in previous volumes. In each case I give the exact page(s) reference and use an abbreviation to indicate where the idea first came up. If you've got a copy of either or both these books around, you can check these references. If not, don't worry; everything covered here stands on its own. *TNF I* is, not surprisingly, *The New Father: A Dad's Guide to the First Year. TEF* is *The Expectant Father: Facts, Tips, and Advice for Dads-to-Be.*

The All-Important Disclaimer . . .

I'm not a pediatrician, financial planner, accountant, or lawyer, nor do I play one on TV. This means that even though all the medical, financial, and legal advice in this book has been suggested by the experts and proven to work by real people (including me, in most cases), you should still check with an appropriate professional before trying it out on yourself and your family.

12-15 MONTHS

Getting Off on the Right (or Left) Foot

What's Going On with the Baby

Physically

♦ By the end of this period, your baby will be most comfortable in a fully upright position. He'll be able to walk by himself and will insist on doing so. And when he's not walking, he'll be climbing.

♦ Your child's favorite activity now is emptying and filling containers of all kinds (although he really is much better at emptying). In a matter of seconds he can empty dresser drawers, kitchen cabinets, refrigerator, and bookshelves. "There seems to be a general pattern in children this age of emptying things that no one else wants emptied," writes child development expert Frank Caplan.

♦ His fine motor coordination is greatly improved. He can turn the pages of a book one at a time and now releases objects as accurately and gracefully as he picks them up—a skill he's finding invaluable when he throws a ball. He can also draw a straight line (if you do one first).

♦ He loves to play all sorts of physical games. Chase me/catch me, rolling balls back and forth, and wrestling are big favorites.

♦ He's trying really, really hard to turn doorknobs. If you're lucky, it'll be a few more months before he successfully puts together grasping and twisting.

Intellectually

♦ In his ongoing attempt to trash your home, your toddler will be picking up, rotating, dropping, tasting, stacking (then knocking over), and throwing everything he can get his hands on, thus giving him a crash course in shape, texture, taste, density, balance, and aerodynamics.

♦ He has a clearer understanding of his own limitations and is getting better at using tools—including adults—to get what he wants. He'll use a stick to get something out from under the couch and will demand that you help him achieve his desire to swing on a swing all day.

♦ He's much better at distinguishing sizes and shapes and has a well-developed sense of how things "should be." He may occasionally put a square peg in a square hole and, if you turn a familiar object (like a book) upside down, he'll turn it right-side up.

♦ His memory continues to improve, and he can now look for an object he hasn't seen being hidden. He's also developing a sense of time: that things (like naps) follow other things (like meals).

♦ He's fascinated by hinged objects—especially books—not so much for what's in them but for the sheer feeling of accomplishment he gets when he turns the pages.

Verbally

♦ According to psychologist Fitzhugh Dodson, there are two phases of language learning: passive language (what you understand) and active language (what you can actually say). Most of the language learning your toddler will do over the course of the next twelve months will be passive.

♦ By the end of the fifteenth month he'll identify upon request his shoes, clothes, and body parts; familiar people and objects; and one or two pictures from a favorite book.

♦ Although he has a speaking vocabulary of fewer than ten words, he's already trying to put them together two at a time: "Bye-bye, Daddy" and "No, baby" are among the first "sentences."

♦ He can also do some pretty good cow, dog, and cat imitations.

♦ He's becoming aware of the expressive function of language and has developed an uncanny ability to pick out—and endlessly repeat—the one swear word you accidentally slipped into a ten-minute-long conversation.

♦ His understanding of the symbolic use of words is growing. If he knows the word *pool,* for example, he may use it when he sees a duck pond, a puddle on the street, or even the ocean. However, he may also call every cat, horse, goat, pig, llama, or other hairy, four-legged animal a "dog."

Emotionally/Socially

♦ He's becoming fiercely independent, demanding to push his stroller instead of riding in it. He'll also insist on feeding himself, but will end up with more on his face, his cheeks, walls, the high-chair tray, or the floor than in his mouth.

♦ Doing things on his own is not all there is to being independent. Your toddler wants to separate himself physically from you as well—but not for too long. Pretending to be on a scouting expedition, he'll stroll a short distance away, casually looking back over his shoulder to make sure you haven't gone anywhere. But independence is a pretty scary thing to a one-year-old, so a second or two after you disappear from his view, he'll scamper back and cling to you for all he's worth. He'll repeat the process of going away and coming back at least until he's through college.

♦ As he slowly becomes secure with the idea that you'll always be there for him, your child's shyness around strangers and his fear of separation should decrease.

♦ As those fears disappear, however, they are replaced by other, even more irrational-seeming ones: the vacuum cleaner and the neighborhood dogs that never bothered him before suddenly terrify him; he now needs a night-light in his room; and he may refuse to take a bath, fearing that he'll get sucked down the drain.

♦ With all the places he has to go and things he has to do, your baby won't want to waste his precious time eating, and may refuse to do so. He will also regard sleep as a major imposition and will probably refuse to nap.

What You're Going Through

Physical Exhaustion

Being a father can be an exhausting proposition, and I'm not talking about sleep deprivation (which has probably passed for the most part by now anyway). Just trying to keep up with a toddler as she careens happily through her day can be enough to drop even a world-class athlete to his knees.

In our prefatherhood days, most of us never did anything to prepare for all the stooping (to get kids into and out of their car seats), bending (to put away hundreds of toys a day), wrestling, pushing (swings or strollers), chasing (to make sure the baby stays out of trouble), schlepping (all those extra bags of groceries in and out of the car), holding (it's fun, but it's hard to keep up for more than a few blocks), and carrying (sleeping children seem to weigh a lot more than awake ones). Not to mention all that extra laundry and housecleaning. Is it any wonder that just about every father I know has a bad back?

It's crucial to take care of yourself physically as well as psychologically. Not doing so can make it impossible for you to take care of anyone else. Here are a few things you can do:

♦ Get plenty of exercise—with a special concentration on stretches and strength-building exercises for your back. And don't forget to eat right, too.

♦ See your doctor regularly.

♦ Don't suppress your emotions. Getting depressed can make you care less—and do less—about yourself.

♦ Treat yourself nicely. Take some breaks, get an occasional massage, buy yourself something special once in a while.

♦ Get some intellectual stimulation. With all the reading you're doing with your baby, don't forget to do some for yourself as well.

What You're Going Through

A Conflict between Separateness and Connectedness

As we will see later in this chapter, your child has been struggling to strike a balance between being dependent on you and independent from you. But your baby isn't the only one in your immediate family who's dealing with separation issues.

As a parent, you are probably struggling with an adult version of separation anxiety: a conflict between wanting to be needed by your child (wanting to keep her a baby), and wanting to push her toward independence.

The great irony here (to me, anyway) is that the attachment that we've tried so hard to achieve with our children is inextricably related to separating from them. In fact, "The task of becoming attached includes beginning to understand separateness," says Ellen Galinsky, head of the Work and Family Institute. It really seems that the stronger your attachment to the child, the more likely you are to be affected by the separation.

There are, of course, two common ways to deal with adult separation anxiety: push the baby to be more independent, or encourage her to be more dependent on you. Adopting either approach by itself will guarantee disaster for your child as well as for your family. As with just about anything else to do with parenting, the trick is to find the balance between the available extremes. And the first step is to become aware of what might be motivating you to take certain steps.

WHY YOU MAY BE PUSHING YOUR CHILD TO BE MORE INDEPENDENT

♦ Your child may be quieter than you'd like her to be.
♦ She may not be as curious as you think she should be.
♦ You may be afraid that your child is too clingy or dependent and that if she doesn't start learning to take care of herself she'll grow up to be a wimp.
♦ You may be afraid that your child is controlling you, that you're losing your independence, and that she's making too many demands on your time and affection. This is an especially common fear among fathers whose kids are temperamentally "difficult."
♦ Particularly if you're a stay-at-home dad or if you're especially involved, you may be afraid that besides having lost your career, you've lost your prestige and your masculinity.

Pushing early self-reliance tends to be thought of as a "dad thing," but mothers are far from immune from trying to make their kids more independent. But before you start worrying about these things, remember this:

♦ If your child seems clingy, there's probably a reason for it. Only when she feels secure in your relationship will she be ready to separate from you.
♦ Learn to take pride in what she does do, rather than in what you think she should do—she's your child, but she's not you and she won't do exactly what you think she should.
♦ If you feel that your baby isn't growing up as quickly as you think she should, you may push her to go places or do things she isn't ready for, says psychiatrist Stanley Greenspan. This can lead to your being further disappointed when the baby fails to live up to your too-high expectations, and to her feeling guilty and inadequate because she can't make you happy.

Some potential negative side effects of pushing independence on your child too much or too soon:

♦ You may suddenly start working longer hours, coming home later, or doing just about anything to stay away from home more.
♦ You might begin distancing yourself from your partner as well as the baby, feeling that you have to make up for all the time you haven't been getting for yourself since the baby came.

*"... and so the princess and the prince lived happily ever after.
The end. Now get some sleep. We want you to be fresh as a daisy for
your first day of college tomorrow."*

♦ You may become less affectionate with your child—especially if you have a
boy.
♦ Your child may come to feel unloved and uncared for, as though you're
trying to get rid of her.

WHY YOU MAY BE SUBTLY ENCOURAGING YOUR CHILD TO BE MORE DEPENDENT

♦ You may be saddened that your baby is growing up so quickly. As young as
she still is, she's already outgrown certain adorable behaviors and gestures,
and you may almost wish that she'd stay this age forever.
♦ You may be afraid of being rejected or abandoned by your toddler. This
feeling tends to arise at times when you really want to sit quietly and
snuggle with the baby and she squirms off your lap and runs away.

Although it is usually thought of as more of a "mom thing," there are plenty
of fathers who are reluctant to let their kids go. If you're feeling this way, think
about this:

♦ Don't think the baby doesn't need you or love you, in fact she needs you more than ever. She needs your support and love to let her know that growing up (which she's going to do whether you like it or not) is okay.

♦ Your feeling that your baby's youth has somehow been "lost" runs parallel to her feelings of exploring unknown territory. Taking pride in her independence and all the "big girl" things she can do is an important part of building her self-esteem and independence.

♦ You may think you want your baby to be a baby forever, but is that what you really want? To be changing this baby's diapers for the next fifty years? I don't think so.

Here are some of the potential negatives of limiting independence:

♦ You can hover too much, never allowing your child to make the mistakes she needs to make in order to learn.

♦ You can be too overprotective and not give the child enough room to explore.

♦ You can limit her contacts with other people, feeling that any free time she has should be spent with you.

♦ You may refrain from setting limits or disciplining your child for fear of driving her away.

♦ You may spoil the child or become excessively aggressive in trying to win her love.

RECOGNIZING YOUR LIMITATIONS

Before Clint Eastwood (as Dirty Harry) was inviting people to "Go ahead, make my day," he was advising people that "a man's got to know his limitations."

In family and parenting experts Phil and Carolyn Cowans' research, one of the factors they found that differentiates fathers from nonfathers is that fathers do a better job discriminating between what they can and can't control. This skill—as absolutely basic as it sounds—is something that can actually take years to develop. "We heard men working on it when they discussed their struggles with wanting it all—job advancement, involved relationships with their wives and children, time for themselves—while accepting the fact that no matter how hard they tried, some things had to be put aside for the time being," write the Cowans. "It is our impression that as a group, men who were not parents had fewer competing demands to balance, were less aware of their limitations, and more invested in maintaining at least the illusion of personal control."

You and Your Baby

Play

The first few months of your baby's second year have been full of dramatic changes, and the ways he plays are no exception. Only a few months ago he depended on you to decide what he'd play with, and he could pay attention to only one object (or person) at a time (see *TNF I,* pages 162–67).

But in just the past few weeks, the baby has begun to assume a less passive role in his playtime. One of the first changes you'll notice is that he will start using "gestures or vocalizations to signal a desire to share attention and to establish the topic of the conversation to follow," says researcher Kim Whaley. At just about the same time, your baby will start putting two playthings together—most likely by giving you a toy and trying to get you to play with him. "The ability to coordinate attention marks a pivotal change in the infant's communicative competence," adds Whaley.

Here are some appropriate toys and activities for the next six months or so:

15–18 MONTHS

TOYS THAT:

♦ The baby can safely chew on (soft plastic or padded blocks, for example).
♦ Can be washed.
♦ Stimulate the senses by incorporating lots of different noises, textures, colors—the more the better.
♦ Encourage manual dexterity by requiring that the baby twist, turn, poke, flick, and/or snap them to get a response.
♦ Encourage the use of both hands: Duplo (the bigger Lego blocks), toy farms with animals, and the like are great.
♦ Have wheels that can easily be pulled, pushed, dragged, or shoved. Lawn mowers, buggies, strollers, and "popcorn poppers" are all good. If your child still isn't very steady on her feet, make sure to get toys that won't fall over, roll away, or collapse if leaned on.
♦ Develop sorting and categorizing skills, such as containers or toy trucks for filling and dumping, measuring spoons, and shape sorters (although it'll be a few months before the baby will be able to get the round block in the round hole very regularly).
♦ Are real. Old telephones (without cords) and even that extra computer keyboard you've got lying around, for example, are more interesting to many kids than their fake counterparts.

◆ Bounce. Just about any kind of ball will amuse just about any kind of kid.

ACTIVITIES THAT:

◆ Promote manual dexterity, such as touching games ("This little piggy went to market . . . ," "Round and round the garden went the teddy bear . . .") and playing ball (this usually means rolling a ball back and forth; the baby will be able to heave a ball in a few months but won't be able to catch one for another year).

◆ Promote awareness of size, shape, color, spatial concepts (in/out, up/down, and so forth). Emptying, dumping, and refilling everything from buckets to bathtubs and kitchen cabinets build awareness of in and out; toys that nest and stack are great for teaching about size and so are large boxes the baby can crawl into.

◆ Continue to teach about consequences. Although we talked a lot about this in *TNF I*, it's still a developing skill. Try tying a string to a favorite toy, handing the other end of the string to the baby, and asking her to get the toy. Will she pull the string? Also, have her turn the lights and the television on and off. Does she understand the connection between flipping the switch and what happens next?

18–21 MONTHS

TOYS: All of the above, plus toys that:

◆ The baby can pound, smack, beat, and smash. Hammer-and-peg boards and sandbox toys are always big hits at this age.

◆ The baby can ride on. Four-wheelers are better (more stable) than trikes. Skip the batteries (the baby hasn't been walking long enough to need a break) and forget the pedals (it's too early).

◆ Encourage sorting. The baby's getting much better at putting the right block in the right hole on her shape sorter. She should also be able to stack a series of increasingly larger rings on a cylinder in the right order.

ACTIVITIES: All of the above, plus those that:

◆ Encourage body-part identification (Where's your nose?).

◆ Continue to encourage turning, twisting, and so on. My older daughter used to entertain herself for hours by locking and unlocking the doors to the car and the house.

◆ Continue to promote awareness of size, color, and spatial relationships.

◆ Promote independence. Let the baby ask you for help before offering any.

See how long it takes her or how many tries she needs to learn new skills. For example, watch as she figures out how to sit down on a baby-sized chair. At first she'll climb on front first. But after a few falls she'll figure out that backing on works better.

♦ Use real tools. Let your baby sweep, push the vacuum, wipe up the floor, and shave you. An electric razor is no problem, but if you use a razor and shaving cream, you might want to leave the blade off the handle the first few times. The lathering is the most fun anyway. Then shave one side of your face and show her the difference between smooth and scratchy.

♦ Continue to promote parent-child attachment. Peekaboo and other hiding games are great.

♦ Promote art awareness. See pages 27–30 for more on this.

♦ Encourage physical fitness, such as dancing to music, chasing, wrestling, and early attempts at gymnastics. For much more on the importance of physical play, see pages 154–56.

PLAYTHINGS TO AVOID FOR THIS GENERAL AGE GROUP

♦ Complicated things. Simplicity is the key here. Your baby doesn't need fancy attachments, cellular phones, fax machines, and the like. Busy boxes are generally unappreciated by kids this age.

"What arrow?"

♦ Antiques. Unless they're exceptionally sturdy, conform to today's more stringent safety standards, and aren't covered in lead paint, leave them in the attic.

♦ Anything with springs, pinch points, or sharp edges.

♦ Anything that has a heating element or an electrical cord (battery-operated toys—provided that the battery can't be accessed by the child—are okay).

♦ Anything with small, detachable parts.

♦ Balloons (the Consumer Product Safety Commission says balloons are the leading cause of childhood suffocation deaths: 110 kids have died since 1973).

♦ Audio tapes. They're great fun to unwind, but not nearly as much fun to get back in the cassette. CDs are at least as interesting to play with (they're shinier, for one thing) and are pretty much indestructible.

♦ Gender-specific toys. There is absolutely no reason why boys can't play with dolls, vacuums, brooms, and kitchen sets, or why girls can't play with cars, walkie-talkies, and balls. In fact, one of my younger daughter's favorite activities is shooting her fifty Hot Wheels cars one at a time down her loop-de-loop track. Don't push any particular toys at your child— just make them available and try to incorporate them into your playtime. If your child sees you using them, he or she will want to do the same.

Computer Readiness

Although your child has been walking for only a few months, it's not too early to begin introducing him to some of the high-tech equipment he's likely to encounter as he grows up. And computers are the place to start.

A lot of parents have some legitimate questions about the sensibility and worthwhileness (and even the danger) of starting kids on computers at a very early age. Here are a few of these concerns:

♦ Will exposing a child to computers make him antisocial or lead to his spending all his time in front of the screen instead of doing other things? Most early childhood experts believe that initially the novelty of the computer may suck children away from other activities, but this is really no different from what happens with any new toy. Your child needs a wide variety of things to play with and learn from. So as long as you don't try to make the computer replace all your child's other toys, it will be just another toy in his toybox within a few weeks.

♦ Can little kids really learn anything from computers? Absolutely. Although computers are not nearly as social as reading, they are far more interactive than television and offer many opportunities for creativity (without, for example, all the mess of finger paints). At this age kids can use computers to learn shapes, colors, and opposites. As they get older, computers can

Hardware—and Software—for Little Kids

Using a standard keyboard and mouse requires a level of hand-eye coordination that your child won't have for another year or so. Fortunately, several companies make child-friendly keyboards and input devices (mice, trackballs, joysticks, and so forth) for younger kids. Perhaps the best of the bunch is the Comfy Keyboard; designed to take a serious beating, this sturdy keyboard has no letters, just buttons with pictures of shapes and colors. It comes with special software appropriate for kids as young as twelve months. My younger daughter was introduced to it at about fifteen months and loved it from the start.

assist them in learning upper- and lower-case letters, word recognition, pattern recognition, spelling, reading, arithmetic, reasoning skills, and hand-eye coordination, says computer expert Mario Pagnoni.

At this age, however, the goal of exposing your child isn't really to teach him anything. It's just another way of getting him involved. Kids as young as fifteen months can turn the computer on, put disks in, and take them out.

Computers are not for all children, of course. Before starting a computer-readiness program at your house, the following five criteria should be satisfied:

♦ You need to have a computer.
♦ You have to be interested in spending some time with the child—you can't just plunk him down in front of the computer and expect him to enjoy the experience. Kids this age can't operate a conventional mouse anyway.
♦ He should be at least twelve months old.
♦ He should have a firm grasp of cause-and-effect relationships (I push the Enter key and something happens on the screen).
♦ He must be interested. One way to increase the chances he'll be interested is to let him watch you work on your computer; another is to let him bang around on an old keyboard (if you don't have one, you can probably buy a used one at a flea market for about five dollars).

Reading

At about fifteen months your baby has put his passive reading days behind him and is taking on a much more aggressive and participatory attitude toward books.

He'll babble along with you now as you read, and make unsolicited (but often appropriate) animal sounds. And if you pause briefly while reading a

---

Poetry for Babies?

In a recent national survey, researcher Ann Terry found that children's taste in poetry is just about as lowbrow as my own. Overall, kids seem to like:

- poems they can understand
- narrative poems
- poems with rhyme, rhythm, and a sense of excitement
- poems about animals or familiar experiences
- limericks of all sorts

They don't like:

- poems with a lot of figurative language and imagery
- highly abstract poems that do not make sense to them or do not relate to their own experiences
- haiku

---

familiar story, he'll often "fill in" a missing word or two—usually the last word in a sentence or rhyme. Over the next few months he'll try to seize control of your reading sessions by pointing to illustrations and insisting that you identify them.

But no matter how great your baby's newfound power, his excitement at his own recently acquired mobility is so consuming that he'll start squirming within minutes after he gets in your lap. Don't be offended or try to limit his movements. If he wants to go, let him. He'll be back soon enough.

To encourage your baby's interest in books and to give him more control over his reading material, consider making a low bookshelf for him, one where the books face cover out, so he can bring you his current favorites. Having a baby-accessible bookshelf will also allow your child the opportunity to pull a few books down and "read" by himself.

Flap books are great for this age, particularly ones with thick pages that the baby can open himself. Before reading a flap book to your baby for the first time, go through it once yourself and test all the flaps; unopened (and hard-to-open) flaps can frustrate even the most eager little fingers. Interactive books and those dealing with real-world themes are also big hits. At this stage babies crave familiarity and will request the same two or three books over and over. For variety— as well as your own sanity—try to slip in a new one every few days.

Whatever you're reading, use a pleasant, conversational manner and be theatrical—adopt a different voice for each character. Your baby won't be interested in plot for a few more months, so don't be afraid to interrupt your reading to "discuss" with your baby what's happening in the story or in the illustrations. Another fun thing to do occasionally is to replace a book character's name with your child's (when reading to my younger daughter, for example, I turned Goldilocks into Talyalocks).

ADDING TO YOUR LIBRARY

Keep reading your child's favorites until either he gets sick of them or they fall apart (but if the latter happens before the former, you might have to go out and buy another copy). Most of the books listed on pages 78–79 and 149 in *TNF I* are still fine for this age. As you introduce new books, though, you might want to consider adding some of these developmentally appropriate titles to your collection:

Airport, Bryon Barton
Are You There, Bear? Ron Maris
Crash! Bang! Boom! (and others), Peter Spier
The Cupboard, John Burningham
Dear Zoo, Rod Campbell
Duck, David Lloyd
Goodnight, Goodnight (and others), Eve Rice
Have You Seen My Duckling? (and many others), Nancy Tafuri
In Our House, Anne Rockwell
Listen to the Rain, Bill Martin, Jr., and John Archambault
Max's Ride, Rosemary Wells
Mommy Buy Me a China Doll, Harve Zemach
My Brown Bear Barney, Dorothy Butler
Toolbox, Anne Rockwell
Two Shoes, New Shoes (and many others), Shirley Hughes
The Very Hungry Caterpillar (and many, many others), Eric Carle

CONCEPTS
100 First Words to Say with Your Baby, Edwina Riddel
In the Morning, Anne Rockwell
I Touch (and many others), Rachel Isadora
Slam Bang, John Burningham

Art

GETTING READY. OR, FRANKLY, MY DEAR, I DON'T . . .
Making art with a toddler can be incredible fun—and incredibly messy. Now that you've been warned, if you don't take the necessary precautions, it's your own fault:

The Basics

◆ **Drawing implements.** Nontoxic markers are the best bet. They come in a wide variety of sizes, colors, and scents. Crayons aren't practical at this age—they crumble and can get ground into carpets and floors. Pencils need too much adult involvement (either to sharpen them or to make sure the baby doesn't stab herself with the sharp point).

◆ **Painting implements.** Use long-handled (8-inch minimum), wide (at least ³⁄₈-inch) brushes. Little kids can't—and won't—do much with anything smaller.

◆ **Paper to draw, paint, or glue on.** Construction (thick) paper is the staple here. It's available at toy, art-supply, and stationery stores. Children's art projects also provide a great opportunity to start a re-cycling program at home and at work. Instead of tossing out all those old reports, flip them over and let your baby create on the other side.

◆ **Things to learn from.** At this age, your child is still exploring the world with all her senses. So give her art supplies that stimulate as many senses as possible, such as scented markers and textured papers.

◆ **Things not to eat.** Make sure everything your baby uses in her art projects is absolutely nontoxic, washable, and too big to be a choking hazard.

◆ Cover every surface—walls, floors, tabletops, chairs—with paper. If you're still concerned, move the whole show outside onto the sidewalk or into the backyard, where you can just hose everything off.

◆ Use an easel or tape paper right to the table. It's far too frustrating for the baby to have to hold the paper steady and draw on it at the same time.

◆ Observe the dress code. Kids this age usually don't like to wear aprons, so have them either work naked (always fun) or wear old clothes that are okay to trash.

◆ Use *tiny* amounts—a thin film of paint or glue on the inside of a shallow container is fine. You can refill it as often as you need to, and if anything falls, there won't be much to clean up.

◆ Dilute. Most of the paint you get at craft stores is quite concentrated. Diluting it 25–50 percent with dishwashing liquid will help the paint wash out of the clothes later (and last longer, too). It also serves to deter kids from putting the paint in their mouths.

◆ Don't give too many choices. Asking "Do you want red or green?" is okay.

Asking "What colors do you want?" is an invitation to a power struggle (unless you're prepared to give in to your child's every demand).

♦ Pay attention. Your child's attention span ranges from about three seconds to fifteen minutes. If you notice any indications of boredom, such as walking away, crying, or eating the supplies, offer another art-related activity or shut things down for the day.

♦ Don't interfere. Showing your baby once or twice how to use a brush or a marker is okay. But telling him which colors to use, showing him where to draw, or making *any* kind of correction is inappropriate. The object here is not to teach art or to create the next little Picasso. It is simply to introduce your child—in a no-pressure, no-expectation kind of way— to the creative process and to the idea that art can be fun.

♦ Monitor your expectations. Even if your child *is* the next Picasso, there's a good chance that she won't create anything remotely recognizable (except perhaps a line, a circle, or a spiral) for another year.

♦ Stop caring. The more concerned you are about the mess or about your child wasting or destroying the supplies (they love to shred paper, put glue in their hair, and use markers as hammers), the less fun you'll let your baby have. So do what you can to prepare. Then take a deep breath, and relax.

Given your child's age, attention span, interest, and level of hand-eye coordination, the range of age-appropriate art projects is fairly limited. Here, though, are some big hits and the supplies you'll need:

♦ Drawing. Paper, markers.

♦ Collages. Objects that will help your baby use all her senses: smelly seeds (fennel, coriander, and so forth); anything that has an interesting shape or texture or that makes an interesting sound when touched; glue; and just about anything you might otherwise be tempted to throw away—egg and juice cartons, cereal boxes, bottle caps, bubble wrap, cotton balls (clean).

♦ Painting. Paint; paper; potatoes or sponges (for cutting out patterns and making prints); toy cars, sticks, or anything else that can be dipped in paint and make an interesting mark on paper.

DISPLAY

Whatever your child creates, be sure to display it someplace—on the fridge, on a bulletin board, taped to the wall. You do not have to compliment the work very much; just having your child's work up where she can see it herself is enough to make her feel proud of herself.

Family Matters

Separation Anxiety

Try to think about things from your baby's perspective for a second: For most of your life you've controlled everything that happened in the world: who and what came and went, how long they stayed, what they did while they were there. But for the past few months, your grip seems to be slipping. Things seem to be coming and going all by themselves. And the people you thought you could always count on to be there for you have developed a nasty habit of disappearing just when you need them most. Even worse, people you *don't* know—and aren't sure you want to know—keep on trying to pick you up and take you away. The universe is clearly in chaos, and given the way things are going you can't really be sure that the people you're most attached to will ever come back.

All this, according to researchers Barbara and Philip Newman, is what separation anxiety is all about. And from your baby's perspective, the best way to put herself back in the driver's seat is to cry. "That's it," she says. "If I cry, my parents won't leave. I just know it."

DEALING WITH SEPARATION ANXIETY

Some babies get it, others don't. Kids who have had regular contact with lots of friendly, loving people will probably have an easier time adapting to brief separations than those who have spent all their time with one or two people.

They'll be more comfortable with strangers and more confident that their parents and other loved ones will return eventually.

In an unusual but far from uncommon manifestation of separation anxiety, many kids about this age develop some sleep problems; they view going to sleep as yet another assault on their ability to control the world. It can also be confusing and frightening for a child to go to sleep in the dark and wake up in the light or to see you wearing one thing when you put her to bed and something else in the morning. Staying awake can seem like a surefire way to make certain that everything (and everyone) stays right where they're supposed to.

Here are some things you can do to help your child manage her separation anxieties:

- **Be firm but reassuring.** Tell the baby where you're going and that you'll be back soon.
- **Don't say you'll miss her.** She'll only feel guilty that she's making you unhappy. She'll also wonder why you would do something to deliberately make yourself unhappy. And finally, if you're sad or upset at leaving her, that's what your baby will think is the appropriate reaction to separation.
- **Don't sneak away.** If you're leaving, say good-bye like a man. Tiptoeing away will undermine your baby's trust in you.
- **Don't give in to crying.** If you're sure the baby is in good hands, leave—with a smile on your face.
- **Don't force.** Let the baby stay in your arms for a while longer if she needs to and don't make fun of her if she wants to bury her head in your shoulder.
- **Try to use sitters the baby knows.** If you have to use someone new, have him or her arrive fifteen to twenty minutes before you go out so he or she can get acquainted with the baby while you are there. Either way, train sitters in your baby's bedtime ritual.
- **Leave while the baby is awake.** Waking up in the middle of the night to a strange (or even a familiar but unexpected) sitter can be terrifying to a child.
- **Be patient.** Don't trivialize the baby's feelings about your leaving. *You* know you'll be back; the baby isn't so sure. So give her plenty of time to adjust to any new situation.
- **Play.** Object-permanence games (see *TNF I*, page 121) help reinforce the idea that things—and especially people—don't disappear forever.
- **Establish routines.** Doing things on a regular schedule (such as dropping the baby off at day care immediately after breakfast or reading two stories right before bed) can help your child understand that some things in life can be counted on.

♦ **Develop a strong attachment.** Singing, playing, reading, and talking together all help build a strong, loving bond between you and your baby and help her feel more secure. The more secure she is, the less she'll worry about being abandoned.

♦ **Ask questions.** You'll have a better chance of finding out what your child is afraid of if you do. The thing that scares most kids the most, for example, is not the dark but being alone. So make sure your child has a favorite toy or other security object at night. And leave a light on so she can see she's not alone.

♦ **Give the baby plenty of space.** If you hover, she'll get the idea that you're afraid of leaving her by herself and that there's actually something to fear from being alone.

♦ **Distract.** Encourage independence by suggesting that the baby play with her train set while you wash the dishes.

♦ **Relax.** Babies will pick up on your mood; if you're nervous they'll figure that they should be too.

♦ **Let the baby follow you around.** This builds a sense of security and confidence that you're there—just in case she needs you.

♦ **Know your baby's temperament.** (For a discussion of temperament, see pages 73–79.) If your child has a low frustration tolerance, she won't want you to leave her and may cry all day after being separated. Your slow-to-adapt child won't want you to leave either, but when you do, she'll usually cry only for a few minutes. She may cry again when you return, though, because your coming back is as much of a transition as your leaving was.

INDEPENDENCE VS. DEPENDENCE

From your baby's perspective, separation anxiety can be a real problem. But from your perspective, it's a positive (albeit frequently frustrating) sign, marking the beginning of your baby's struggle between independence and dependence. It's a scary time for the baby, and you can see his ambivalence dozens of times every day as he alternates between clinging and pushing you away.

At this stage, says British child-care expert Penelope Leach, "his own emotions are his worst enemy"—just when it seems that your baby should be needing you less, he actually needs you more. You're the grown-up, so it's up to you to help your baby make some sense of his conflicting emotions, as well as to nurture his independence while supporting his dependence. But beware: it's extremely easy to get trapped in a vicious circle of dependence and independence. Here's how:

IF YOU . . .	HE FEELS . . .	WHICH, IN TURN, MAKES HIM FEEL . . .
Interfere with his independence and his developing ego	frustration, anger, and hate	anxious and afraid
Interfere with his need to be dependent on you and his desire to cling	anxiety and fear	angry, hateful, and frustrated

Safety Update

Now that your child is vertical, he can get into a lot more trouble much more quickly than just a few months ago. That means that in addition to childproofing your home (see *TNF I*, pages 138–41) you're going to need to take some extra safety precautions.

ESPECIALLY IN THE GARAGE, BASEMENT, WORKSHOP, AND OUTSIDE

♦ Keep all dangerous chemicals, paints, thinners, gas, oil, weed killers, fertilizers, and so forth securely locked up.

♦ If you have an extra refrigerator or freezer, make sure it is locked (not just shut). It's easier than you think for a toddler to pull open the door, climb in after something particularly attractive, and get stuck inside. If the refrigerator/freezer isn't being used, take the doors off.

♦ Be particularly careful when backing out of the garage or driveway. Your baby might run after you to say one more good-bye or to get one more kiss and. . . .

ESPECIALLY AROUND SWIMMING POOLS

♦ Put a fence around it, although not an electrified one. (Don't laugh; I actually heard of a couple who installed an electrified fence around their pool to keep the dog out, but succeeded in electrocuting one of their children.)

♦ Keep furniture, plants, toys, or anything else that can be used to climb on away from the fence.

♦ Get a pool cover that is strong enough for an adult to walk on.

♦ Make sure you have the proper poolside safety equipment (life preserver, poles, and so on).

"Do you know where the fire extinguisher is, Dad?"

♦ Keep a phone nearby for emergency purposes.

♦ Never let your child in the pool area without at least one adult present.

GENERAL SAFETY

♦ Scuff up the soles of any new shoes with sandpaper. Slippery shoes and slippery floors aren't a good combination.

♦ Be cautious around strange—and even familiar—pets. Animals may not be as responsive to your child's hugs and kisses as you'd like them to be.

♦ Remember the twelve-inch rule. To keep babies from grabbing things from counters and tabletops, pediatrician William Sears suggests making sure that objects are at least twelve inches from the edge. That way, your curious baby won't be able to reach them.

♦ Keep all automatic or self-closing doors either locked or secured in the open position. Kids can (and do) get stuck.

♦ Reminder: Never leave your child alone—or with another child less than eleven years old—in or near water, even if he seems to be sitting up nicely by himself in the bathtub. And while we're on the subject, be sure to dump the water out of any buckets or pans you happen to have standing around. A lot of horrible things can happen in just one second.

15-18 MONTHS

Keeping Communication Open

What's Going On With the Baby

Physically

- As if making up for the lull in motor development of the past few months, your toddler will be a blur of activity, rushing from room to room investigating everything.
- Early in the second quarter of your toddler's second year, her walking will still be somewhat clumsy: getting herself into motion is difficult, her legs will move stiffly, and she'll hold her arms away from her body for balance. Most of the time she'll stop by falling.
- By the end of this quarter starting and stopping will be no problem (although she'll still have a tough time negotiating corners upright).
- Her balance is also improving. If she holds on to something, she can actually stand on one foot.
- She loves to show off her strength, often grunting theatrically as she struggles to pick up or push around the biggest things she can get her hands on.
- She may be able to throw a small ball, but can't catch. And although she'd like to kick a ball, more often than not she ends up stepping on it instead. *Note:* If your child isn't walking unassisted by the end of her eighteenth month, check with your pediatrician.

Intellectually

- Most of your child's development in this period will be physical rather than intellectual.

♦ She'll continue to use trial and error to solve problems and will expand her use of tools to retrieve out-of-reach items. (If a toy is on a blanket, for example, she may pull the blanket toward her instead of walking over to get the toy.)

♦ She still struggles with the conflict between autonomy and dependence— refusing your requests to do even the most basic things, but wanting to keep you well within sight as she explores new places.

♦ She has a very short attention span and may flit from activity to activity. Expecting a lot of rational thought from a child this age is a waste of time, as is giving her long explanations of whys and why nots.

♦ Toddlers love routines and rituals. Establishing patterns now, such as bath-story-bedtime and park-lunch-nap, will help you minimize some of the problems you're likely to encounter later on.

♦ She's developing an imagination. She'll crawl on the floor, pretending to be a dog, and she'll "eat" food pictured in a book. The downside to this is that if your child continues imagining things even after she falls asleep (and most do), she may begin to have nightmares. Since kids can't really tell the difference between dreams and reality, nightmares at this age can be particularly frightening.

Verbally

♦ Your toddler continues to discover the power of language. She tries as often as possible to combine words, and she knows that phrases like "up me," "gimme ba-ba," and "book read" will get her picked up, fed, or read to.

♦ Her mimicking skills are moving into high gear, and she'll try to repeat any word you can throw at her.

♦ She loves singing and will join in on familiar songs wherever and whenever she can. Although far from fluent, your baby is beginning to understand the humorous uses of language. My younger daughter had the "moo-moo," "woof-woof," "quack-quack" parts of "Old MacDonald's Farm" down at fifteen months, but insisted that the chorus was "E-I-E-I-EEEEEEEEE."

♦ She may also sing, hum, and bounce to music when she's alone.

Emotionally/Socially

♦ The first half of the second year may be marked by great frustration and contradictions, feelings that frequently result in tantrums. Unable to express their wants in words, kids this age often become enraged. They also "get angry both when their parents withhold help and when they proffer needed assistance," writes child development expert Frank Caplan. Overall, "they get angry because they are not big or strong enough for the tasks they set for themselves." Some tantrums, especially the ones that involve breath-holding, can be quite spectacular. (See pages 70–71 for more on this.)

♦ Most of the time, however, your toddler is a pretty happy soul. Her sense of humor is developing nicely, and she's truly amused by her own movement— sliding, dropping things, falling down on purpose.

♦ She can also understand verbal humor, particularly when it deals with incongruities. For example, after emphatically refusing your lunchtime offer of a banana, a bowl of cereal, or a cheese sandwich, she may laugh hysteri-cally if you suggest a spoonful of dirt.

♦ She still plays alongside, not *with*, other toddlers. In fact, the only people she really wants to socialize with are her parents. During this period she may begin bringing you favorite books so you can read to her.

What You're Going Through

Thinking About Sex

Sex may mean very different things to you and your partner:

YOU MAY . . .	SHE MAY . . .
♦ See sex as a way of setting the stage for verbal intimacy.	♦ See verbal intimacy as a way of setting the stage for sex.
♦ Want sex as a way of feeling closer to her.	♦ Want sex when she's already feeling close to you.
♦ Need sex to establish an emotional connection with your partner.	♦ Need an emotional connection with you before being interested in sex.

POTENTIAL CONFLICTS

YOU MAY . . .

♦ Complain about the actual sex more than your partner, says psychologist Aaron Hass: the quantity, the quality, her lack of seductive behavior, her lack of taking the initiative.

♦ Be feeling excluded from your baby by your partner and may want to have sex as a way of reconnecting with your partner.

♦ Be embarrassed to admit that you feel too exhausted, unsure, overwhelmed by family responsibilities even to think about sex.

♦ Find it difficult to contemplate sex—especially oral sex—after remembering all the blood from the birth. You may be feeling that she's somehow been disfigured and get turned off as a result.

♦ Feel guilty about what pregnancy did to her body.

♦ Feel guilty about the pain she was in during pregnancy and be afraid of having her go through the same thing again (this is a common fear, even if you're using birth control).

♦ Feel that your partner prefers the baby to you if she rejects your advances.

SHE MAY . . .

♦ Complain that you don't talk to her, you aren't affectionate enough, you take her for granted, you don't understand her or her feelings. "Sexual excitement is very much a function of the strength of her loving feelings for her man and her perception of his love for her," says Hass.

♦ Be withholding sex as a way of getting back at you for not sharing equally in the distribution of household labor or for escaping into work.

♦ Be "affectioned out" from taking care of the baby all day.

♦ Be too sleep-deprived to show much sexual interest in you.

♦ Have less interest in sex, find intercourse painful, or have difficulty reaching orgasm. Twenty percent of women suffer from one or more of these problems longer than a year after the baby, says Dr. Dwenda K. Gjerdingen of the University of Minnesota.

♦ Not be feeling enough of a connection with you: after focusing predominantly on the baby, she may not know what she and you have in common anymore.

♦ Think that you find her less attractive than you used to. She also may find *herself* less attractive.

♦ Be more comfortable interacting with a child because the child expects less of her.

BOTH OF YOU MAY . . .

♦ Find it hard to admit to the other your basic need for support, comfort, love. The result can often be mutual blaming and resentment.

♦ Be reluctant to allow yourselves to get aroused. You might be afraid of being interrupted by the baby or you might feel guilty about satisfying your own needs when you should really be doing something to take care of the baby.

(A recent survey by *Parenting* magazine found that parents kiss their children twice as much as they do each other.)

♦ Have stopped touching each other because you're afraid that a stroke or a touch might be misinterpreted as a sexual overture (see *TNF I*, page 51). A new mother "may think her mate is obsessed with sexual desires," says Hass, "when what he really needs is reassurance that she still loves him and he has not been replaced by the baby." Sounds silly, but it isn't.

SOLUTIONS

♦ Make sure there are opportunities for verbal as well as sexual intimacy. And while you're at it, get rid of the idea that there's always a connection between the two.

♦ Eliminate sex (for a while). Spend some time getting used to each other in a nonsexual way.
  ◊ hold hands
  ◊ stroke her hair

The Ultimate Aphrodisiac

According to Aaron Hass, the most frequent complaint from wives about husbands is that they aren't involved enough with the children. And—from her point of view, anyway—if you don't love the kids, you don't love her. "A man, therefore, who does not actively father will inevitably trigger his wife's resentment," says Hass.

The solution? Be an active, involved father.

"There is no more powerful aphrodisiac to a mother than to see her husband lovingly engaged with their children," says Hass. "When your wife sees your involvement with her children, she will want to see you happy. She will, therefore, want to satisfy your sexual desires. She will be more likely to suggest that just the two of you get away for a night or a weekend so that you can have more intimate time together. She will be more open to sexual experimentation. . . . She will be more sexually creative. She will take pains to make sure the children are tucked away early in the evening so that you can have uninterrupted time together. And, of course, when your wife is happier, her own libido is more likely to assert itself."

Whew! If that doesn't make you want to quit your job and take care of your children, nothing will.

◊ kiss her when walking through the kitchen

◊ give each other massages, back rubs, and so forth

◊ make out

♦ Schedule sex—it doesn't have to be spontaneous like it was (see page 51 for more on this).

♦ Go on dates.

Dating Your Partner: A Few Requirements

♦ Don't try to make up for lost time. Packing too many things into a single evening can put a lot of pressure on both of you.

♦ Make it clear that there are no strings attached. Either of you may be suspicious that the "date" will be used as a way of getting the other in the sack.

♦ Don't talk about the baby. Let's be realistic: the baby is the one you and your partner are trying to get away from, the one who has consumed so much of your time that the two of you have neglected each other.

You and Your Baby

Dealing with Your Baby's Fears

Even though your baby's world is growing at an incredible clip, it's still a fairly small, well-managed, and—above all—safe little place. But the more she separates from you and the more independent she becomes, the scarier the world gets.

Babies may seem fairly unpredictable to us, but they are essentially creatures of habit who crave familiarity and routine. And just about everything your child will fear in her first three years of life will be the result of a break in her routines or an unfamiliar, unanticipated, or surprising event.

Stranger anxiety (see *TNF I*, pages 149–50) and separation anxiety (pages 30–32) were undoubtedly your baby's first fears. At about fifteen months, fear of the bath and of getting their hair washed top most kids' lists (see the chart on pages 42–45 for a list of some of the most common early-toddlerhood fears, a little about what they might mean, and a few suggestions for handling them). And by the time they're twenty-one months old, they've graduated to being afraid of dogs, the dark (and associated monsters), and loud noises (sirens, vacuums, car backfirings, and so forth)—in that order.

Many of your child's fears, writes child psychologist Selma Fraiberg, are "essentially a fear of his own impulses which are transferred to objects or phenomena outside himself. . . . Normally the fear will subside when the child has learned to control successfully the particular impulse which is disturbing him."

FIGHTING FEARS

Here are some general guidelines for helping your child deal with her fears.

TRY TO DISCOVER THE CAUSE

Starting when she was about eighteen months old, my younger daughter suddenly started crying hysterically every time I put her down on the sidewalk. After a few months, I figured out that she was afraid that the cars would hop the curb and run us down—a perfectly reasonable fear. My wife and I explained to her many, many times that cars live in the street and that they aren't allowed where people walk. That seemed to take the edge off the fear. But a few days later when we were out for a walk a car pulled into a driveway right in front of us, and my daughter went ballistic again. In her view, I'd been lying to her and cars really were after her.

Once you've figured out what's troubling your child, keep the following in mind:

- Acknowledge that your child's fears are real. Let her know that everyone has fears and that being afraid is perfectly normal. You might want to tell your child about some of the fears you had when you were a kid.
- Read. There are plenty of good books about how kids triumph over all sorts of potentially scary situations.
- Don't tell her she really isn't—or shouldn't be—afraid of some thing, place, or person. Instead, comfort her, tell her you'll always be there to help her.
- Never force your child to confront her fears (gently demonstrating that vacuums and baths really won't hurt the baby is okay, but don't push). And never laugh at or tease a fearful child; this will only make things worse.

CONTROL YOUR OWN REACTIONS

Thrust into a situation she's never been in before—especially a scary one—your baby probably won't know how to react. So she'll look to you for some visual or verbal cues as to how *you* think she should respond.

In one recent study, researcher James Sorce and his associates conducted a fascinating experiment designed to see whether parents' facial expressions—happy, fearful, interested, or angry—have any influence on their children's behavior in potentially dangerous situations. Sorce placed the babies and one of their parents on opposite sides of a "visual cliff"—a long, piece of sturdy but transparent Plexiglas that traversed a dangerous-looking (to the babies,

THE FEAR	WHAT IT MIGHT MEAN	WHAT TO DO ABOUT IT
Bath/hair washing	◆ Fear of getting washed down the drain and thrown away (if soap suds go down the drain, the hair can go too, and if the hair goes, why not the whole body?). ◆ Fear of the noise of the water. ◆ Fear of the hot water. ◆ Fear of getting things in the eyes and losing vision—if you can't see the world, you can't control it.	◆ Get a special toy that your baby can play with only in the bathtub. ◆ Take baths with your baby. ◆ Show her that big things (like you and she) can't go down the drain. ◆ Have her get in one toe at a time, then a leg, then the bottom. ◆ Wash her with a washcloth instead of sticking her head under water.
Vacuum cleaner	◆ Fear of being disposed of just like the dust (similar to fear of baths, above). ◆ Fear of loud noises, of being yelled at.	◆ Have the baby explore the vacuum, and perhaps even push it around a little while it's off. ◆ Have one of the baby's toys go for a "ride" on the vacuum. ◆ Hold the baby while vacuuming. ◆ Let the baby turn it on and off, thus giving her control over the noise.
Haircuts	◆ Fear of being disposed of (same "logic" as getting rid of soap suds).	◆ Have the baby check out the barber first, and watch a few strangers get haircuts. ◆ Take the baby (with another adult) to watch you get a haircut. ◆ Find a child-friendly barber who has lots of experience with kids.

THE FEAR	WHAT IT MIGHT MEAN	WHAT TO DO ABOUT IT
Haircuts (continued)		◆ Learn to cut hair yourself. ◆ Let your child cut the hair of her dolls, bears, and so on to practice. ◆ Have her sit in your lap during the haircut. ◆ Skip the hair washing—too many fears combined.
Monsters	◆ Fear of the unknown. ◆ Fear of being separated from you. ◆ Fear that there is something so powerful and unpredictable that even *you* (the all-powerful parent) can't control it.	◆ Write a "No Monsters Allowed" sign (or one warning of a monster-eating kid inside the room). ◆ Check under the bed and in closets for monsters. ◆ Watch out for mixed messages. Telling your child monsters don't exist and then putting up signs or looking under the bed can be confusing. Try a compromise approach, such as, "There really aren't any monsters, but if there were, they would read this sign and stay out." ◆ Have a large, sturdy toy "stand guard" over the baby's room. ◆ Give the baby a magic wand or a special magic button to push that makes monsters disappear instantly. ◆ Cut down on prebedtime scary things (including stories, growling, and making faces). ◆ Leave on a night-light.

(continued on page 44)

THE FEAR	WHAT IT MIGHT MEAN	WHAT TO DO ABOUT IT
Sleep or dark	♦ Fear of losing control. ♦ Fear that loved ones and loved things won't be there later.	♦ Establish a comfortable bedtime routine. ♦ Emphasize the big-kid bed. ♦ Tell baby that everyone else she knows is sleeping (name them one at a time). ♦ Tell baby that you—and everyone else—will be there in the morning. ♦ Leave a light on.
Scary stories	♦ Similar to monsters, night, dark.	♦ No scary stories before bed or, if the problem is severe, no scary stories at all, even during the day. ♦ Cuddle while reading. ♦ Edit or cut out the scary parts. ♦ Make sure she knows the story isn't real. ♦ Use a night-light.
Animals	♦ Fear of the unfamiliar (not human). ♦ Fear of being eaten. ♦ Fear of being bitten. ♦ Fear of not being able to control her own impulses or live up to her parents' expectations.	♦ Read lots of books about friendly animals (the *Carl* books, by Alexandra Day, are great for this). ♦ Teach baby the proper way to behave with pets: no fingers in animals' noses, and so on. Take her hand and show her the right way to pet an animal. ♦ Teach baby to recognize inviting and hostile animal gestures.

THE FEAR	WHAT IT MIGHT MEAN	WHAT TO DO ABOUT IT
Animals (continued)		♦ Ask pet owners if their animal is friendly before letting your baby anywhere near it. ♦ Hold your baby's hand near unfamiliar pets. ♦ Never force the baby to touch animals if she doesn't want to.
Doctors/ dentists	♦ Fear of strangers. ♦ Fear of new situations, smells, sights. ♦ Fear of pain. ♦ Fear that there's really something wrong (you wouldn't go to the doctor if there weren't, right?).	♦ Talk about the doctor, about how pediatricians love kids and want to make them feel good. ♦ Play through it (see below)—have baby do to her stuffed animals what the doctor will do to her. ♦ Do *not* lie—don't say there won't be shots or that the shots won't hurt. ♦ Schedule appointment for noncranky times. ♦ Switch to a same-sex doctor (don't worry about offending yours, he or she is very familiar with these requests).

anyway) surface. He then induced the babies to crawl across the "cliff" to retrieve a tempting toy from the parent. The results were illuminating: of the seventeen children who saw a fearful expression, *none* crossed the cliff. And only two of the eighteen confronted with an angry expression did. Of the nineteen who saw happy faces, however, fourteen crossed, and so did eleven of the fifteen whose parent's expression was one of "sincere interest."

Your reactions influence your baby in other areas as well. When she's learning to walk, for example, she'll probably fall down twenty times a minute and get right back up without the slightest complaint. But if you gasp and lunge across the room to "save" her, she'll probably start crying, thinking that since you're scared, she should be too. And in just a few years she'll be able to over-react on her own, without your help: when you were a kid you could probably take a pretty good tumble, get right up, and forget all about it. But if you saw blood, you'd start crying.

WATCH WHAT YOU SAY

Like your physical reaction, your verbal reaction can have a great influence on how your baby deals with fear.

♦ Bring up and discuss potentially scary situations in advance. Say things like, "We're going to . . . but . . ."

♦ Well-intentioned warnings such as, "Oh, there's nothing to be afraid of," usually backfire. In your baby's mind, if there really wasn't anything to be afraid of, you wouldn't have said anything at all.

♦ Also, don't say things like, "Be careful, this might be a little scary." Your baby will actually think you want her to be scared.

♦ Don't go overboard on safety issues. Warnings like the ones you heard from your parents ("Don't talk to strangers," "Don't take candy from strangers," "Don't get into a car with strangers") can give a child a nearly irrational fear of, well, strangers.

♦ Think about potential mixed messages: now that you've got your baby scared away from the hot stove, do you think she's going to be happy about eating some hot breakfast cereal or, even worse, getting into a bathtub filled with hot water?

PLAY IT OUT

One of the things infants and toddlers are most afraid of is being out of control. Letting them play through scary situations—either ones that just happened or ones they're anticipating—can help them regain that important feeling of being in charge. So, if your child is afraid of doctors, get her a toy doctor's kit, complete with stethoscope and syringe, so she can examine— and give shots to—all her stuffed animals. If she's afraid of *real* animals, try a small but ferocious-looking stuffed one she can tame.

EXPECT THE IRRATIONAL . . . AND TRY NOT TO LAUGH

A friend of mine told me about taking her two-year-old daughter, Arielle, to the barber for her first haircut. They'd talked things over, read some books about haircuts, given the stuffed animals trims, and everything was going fine—until the barber made the first cut. All of a sudden Arielle winced and let out an incredibly loud "Ouch"—a wail she repeated with every snip of the scissors. There wasn't anything wrong, but little Arielle, who knew that cutting her finger hurt, figured that cutting her hair would hurt too.

SECURITY OBJECTS

About half of all kids need, want, use, or demand some kind of security objects: blankets, pacifiers, toys, and so on. Don't discourage this—she'll give it up when she's ready to. Trying to break a security-object habit can make your baby feel even more needy than before, creating a pattern that may result in her using, in later years, such "adult" security devices as alcohol and drugs.

So if you think your child is developing a real fondness for a particular object, go out and buy one or two more identical ones to keep in the closet. The first one might get lost, shredded, or so filthy that it can't be salvaged.

Nutrition Update

BALANCED MEALS? GOOD LUCK!

Getting your baby to eat balanced meals is one of the most frustrating tasks you'll have during his second year of life. For a week it may seem that no matter what kind of delicacies you prepare, he won't eat anything but plain rice and soy sauce. Then, all of a sudden, he'll refuse to eat rice and won't be satisfied with anything but macaroni and cheese. Believe me, this happens all the time.

Part of the problem, of course, is that you and your baby haven't agreed on what, exactly, a balanced meal is—and you won't for quite a few years. Fortunately, you don't have to. In a classic study, Dr. Clara Davis allowed a group of year-old babies to choose freely from a sampling of foods (that carefully omitted high-sugar foods, candy, cookies, and soft drinks). She found that on a

MOST ALLERGENIC FOODS	LEAST ALLERGENIC FOODS
◆ Egg whites	◆ Rice
◆ Wheat and yeast	◆ Oats
◆ Milk and other dairy products	◆ Barley
◆ Citrus fruits	◆ Carrots
◆ Berries	◆ Squash
◆ Tomatoes	◆ Apricots
◆ Chocolate	◆ Peaches
◆ Nuts	◆ Apples
◆ Shellfish	◆ Lamb

"Because I'm a sovereign, and a sovereign is allowed not to eat his spinach if he doesn't want to."

day-to-day basis the babies' diets were indeed out of balance. But over the course of a few months—a far more critical time frame—their diets were actually quite well balanced.

Still, having a kid eat nothing but bananas for two weeks at a stretch (as my younger daughter did) can be a little disconcerting. The only time this kind of eating truly is a problem is if the baby has absolutely no fruits or vegetables for more than a week—a situation that's probably more your fault than the baby's. If this happens, call your pediatrician; he or she may be able to suggest some alternate sources of those crucial nutrients.

Overall, you probably won't be able to do much to change your baby's eating habits. But if you're really worried, here are some suggestions that might help:

♦ Introduce a wide variety of foods—even if the baby won't touch any of them.

♦ Serve small portions; large ones can be a little scary.

♦ Keep a log of what the baby eats over the course of a week—just to see how he's doing.

♦ Don't give up after only one try.

♦ Don't make a huge battle out of it.

Diagnosing Food Allergies

Correctly diagnosing food allergies is tricky, even for professionals. Since trace amounts of the most common allergens are present in many foods, pinpointing the single offending ingredient is extremely difficult. Casein (a milk protein), for example, is sometimes found in tuna and even in nondairy ice creams. Chili recipes often include peanuts, and just try to find a packaged product that doesn't contain corn, or at least corn syrup.

If you suspect your toddler is allergic, but her reactions aren't severe, keep a diary of everything she eats and all her symptoms for at least two weeks. This may seem like a real pain, but the diary will help you and your pediatrician identify the source of the problem.

Because the only proven way to treat food allergies is to avoid the offending foods, your pediatrician may, after reviewing the diary, prescribe an elimination diet. These diets typically last two weeks and include only the least allergenic foods possible (see page 47). If the symptoms don't improve after a few weeks, you can assume your child doesn't have a food allergy. But if the symptoms do improve, other foods are introduced, one at a time, a few days apart. If a reaction occurs, the new food is eliminated again and reintroduced after the symptoms have subsided (to make sure the first reaction wasn't just a coincidence). Because most allergies are eventually outgrown, however, many doctors recommend reintroducing previously eliminated foods every three months or so.

Elimination diets may sound simple, but don't start one without your doctor's supervision. Too many parents misdiagnose food allergies and eliminate too many foods. "Most kids are allergic to only one or two foods," says Ann Muñoz-Furlong, who founded the Food Allergy Network. Muñoz-Furlong warns that pulling kids—toddlers in particular—off too many foods can lead to an unbalanced diet or even malnutrition.

A word of caution: if your pediatrician immediately recommends diagnostics such as skin-prick tests, or treatments like immunotherapy, get a second opinion. A lot of these tests are inconvenient, expensive, and, worst of all, ineffective.

To get more information on food allergies, call the Food Allergy Network at (703) 691-3179.

- Don't beg; it will just give your baby an inflated view of her own abilities to control you.
- Don't punish the baby for not eating what you serve.
- Go along with the craziness; let the baby knock himself out.
- Don't use dessert as a bribe (for more on this, see page 132).

Be sure to read the "Food and Your Child's Temperament" section on page 133.

Family Matters

Communication

MORE CH-CH-CH-CHANGES

Nearly all the couples in Jay Belsky's exhaustive studies of new parents experienced a drop in the quality of their communication. Half the time it was permanent. Here are some factors Belsky and several other researchers have identified as contributing to a decline in couples' communication skills:

- "A new child deprives a couple of many of the mechanisms they once used to manage differences," says Belsky. For example, a couple that had disagreements about who did what around the house might solve the problem by getting a housekeeper. But once the baby arrives, strained finances might preclude a cleaning person and the once painless who-does-what disagreements now need to be confronted.
- The lack of spontaneity. Before your baby was born, if you wanted to go to a movie or just sit around and talk, you could just do it. But now, as parents, you don't have that luxury. If you want to go out, you have to get a sitter a day or so in advance, make sure the baby is fed, and be back at a certain time.
- Physical exhaustion. Even if you and your partner stay home together, there's a better than even chance you'll be too tired to stay awake for an entire conversation.
- There's a general decline in intimacy-promoting activities such as sex, getting together with friends, and so forth.
- With so much time and energy focused on the baby, you and your partner may find that your pool of common interests is shrinking fast.
- There's a lot less time and money left to pursue individual interests and activities outside the home. As a result, many new parents find that their communication skills have "rusted." They don't have nearly as many new things to talk about and they've lost (partially, at least) the ability to hear and understand each other.

♦ If you or your partner has left the workplace, you've lost a rich source of conversational topics; there are now a lot fewer stories to tell about people at the office.

Here are some things you and your partner can do to keep (or get) your communication on track:

♦ Get a family calendar. This can keep double-booking and scheduling miscommunications to a minimum.

♦ Set aside at least fifteen minutes a day to talk about things other than the baby. It's harder than you think. See the "(Re)Learning to Talk" section below for more.

♦ Go out on dates (with your partner, of course). Spending time alone with your partner is absolutely critical to the long-term health of your marriage. Get a sitter if you can, or ask friends or relatives to step in. You might also want to set up an informal baby-sitting cooperative with a few other parents in your neighborhood; they need to get out as much as you and your partner do (see page 40 for more on this).

♦ Do something special for each other. But be flexible and understanding. If you've made surprise plans and your partner is too exhausted, it doesn't mean she doesn't love you. Try again another night or put the "surprise" on the calendar.

♦ Schedule sex. It sounds terribly unromantic, but just having the big S on the calendar may actually make it *more* fun. And anyway, if you're still interested, this may be the only way it's going to happen. Weekdays may be out, but if you use your weekends wisely, you should still be able to rechristen every room in your house.

♦ If your partner is at home with the baby during the day, try to give her some time every day when she can be completely alone and doesn't have to take care of anyone but herself. If you're the primary caretaker, do the same for yourself.

♦ Don't blame the baby for your troubles. Too many couples interpret their communication problems as a sign that the baby pushed them apart and that they shouldn't have become parents.

♦ Talk to other people. Talk to other couples with kids to find out what they've been through, what works, and what doesn't. You might also join a new parents' or new fathers' group.

(RE)LEARNING TO TALK

"I get the picture sometimes of two people who may be very much in love and very much together, having private dreams that shape their lives, but not letting each other know the content," says Phil Cowan. Frequent, open, and honest communication is "the key to an effective transition from couple to family," he adds. But because so many couples seem to forget how, let's go over the basics:

♦ **Open your mouth.** Although many men have been socialized into thinking that we don't have strong feelings or emotional needs, this obviously isn't true. Nevertheless, many men are reluctant to talk to their partners about their needs and feelings, fearing that they'll seem weak in the eyes of their partners and will be letting them down.

♦ **Close your mouth and open your ears.** One of the most widespread stereotypes about men and women is that women are more open than men about discussing their feelings and emotions. If your partner is a natural talker, great. But plenty of new mothers need some gentle, supportive encouragement. "A great deal of needless suffering goes on because mothers and fathers are ashamed to express feelings they have that seem 'unmotherly' or 'unfatherly,'" writes Phil Cowan. So encourage her to talk, ask her about her deepest feelings about the baby, tell her you love her, reassure her that you'll be there for her.

♦ **Speak the same language.** Sounds silly, but it's not. Some of the biggest communication breakdowns come because people don't (or can't or won't) agree on the definition of some very basic words. For example, does the word *love* mean the same thing to you and your partner? Do the two of you express your love for each other in the same way? Probably not. Men commonly express love for their partners (and other people) by *doing* things (that may be how the whole "good provider" thing got started). Women, however, are more likely to express their love *verbally*. Unfortunately, most people want to be communicated with in their own language. Consequently, what you *do* may not be loving enough for your partner and what she *says* may not be enough for you. Learning to understand and express love differently is like learning a new language. Granted, it's a little more complicated than high school French, but it can be done.

Here are some ground rules for putting your newly polished communication skills to work:

♦ Schedule a special time and place for your discussions. Let's face it: if you can't have sex without a schedule, you won't be able to have a serious conversation without one either.

♦ Tell her what's on your mind. Tackle one issue at a time and stay away from phrases like "you always . . . ," "you never . . . ," or anything else guaranteed to put a quick end to your conversations.

- Ask her to tell you what she heard you say. Just saying, "I understand what you're saying" isn't enough here. It's important to have your partner tell you in her own words what you've just told her.
- Confirm for her that she heard you correctly. Tell her again if she didn't.
- Go back to Step 2, but switch roles: she talks, you listen.
- Learn to compromise. Understanding each other's concerns is a great place to start, but it doesn't do much good if you can't figure out how to bridge the gaps.
- Get professional help if you need it. Set up a monthly or quarterly appointment with a marriage counselor to give you and your partner a safe place to discuss your relationship, differences, problems, worries, and so forth.

FIGHTING CAN BE A GOOD THING . . .

Parenting approaches are the source of just about as many marital spats as money and division of labor. Naturally, you should avoid having huge fights in front of your children. (Kids are scared and confused when their parents yell at each other, and researchers have found that the angrier the parents, the more distressed the children.)

But this doesn't mean that whenever the kids are around, you and your partner always have to see eye to eye (or at least seem to). In fact, just the opposite

"They're playing the blame game."

"Repression and denial have always worked for Dad."

is true: "Children of parents who have regular and resolved fights have higher levels of interpersonal poise and self-esteem than those whose parents have chronic unresolved fights or those whose parents appear not to fight at all," writes psychologist Brad Sachs.

Children can also learn plenty from watching their parents disagree—provided they do it civilly. "Occasionally divided ranks will encourage and stimulate a child's capacity to negotiate, bargain, and present her own case against the opinions of others," writes child-rearing columnist Lilian Katz.

So let your child see you and your partner squabble about easily resolvable things and schedule weekly or, if necessary, daily meetings away from the kids to discuss the bigger issues.

Big or small, if you do ever have a disagreement in front of your child, pay close attention to how you make up afterward. "It is probably useful for young children to observe how adults renegotiate their relationship following a squabble or moments of hostility," says Katz. "These observations can reassure the child that when distance and anger come between her and members of the family, the relationship is not over but can be resumed to be enjoyed again."

GO AHEAD, GET ANGRY

Don't go too far out of your way to avoid fighting with your partner. In fact, you may be far better off releasing some steam in her direction (in a reasonable way) than suppressing it. "In trying to avoid conflict, we may create even more," says Sachs. "What we risk by venting our anger out loud is generally far less threatening than what we risk by suppressing it," says Sachs. "Internalized anger causes emotional and physical symptoms like depression, alienation, ulcers, fatigue, backaches, and high blood pressure. Also, we have to remember that if we don't express it directly, it will come out anyway, but sideways, in a way we can't control. The phone message that we forget to deliver to our partner, the medicine we forget to give to the baby, the check we forget to deposit, can all be passive aggressions directed against our spouse when we're afraid of what we're feeling."

18–21 MONTHS

Still Wild (or Mild) after All These Months

What's Going On with the Baby

Physically

- No longer content just to walk forward, your toddler can now walk backward and sideways. He may even be able to run. (Well, sort of. It really looks more like a clumsy speed walk.)
- He can kick a ball without stepping on it and can, at long last, throw overhand.
- As his hand-eye coordination improves, your toddler loves piecing things together. He does simple puzzles (in which each piece fits in a separate hole) and can build a tower five or six blocks high. He'll also put blocks or Duplo or Lego pieces together to make long, straight walls. There's still room for improvement; when hammering, he finds it nearly impossible to keep the head of the hammer straight and, more often than not, it lands sideways.
- All his block building, besides improving his coordination, is teaching him about balance. Will a big block stay on top of a little one?
- He's getting really good at undressing himself. But his dressing skills—if he has any at all—are still pretty much confined to not squirming for a few seconds and allowing you to slip something on him.
- He's experimenting with using forks and spoons, but not the way you'd hoped. He holds his fork in one hand, picks up a piece of food and pushes it onto the tine with the other.
- He still has trouble turning the pages of a book one at a time.

Intellectually

♦ Despite the major intellectual advances he's made over the past eighteen months, your toddler is still a fairly egotistical little creature, believing that he is the source of all action. Child psychologist Selma Fraiberg beautifully describes his attitude about the world: "The magician is seated in his high chair and looks upon the world with favor. He is at the height of his powers. If he closes his eyes, he causes the world to disappear. If he opens his eyes, he causes the world to come back. . . . If desire arises within him, he utters the magic syllables that cause the desired object to appear. His wishes, his thoughts, his gestures, his noises command the universe."

♦ Despite his self-centered view of the world, your toddler is beginning to become aware of the ownership of objects. He can (but may not want to) distinguish between "mine" and "yours."

♦ His sense of object permanence is becoming more sophisticated, and he now anticipates where objects "should" be. If a ball rolls under the couch, for example, he'll run to the back of the couch, knowing the ball will be there soon. And as you pass the gas station down the block from your house and turn onto your street, he'll begin to get excited, knowing he'll be home soon.

♦ Your toddler has been getting increasingly negative and contrary lately: the first word out of his mouth in any given situation is usually "No," he'll refuse to do almost anything you ask, and he deliberately dawdles when he knows you're in a hurry. For a toddler to do just the opposite of what you want him to do "strikes him as being the very essence of his individuality," writes Selma Fraiberg.

♦ He still has some difficulty with time concepts: "now," "later," "yesterday," and "tomorrow" mean nothing to him.

Verbally

♦ Although your toddler knows between ten and forty words (girls are usually more articulate at this stage than boys), "No" is by far the most popular.

♦ He now makes a serious effort to repeat what you say, using a kind of shorthand. For example, if you say, "No, you can't pour your milk on the floor," he'll probably reply, "Pour milk floor." Language expert James Britton has found that toddlers repeat the words that carry the most information, while omitting the less important words.

- He will frequently ask you to identify unfamiliar (and sometimes quite familiar) objects. And when you're reading to him, he can name a few objects from a favorite book.
- Kids this age are beginning to grasp the concept of pronouns and can make subtle distinctions: "don't hit him" is different from "don't hit her."
- For the first time, you toddler is now capable of engaging in "conversation." Instead of responding physically to your questions (by going somewhere, pointing to something, or doing something), he may use words.

Emotionally/Socially

- He still can't really differentiate between inanimate objects and people, and treats other toddlers accordingly—poking, hitting, biting, and pushing them. This kind of behavior is usually not hostile—your toddler is learning some valuable lessons about actions and reactions.
- Although he is expressing some interest in interacting and socializing with other kids, your toddler still usually plays alone, pausing once in a while to defend his property rights or to snatch something away from a "playmate." Despite his seeming lack of interest, he is learning a massive amount by imitating his friends (they, presumably, are also learning from him).
- If they haven't already, this is about the time when girls discover their vaginas and boys their penises. Boys may even get, albeit rarely, an erection. This is absolutely normal for kids this age, and every attempt should be made *not* to make a big deal of it (see pages 174–75 for more on this).
- Still plenty of tantrums.
- Your toddler may exhibit an early interest in toilet training by occasionally letting you know when he has a wet or soiled diaper.

What You're Going Through

A Fear of Being Rejected by Your Baby

One of these days, you're going to run to comfort your crying child. Oh, you've done it before, but this time it'll be different. This time, instead of running to meet you, your child will see you and scream, "No! I want Mommy!" or "I Hate you," or "You're a bad daddy!"

There's not really anything I or anyone else can say that will make you feel any less rejected or despised when those horrible words pop out of your child's mouth. The first time (and the tenth and the twentieth) my older daughter said something like that to me, I nearly cried.

Remember, though, that your child has no idea that he's hurting you with his words. Feelings are still something new to him, and he may just be experimenting to see how you'll react. Rather than withdraw completely or punish your child (even subtly) for wounding you, here are a few other approaches:

♦ Acknowledge that your child is upset. Say something like, "You're really mad, aren't you?"

♦ Reassure him that you love him.

♦ During a calm moment much later, talk with him a little about how it feels when your feelings are hurt. But don't go on too long about this; the last thing you want to do is put your child in charge of your self-esteem (or to make him feel as though he's in charge of it).

♦ Try some sarcasm. Saying, "Yep, you're right. I'm the world's worst father and everyone hates me," may shock your child so much that he'll rush to your defense.

Eventually, you'll learn to ignore (or at least pay less attention to) your child's slings and arrows. And you'll find that things have a way of coming full circle. When my younger daughter was about eighteen months old, she went through a stage when she wouldn't let me put her down. In fact, she wouldn't let anyone else—my wife included—pick her up. On one occasion, after carrying her around for about eight hours straight, my legs and shoulders had gone completely numb and I had to take a break. So I told my daughter I was going to take her to mommy for a while, and I did exactly that. The hand-off went fairly well, but the moment I turned to walk away my daughter shrieked, "Daddy! Help me, Daddy! I need you!"

Being a Father Can Make You Smarter . . .

Well, maybe not, but there's no question that becoming a parent can have a major impact on the way you think. According to researchers Newman and Newman, parenting:

♦ Has the "potential consequence of expanding the realm of consciousness." It can increase your capacity to put the past, present, and future into the proper perspective.

♦ Makes you think more flexibly. The need to protect and nurture their children requires parents to develop skills in anticipating—and preparing for—the future, including making appropriate contingency plans.

*"I know what you're going through. I, too, spent several years
as a small child."*

♦ Gets you to put together a consistent philosophy of life and to seek to raise
your children according to your central values and goals.

♦ Makes you a bit more forgiving of people's weaknesses and perhaps look a
little harder to find their strengths and potential.

♦ "Requires and promotes the capacity to hold two or more opposing ideas in
the mind at the same time." For example, most new couples say that having
children brought them closer together. At the same time, though, they say
that labor around the house has been divided along traditional lines,
causing fights about the division of labor.

Themes of attachment and separation are another area where adults can
have two opposing ideas at the same time, say psychologists Barbara and
Philip Newman. Most parents want to remain close to their children. They
continue to have a strong bond of affection for their children, and they worry

about their children's safety and welfare. At the same time, they take pride in signs of their children's independence and encourage their children to be self-sufficient.

The capacity to hold two or more opposing ideas in the mind at once is widely considered to be one of the characteristics of adult cognition.

You and Your Baby

Play

In the last few months of your baby's second year, three major play-related developments occur, usually in rapid succession:

♦ He learns to play with others his own age.

♦ He learns to play alone.

♦ He learns to tell the difference between what's pretend and what's real.

PLAY WITH PEERS

If your child has been thinking of himself as the center of the solar system, he certainly considered you and your partner to be nearby planets, orbiting around him contentedly. The gravitational pull connecting you to your child was so strong that, in the words of Bruno Bettelheim, "in the long run he can have pleasure only if his delight is validated for him by that of his parents."

But just recently he's realized that there are other objects floating around out there. And some of them seem to be stars—just like him.

Several researchers have analyzed infant-parent interaction with and without a peer present. When both parent and peer were in the room, the children paid more attention to the peer than to the parent, says Whaley. The researchers suggest that toddlers relate to peers better because they share more common play interests than parents are likely to.

PLAYING ALONE

"By twenty-one months, the child is well aware that he or she influences behavior and has now become his or her own source of stimulation rather than relying on adults," says Whaley. Ordinarily, being ignored isn't considered to be a compliment. But if you and your baby are together and he wants to spend some time playing by himself, consider yourself praised: if he wasn't absolutely sure he could count on you to be there in an emergency, he'd never take his eyes off you.

A Few Fun Educational Activities for Kids This Age

♦ Take a nature walk. Pick up things and discuss them. You'd be amazed at the variety of stuff there is just lying around and at the variety of educational opportunities. (Picking up a leaf, for example, can spark a great discussion about how nutrients get from the root of the tree to the leaves and about the difference between deciduous and evergreen trees). Activities like nature walks also encourage observation skills, and you'll probably find that your child is spotting a lot more interesting things than you are.

♦ Play matching games. Cut postcards in half and have the baby match the halves. Or, in a more advanced version, match playing cards.

♦ Cook. Make simple edible recipes together, or just make some Oobleck—a kind of moldable dough that kids love to play with. (Mix 1 pound of cornstarch, 1½ cups of cold water, and some food coloring together until smooth. That's it.) Besides teaching all sorts of great things—measuring, textures, how things change shape and form when heated or cooled—cooking with your child will subtly teach him some valuable lessons about men's and women's roles in society. But best of all, it's a lot of fun. (See pages 159–65 for more on cooking with kids.)

♦ Build a fort out of chairs and blankets. Learn about structure, balance, privacy, light, and dark.

"See, son? He's not gone. He just turned into 'Splashy the Puddleman.'"

A Few Equipment-Buying Tips

♦ Make sure anything you buy for use by your child can be easily used. For example, if you have a minibasketball hoop, make sure the child—not just you—can hit a few jumpers. If it's too high, she'll get frustrated and quit.

♦ Chairs should be wider at bottom than at top to reduce the chance of their tipping over. They should also be low enough so that the baby can get up and sit down without having to ask for help.

♦ Tables should be high enough to fit comfortably above your child's knees while she's sitting on her chair.

The capacity to be alone is a critical sign of emotional maturity, says English pediatrician and psychoanalyst D. W. Winnicott. And as usual, your role as a father needs to be adjusted in response to your child's growth and development. "Toddler learning now depends in part on the freedom a child is given to explore the environment," says Whaley. "There is now a shift from adult as participant to adult as audience."

Although your child may be playing alone, he'll often accompany himself by singing, humming, laughing, or squealing. "Children as they exercise their bodies feel such an exuberance that they often cannot remain silent but loudly express their joy in what their bodies can do, without knowing that this is its cause," says Bruno Bettelheim. The bottom line is that they've just begun to discover some of the wonderful things their spry young bodies can do, and it feels incredibly good. And anything that makes him feel good enough to squeal is worth doing again.

According to Bettelheim, learning to take pleasure in our own bodies is an important developmental stage. "The pleasure we derive from the experience that our bodies and minds are operating and serving us well," he says, "forms the basis for all feelings of well-being."

PRETEND PLAY

"Pretend play actually fosters cognitive and social development," says Bettelheim. Children who have well-developed pretending skills tend to be well liked by their peers and to be viewed as peer leaders. This is a result of their advanced communication skills, their greater ability to take the point of view of others, and their ability to reason about social situations. "Children who have been

Thinking Music

Ever since you were just a few years old, you've been able to summon up images of objects or people, or imagine words and sentences or entire conversations without actually speaking a word. That's what *thinking* is.

In music, the same basic process is called *audiation*. "To audiate is to hear and comprehend music that is not physically present, just as to think is to hear and give meaning to language, the sound of words not physically present," write Richard Grunow, Edwin Gordon, and Christopher Azzara. Just as you can't develop as a person without thinking, "without audiation, no musical growth can take place," they add.

Sound complicated? It really isn't. Think of all those times you haven't been able to stop humming a particular melody, or the times you've taught someone else a song. That's audiating.

One of the best things you can do to help your child build her audiating skills is to expose her to music without words. Because language development receives so much emphasis in our culture, the words of a song may distract your child from being aware of the music itself. In the case of kids with limited language skills, the words can actually slow down musical development. If a child's "language has not developed well enough to sing the words of the song," writes Gordon, "she may not attempt to sing the song at all."

Please remember that as important as it is to expose your child to music, having the stereo going twenty-four hours a day isn't necessary or helpful. Learning to listen to and appreciate silence is important too. It is during periods of silence that your child has the opportunity to exercise her developing powers of audiation by remembering, thinking about, and experimenting with the music she has already heard.

encouraged in a playful, imaginative approach to the manipulation and exploration of materials and objects through fantasy show more complex language use and more flexible approaches to problem solving," Bettelheim says.

Encourage your child's pretending any way you can: play imitation games, act out stories with your child and his toys, or write your own plays. If your child develops an interest in toys traditionally associated with the opposite sex, don't make a big deal of it. (When my older daughter was nearly two, she decided that she was Oliver Twist. She responded only when addressed as

Oliver, and insisted that my wife and I act the parts of the various villains and heroes from the movie. This little phase lasted well over a year and a half.)

Making Music

"In general, the more you and your child have become actively involved in music . . . the more your child's attention span and appetite for music will increase," writes music educator Edwin Gordon.

Even if you haven't done much more than sing a couple of lullabies or leave the radio on a few hours a day, you'll notice that your baby has become a much more active music listener than he was in his first year (see *TNF I*, pages 176–78). He clearly recognizes familiar songs and tries to sing along. At this stage, he won't be able to get more than a note or two—usually the last one in the song or phrase—the "O" in "E-I-E-I-O," for example. But he's delighted to be able to do even that.

By the time he's about two and a half, he'll add the first few notes and an occasional short phrase in the middle of a song as well (all of "E-I-E-I-O," perhaps, or maybe even "Yes, sir. Yes, sir. Three bags full").

If you haven't done so already, make singing part of your everyday routine. Since your child is taking a more active role in singing, select songs that are short and repetitive, and change your focus from singing *to* the child to singing *with* him. Encourage him to make up his own songs and have him teach you the words or melody.

If you'd like a little help selecting music, several companies produce sets of developmentally appropriate tapes that are aimed at children but that you'll like too. A few are listed in the Resources guide on page 216.

You'll also notice that the way he moves to music is quite different now. Just a few months ago, his arm and leg movements seemed almost random. But now, just before his second birthday, he has adopted his very own, unique rhythmic "gestures"—shaking, wiggling, half-crouching, or bouncing up and down— that are different from those of every other child his age. As before, your child's movements—which now come in groups of three to seven "pulses"—may not seem to have much to do with the music he's hearing. They are, however, definitely in response to the music and are internally very consistent, meaning that you can almost set your watch by the pulses.

The way your child moves to music is an expression of some primal part of his personality. So let him do what he wants—don't tell him how to move, show him new routines, or move his arms or legs for him. That's the surest way to stifle his budding self-expression.

"Do we have something with more of a chararcter driven plot?"

Keep on Reading

DEALING WITH BOREDOM

After reading the same book six times at a single sitting (or several hundred times over the course of a few months), you might find yourself less than completely enthusiastic about reading it again. If (when) this happens, spice things up by making some deliberate mistakes in the text, just to see if your baby is on the ball: switch characters' names, say "in" instead of "out," and so forth.

YOUR ATTENTION, PLEASE

The average almost-two-year-old's attention span is about three minutes, so try to get in at least three or four reading sessions each day. But be prepared: the range varies enormously. When my older daughter was this age, she could easily spend an hour listening, but at the same age my younger daughter wouldn't sit still for more than thirty seconds at a stretch. Please also remember that attention span is *not* an indication of intelligence. Despite her seeming indifference, my younger daughter still ran around the house most of the day demanding to be read to and still managed to memorize at least as many books as her seemingly more attentive peers.

ADDING TO YOUR LIBRARY

If your child is still interested in the same books that interested him a year ago, don't worry. And don't push him to give up old favorites. "When a child has gotten all he can from the book or when the problems that directed him to it have been outgrown," says Bruno Bettelheim, "he'll be ready to move on to something else."

This doesn't mean, though, that you can't introduce new titles. Big hits for this age group include books that introduce numbers, sizes, shapes, colors, opposites, special concepts (up, down, in, out), and that discuss body parts. Here's a short list of some of my developmentally appropriate favorites for this age:

Across the Stream (and many others), Mirra Ginsburg

Can't You Sleep, Little Bear?, Martin Waddell

Caps for Sale, Esphyr Slobodkina

Each Peach Pear Plum, Janet Ahlberg, Allan Ahlberg

Freight Train, Donald Crews

Golden Bear, Ruth Young

A Good Day, A Good Night, Cindy Wheeler

Holes and Peeks (and many others), Ann Jonas

How Do I Put it On?, Shigeo Watanabe

Jesse Bear, What Will You Wear?, Nancy Carlstrom, Bruce Degen

Jump, Frog, Jump, Robert Kalan

Kitten Can . . . , Bruce McMillan

Little Gorilla, Ruth Borenstein

Lunch, Denise Fleming

Mouse Paint, Ellen Walsh

Owl Babies, Martin Waddell

Planting a Rainbow (and many others), Lois Ehlert

Ten, Nine, Eight, Molly Bang

What Do You See?, Bill Martin, Jr.

Where Does the Brown Bear Go?, Nicki Weiss

Wynken, Blynken and Nod, Eugene Field

CONCEPTS

Becca Backward, Becca Frontward: A Book of Concept Pairs, Bruce McMillan

Who Said Red, Mary Serfozo

On Market Street, Arnold Lobel

One Wolly Wombat, Rod Drinca, Kerry Argent

(For more concept books, see pages 109–10 and 152.)

POETRY

A Child's Garden of Verses, Robert Louis Stevenson

Jamberry, Bruce Degen

Rainbow in the Sky, Louis Untermeyer (editor)

(For more poetry books, see pages 110 and 153.)

Family Matters

Tantrums

WHAT CAUSES THEM

In some cases as early as twelve months, but most frequently between fifteen and eighteen months, almost all kids begin having regular tantrums. According to pediatrician T. Berry Brazelton, toddler temper tantrums are perfectly normal and are the result of the child's "inner turmoil."

One of the major sources of turmoil is the frustration that results from the child's inability to use his limited verbal skills to express his specific needs and wants. Generally speaking, the more verbal the child (hence the better able to explain his needs), the less he'll be frustrated and the fewer tantrums he'll have. Many kids, however, are frustrated by their body's inability to respond to their mind's rather sophisticated requests or desires.

Either way, frustrations build up over the course of a day or two until the child finally is no longer able to control herself and explodes. Just to put this into perspective, consider this: nearly 15 percent of twelve-month-olds and 20 percent of twenty-four-month-olds have two or more tantrums *per day.*

Besides frustration, of course, there are a variety of other factors that may account for tantrums:

♦ Your child is trying to assert herself. She may feel she's lost your attention and will do whatever it takes to get it back.

♦ She may be frightened at how angry her frustrations make her, and may be trying to attract your attention, hoping you'll help her regain control over her life and emotions.

♦ Illness, hunger, exhaustion, overstimulation.

♦ Too much discipline. You may have set too many limits, laid down too many rigid or inconsistent rules.

♦ Not enough discipline. You may have imposed too few rules or established erratic or inconsistent limits. Tantrums may be, in a sense, a plea for more effective limit setting.

- Temperament. Low-frustration-tolerance, slow-adaptability kids are much more susceptible to tantrums (see pages 73–79 for a discussion of temperament). This susceptibility to tantrums can also result in parent-child personality clashes.
- Family stress. Divorce, separation, or even a major change in work schedule or lifestyle can be tough for kids to deal with.

WHAT TO DO ABOUT THEM

When your child is in the midst of a tantrum, he is no longer a member of the human race. So reasoning, shouting, hitting, and punishment will have little (if any) effect. Here are a few things that may work to minimize the tantrum and its effect on everyone:

- Don't panic. That's just what your child is trying to get you to do. If you get upset and rant, you'll only make things worse.
- Use humor. Say something completely silly. If that doesn't work, get down on the floor and thrash around in your own tantrum. This may snap him out of it by showing him how ridiculous a tantrum looks.
- Walk away. In many circumstances, no audience equals no performance.

Breath Holding/Passing Out

Starting at about eighteen months, babies who have finished in the top 10 percent of Tantrums 101 are invited to get advanced training, this time in how to scare the hell out of their parents by holding their breath and passing out.

The bad news about breath holding is that it is incredibly frightening (how could a child's turning blue and keeling over *not* be?). But the good news is that besides taking ten years off your life, it isn't all that dangerous. What usually happens is that the child starts to cry, takes a huge breath— and holds it. If he holds it long enough, he may lose consciousness, but the moment he does, he'll start breathing immediately and usually recover within seconds.

So why do kids really hold their breath? "When all else seems to fail in battling for control," says temperament researcher Jim Cameron, "holding one's breath becomes the ultimate stronghold—no one can make you breathe."

Breath holding is more common among active, intense, slow-adapting-to-change toddlers (see pages 73–79 for more on this). According to Cameron, "The more energetic they are, the less they want to stop what they're doing or to shift to things you want them to do." In addition, since active kids spend

♦ Stand firm. If the tantrum is the result of some disciplinary measure, tell your child that the rule still stands and will continue to do so until he calms down.

♦ Explain. Say things like, "I know you're upset because you really wanted to read that story. . . ."

♦ Time out. If things are really getting out of hand, put the child by himself someplace and explain (privately) that he won't be able to be with other people until he calms down. Again, the no-audience-equals-no-performance theory applies here.

♦ Protect your child. Kicking, swinging, and throwing things can hurt not only other people but the child as well. Holding him firmly but calmly often calms an out-of-control kid.

♦ *After* the tantrum, reassure the child that you're still there for him, that you still love him. But *do not* reward him for stopping.

more time practicing large motor skills (running, crawling, and so on) than other kids, the joy of doing these things is greater. "They can become addicted to the pleasure of imposing their newfound abilities in any possible situation so they don't want to stop," says Cameron. They also may be a little behind in verbal skills, making it harder for them to argue with you.

If your child has started holding, or trying to hold, his breath, some special handling is required:

- Give him extra time to adjust to change. Instead of one ten-minute warning, give notice at ten, five, three, and one minute.
- Don't react intensely to your child's reactions. The bigger your reaction, the more likely your child will make breath-holding a regular part of his anger routine. Also, don't become overly permissive out of fear of triggering another breath-holding episode.
- Talk, talk, talk. Encourage your child to use words. As frightening as these fits are, they won't last forever. The more verbal your child becomes, the faster they'll fade.
- Do not attempt to "shock" your child back to reality by slapping him or throwing water in his face. According to Cameron, this can "leave a kid feeling defeated and helpless, feelings which can lead to other problems later on." Instead, hold your child.

WHAT *NOT* TO DO

- Don't shout. Any big reaction proves that the tantrum was the right approach.
- Don't try to argue with a kid who's in the middle of a tantrum. You'll be wasting your breath.
- No physical punishment. Another waste of time, since most of the time your child isn't in control of the tantrum anyway.
- Don't give in. Doing so offers kids conclusive evidence that tantrums do, indeed, work.

HOW TO PREVENT THEM

There's nothing you can do to prevent tantrums completely. But there are a few preemptive steps you can take that should greatly reduce the frequency and severity of these little outbursts:

- Be a reliable source of help and support.
- Know—and pay close attention to—your child's temperament (see pages 73–79). Don't try to force an irregular child to be regular, or a slow-to-warm child to warm quickly.
- Give your child plenty of opportunities throughout the day to let off steam—physical play, running around, and so forth—as well as some occasional periods without rules (or with as few as possible).
- Encourage your child to talk about the things that make him angry. And be supportive and empathetic when he does.
- Make sure your child gets enough food and sleep. Shortages of either can make kids cranky and more susceptible to having tantrums.
- Think carefully before you say no. Is what you're rejecting really that big a deal? Giving in—perhaps partially, with some conditions or time limits—can give kids more control, thus reducing tantrum possibilities.
- Compromise as much as possible. Offering a *firm* "two more minutes," gives the child a lot more control than insisting on his doing what you want him to do immediately.
- Avoid yes/no questions and open questions ("Which pair of socks do you want to wear?"). Give choices instead: "Do you want the red ones or the blue ones?"
- Compliment good behavior regularly. Tell your child you understand that doing some things is hard and frustrating, but that you appreciate his efforts.

Public Tantrums

Sometimes I'm absolutely convinced that my children subscribe to some kind of special, underground newsletter filled with super-secret techniques they can use to drive adults nuts. And I'm sure one of the most popular features is "Tantrums in the Produce Section, or 25 Surefire Ways to Embarrass Your Parents into Giving You What You Want NOW!"

Besides the techniques described above, there are a few special ways of handling public tantrums:

- Isolation. Take the child to the bathroom, outside, to the car—anywhere you and he can be more or less alone.
- Ignore the audience. You'll be mortified at what your child is doing—and even more mortified at what spectators will think *you're* doing to the child. If your child is particularly theatrical, he's liable to attract quite a crowd. If the peanut gallery gets overly aggressive or hostile, Brazelton suggests that you ask for volunteers to take over for you.

"Rachel! *If you can't even stay focused on spreading* peat *moss, how do you expect to get into* law *school?*"

♦ Give clear, concise warnings. "Daddy and Mommy are going out later, and Grandpa will be baby-sitting. We'll be there when you wake up." Or, "Five more minutes, then we have to start cleaning up." I've found that setting a timer helps a lot: "When the buzzer goes off, we'll have to . . ."

Temperament

As we discussed in *TNF I*, pages 89–96, your child's temperament will remain fairly constant throughout his life. But now that he's no longer an infant, you should take a look at the kind of emotional and behavioral characteristics you're likely to see in the toddler years.

The nine basic temperament traits we covered in that volume are pretty much the same. However, because your child's emotions are so much more sophisticated than they were a year ago, I've taken the advice of the folks at the Center for Human Development in Oregon and divided the Sensitivity category into two related but separate categories: Emotional Sensitivity and Sensory Awareness. The ten categories they suggest are outlined on pages 74–77.

The Ten Temperament Traits of Toddlers

1. **Approach/Withdrawal:** Your child's initial reactions to new experiences, meeting new people, tasting new foods, being in new situations, and so on.

APPROACHING TODDLERS
- are the opposite of shy
- lack fear in potentially dangerous situations
- may be friendly with strangers
- separate easily from parents; may get lost in crowds or stores
- may be impulsive
- approach new situations with great interest

WITHDRAWING TODDLERS
- are usually shy
- need time to warm up to new experiences
- say they don't like things before trying them
- may be picky—eating only certain foods, playing with only certain toys
- usually have difficulty separating from parents
- show fear in seemingly safe situations
- are cautious
- hesitate before investigating strange sounds
- stand back and watch when first entering a playground

2. **Adaptability:** Similar to Approach/Withdrawal, but deals with your child's longer-term reactions to changes in routines or expectations, new places, or new ideas.

FAST-ADAPTING TODDLERS
- are usually compliant
- tend to "go with the flow" when new changes are imposed
- may lack assertiveness
- like change and may get bored when there isn't enough change taking place
- can be compliant with peer pressure

SLOW-ADAPTING TODDLERS
- often refuse to comply with almost anything
- need time to adjust to imposed transitions and ideas
- like to follow their own agendas, and can be bossy and stubborn
- may be quick to anger and slow to get over being angry
- get "locked in" on what they are doing
- may be judgmental
- protest loudly against taking medicine
- may have trouble getting to sleep in unfamiliar places

3. **Intensity:** Your child's overall volume level, both when happy or unhappy.

LOW-INTENSITY TODDLERS
♦ are "hard to read"—they have emotions, but it is difficult for others to notice
♦ may seem apathetic
♦ are sometimes mistakenly viewed as uninvolved, low in motivation or intelligence

HIGH-INTENSITY TODDLERS
♦ put a lot of energy into their emotional expressions
♦ shout instead of speaking
♦ may scream so loudly it hurts your ears
♦ are emphatic in voice and physical gesturing
♦ have intense reactions to new toys

4. **Mood:** Your child's dominant outlook—optimistic or pessimistic—over the course of a typical day.

POSITIVE-MOOD TODDLERS
♦ are rarely bothered by anything
♦ can be described as happy-go-lucky
♦ may lack seriousness
♦ may be easily taken advantage of
♦ tend to trust easily
♦ expect goodness/success

NEGATIVE-MOOD TODDLERS
♦ are often in a negative mood, angry, depressed, disappointed, and so on
♦ unlikely to be conned
♦ may be skeptical
♦ extend trust slowly
♦ expect the worst
♦ complain when given a bath
♦ don't like traveling in a car or stroller
♦ cry often and easily

5. **Activity level:** Your child's overall preference for active or inactive play; his overall energy level throughout the day.

LOW-ACTIVITY TODDLERS
♦ may take a long time to complete tasks
♦ may avoid activities that require a lot of physical energy
♦ may dislike active family pastimes
♦ may nag parents to keep them entertained
♦ seem to absorb a lot of info by watching quietly

HIGH-ACTIVITY TODDLERS
♦ are often extremely active—running wildly, talking incessantly
♦ are usually *not* clinically hyperactive
♦ may be aggressive during play
♦ are often fidgety or restless
♦ may, however, be able to sit quietly in front of video or TV for extended period
♦ have to be watched carefully to prevent accidents

(continued on page 76)

6. **Regularity:** The day-to-day predictability of your child's basic biological functions: hunger, sleep, and elimination. Each should be rated on its own scale.

HIGHLY REGULAR TODDLERS
+ may be easy to train if bowels are predictable
+ adjust easily to regular eating and bedtime schedules
+ are so regular you can set your clock by them
+ struggle with changes in eating and sleeping routines

IRREGULAR TODDLERS
+ may be difficult to potty train
+ have bedtime struggles due to irregularity in sleep patterns
+ may not be hungry at meals, but want food at a different time every day
+ have highly irregular sleep/nap patterns

7. **Emotional Sensitivity:** The ease or difficulty with which a child responds emotionally to a situation. This trait has two subcategories: one for sensitivity to his own feelings, and one for sensitivity to others' feelings.

EMOTIONALLY INSENSITIVE TODDLERS
+ rarely display emotions
+ can be "instigators" who like to start a little trouble now and then
+ can be budding con artists who enjoy manipulating a situation to their advantage
+ can have what seems to be a mean or cruel streak
+ often are oblivious to others' feelings
+ don't seem bothered by others' insensitive behavior

EMOTIONALLY SENSITIVE TODDLERS
+ tend to be fearful
+ get upset when teased
+ are sensitive to how others are treated
+ seem particularly tuned in to others' feelings
+ may worry a lot
+ may cry easily
+ may be "people pleasers"
+ get their feelings hurt easily

8. **Sensory Awareness:** Your toddler's sensitivity in each of his sensory areas: pain, touch, taste, smell, hearing, and sight. Each channel is rated on a separate scale. *Note:* it's quite possible for a child to be very aware in some areas and quite unaware in others.

LOW-SENSORY-AWARENESS TODDLERS
+ may have dull senses
+ can miss a lot of things going on around them—they just don't seem to notice
+ can have excellent concentration; aren't distracted by sensory input

HIGH-SENSORY-AWARENESS TODDLERS
+ may have sharp senses
+ may be distracted by sensory input
+ can be picky, finicky, or particular
+ sometimes complain about things others don't notice, such as temperature changes or itchy clothes

9. Distractibility: The ease with which your toddler is distracted by all the things going on around him.

LOW-DISTRACTIBILITY TODDLERS
♦ tend to stick with tasks until they are completed
♦ often have terrific memories
♦ may become caught up in their own world, not noticing things going on around them
♦ can be excellent naggers who challenge the parents' ability to not give in
♦ when upset, can be calmed by only one or two people

HIGH-DISTRACTIBILITY TODDLERS
♦ have short attention spans
♦ notice things easily
♦ may have trouble concentrating on complex tasks
♦ may leave belongings scattered everywhere
♦ tend to be forgetful
♦ when learning something new, will stop when hearing people or sounds

---

10. Persistence: Similar to Distractibility, but goes beyond the initial reaction and concerns the length of time your child will continue to make an effort—even when the task gets hard.

HIGH-PERSISTENCE TODDLERS
♦ rarely give up on difficult tasks
♦ take on challenges well beyond their skill level
♦ sometimes persist at things that are unimportant
♦ may tend to do things the hard way because they don't like to ask for help
♦ may take things too seriously
♦ may be perfectionists
♦ may have long attention spans
♦ may want to stick with a game long, long, long after you're ready to quit

LOW-PERSISTENCE TODDLERS
♦ are frustrated easily, even by simple tasks
♦ may throw tantrums in response to frustration
♦ if interrupted, won't return to original task
♦ may get angry and give up
♦ may demand help from parents, grandparents, and other caregivers
♦ may struggle to master self-care skills such as toilet learning and dressing
♦ tend to stick with things they are naturally good at, and can look highly persistent when not frustrated
♦ tend to "let go" easily
♦ won't play in playground for more than five minutes at a stretch

Again, because your child is far more sophisticated than a year ago, the rating system is too. Here's the rating scale suggested by the Center for Human Development.

TRAIT	RATING		
APPROACH/WITHDRAWAL	Outgoing	1 2 3 4 5	Slow-to-warm
What is your child's first and usual reaction to new people, situations, places?			
ADAPTABILITY	Easy-going	1 2 3 4 5	Strong-willed
Does your child adapt quickly to new ideas, new places, changes in routine or schedule?			
INTENSITY	Mild reactions	1 2 3 4 5	Dramatic reactions
How loud or physically dramatic is your child when expressing strong feelings?			
MOOD	Happy-go-lucky	1 2 3 4 5	Serious, displeased
Is your child primarily an optimist or a pessimist? Lighthearted or serious?			
ACTIVITY LEVEL	Calm and slow-moving	1 2 3 4 5	Wild and quick-moving
Left to his own devices, would your child be on the go or idle?			
REGULARITY			
Hunger	Wants food at same time every day	1 2 3 4 5	Irregular eater
Sleep	Tired on schedule	1 2 3 4 5	No schedule
Toileting	BMs at same time every day	1 2 3 4 5	Try and guess
Does your child normally eat, go to bed, wake up, and have bowel movements at the same time every day?			
EMOTIONAL SENSITIVITY			
Own feelings	Unaware of emotions	1 2 3 4 5	Feels emotions strongly
Others' feelings	Doesn't notice others' feelings	1 2 3 4 5	Highly sensitive to others' feelings
Does your child often get upset over nothing, or does he rarely get upset even when circumstances suggest that he could? Does your child feel sympathy or empathy for others?			

TRAIT		RATING	
SENSORY AWARENESS			
Pain	What nail in my foot?	1 2 3 4 5	EEEOOWWWWHH!!
Touch	No reaction to contact	1 2 3 4 5	Easily irritated or pleased by contact
Taste	Can't make subtle distinctions	1 2 3 4 5	Notices tiny variations
Smell	Doesn't notice odors	1 2 3 4 5	Human bloodhound
Hearing/Sound	Noise is no problem	1 2 3 4 5	Sensitive to sounds
Vision/Lights	Visually sensitive	1 2 3 4 5	Visually insensitive
DISTRACTIBILITY	Not easily diverted	1 2 3 4 5	Easily diverted

Is your child very aware and easily distracted by noises and people? Can you distract him from upset feelings by redirecting his attention?

PERSISTENCE		Hard to stop	1 2 3 4 5	Stops easily

Does your child stick with things even when frustrated? Can he stop an activity when asked to?

After you've evaluated your toddler, take a quick look at your own temperament and see how the two of you compare. If you'd like a much more detailed analysis of your child's temperament, contact Temperament Talk (see Resources guide, page 217).

What Are Daddies Made Of?

What's Going On with the Baby

Physically

+ Now that your toddler has fairly good control over her legs, she's decided to use them all the time.
+ She runs (but still has some problems slowing down and turning corners), jumps forward with both feet, kicks a ball without stepping on it, rarely falls anymore, stands on her tiptoes, climbs stairs by herself (holding on to a railing), can push herself along in a toy car, and may even be able to pedal a small tricycle.
+ And she hasn't forgotten about her arms and hands: she draws nicely controlled straight lines, throws a ball into a basket, makes beautiful mud pies, spends hours opening and closing screw-top containers, can put together more complex puzzles, and still stacks, piles, tears, and pours anything she can get her hands on. She can even unzip her pants (but can't zip them up), and can put her shoes on (but can't lace them).

Intellectually

+ Although time still doesn't mean much to her, she's learned about sequences (first we'll put on your shoes, then we'll go for a walk), and can differentiate between "one" and "many" (although she'll probably say "two" for anything above one).
+ She's expanding her knowledge of spatial concepts—climbing into boxes, climbing (or being held) as high as possible, pouring things back and forth.

- She now thinks through possible solutions to problems instead of physically acting them out. For example, if an object is out of reach, she won't jump up to get it and probably won't try to knock it down with a stick. Instead, she'll bring a chair over, climb up, and grab what she wants.
- She's learning to tell the difference between animate and inanimate. She spends a lot of time staring at and comparing objects that move by themselves (dogs, people, fish) and those that need some outside intervention (blocks, bikes).
- She still has a tendency to regard everything—animate or not—as her personal property.
- She also deliberately imitates your every activity (sweeping, washing dishes, brushing teeth), but *only while you're there with her.*

Verbally

- She uses longer, more complex sentences and is beginning to use language in situations where she once used emotions: she'll ask for desired objects by name and say "change my diaper" instead of crying.
- She also delights in the power that naming objects gives her, and labels everything she possibly can.
- She likes nursery rhymes and, if you pause for a few seconds, she'll fill in the last word of a couplet ("Hickory, dickory, dock/ The mouse ran up the _____"). And if you're reading a familiar book and make a mistake, she won't let you get away with it.
- She's tightening her grasp on pronouns, correctly using "I," "mine," "his," and "hers." But she may get confused when trying to use two pronouns in the same sentence: "I want to do it yourself," for example.

Emotionally/Socially

- The contrary, negative, temper-tantrum phase is passing, and your toddler is getting more cheerful and more cooperative. She'll come when you call her and may even put away some of her toys (if you ask really, really nicely).
- Nevertheless, she's still easily frustrated, often to tears, by the internal conflict between independence and dependence. She still walks away from you but comes flying back for reassurance that you're still there; she truly wants to please you by doing the "right thing," but she still needs to test your limits by disobeying.
- Perhaps as a result of this conflict, your toddler is also developing a lot of fears of things she may have loved before: night, dogs, bugs, vacuum cleaners.

She may also be getting more fearful of things that she was only slightly afraid of before: loud noises, big trucks, and people (especially doctors).

♦ She's developing a wider range of emotions: she's now quite affectionate with her friends, family, stuffed animals, and even pictures in books. She loves to "baby" her dolls (and even her parents), covering them with blankets and putting them to "bed." Her whole body lights up when praised and her feelings are genuinely hurt when criticized.

What You're Going Through

Your Changing Identity

There's an old saying in the Talmud that a man has three names: the one his parents gave him at birth, the one that others call him, and the one he calls himself. A person's identity, according to the rabbis, is a rather amorphous thing. What the rabbis don't talk about is that all three of those names are subject to change over time—especially the one you give yourself. The way you view yourself today may have nothing to do with how you'll see yourself tomorrow.

This point is nicely illustrated by what family researchers Phil and Carolyn Cowan call the "pie chart." Over a period of nearly two years, the Cowans asked a large number of men to draw a circle and divide it up into sections that reflect how important each aspect of their life actually felt—not simply the amount of time in the role.

Over the duration of the study, "Men who remained childless showed a significant increase in the 'partner/lover' aspect," said the Cowans. "New fathers, however, were squeezing 'partner/lover' into a smaller space to accommodate the significant increase in the 'parent' piece of the pie."

The Ambivalent Father

Over the course of my writing career, I've written only a few things that I'm not sure I want my kids to see, and this section is one of them. But you can read it if you promise not to tell them.

Throughout this book (and the others in the series) we've talked a lot about the joys, anxieties, fears, and intense feelings of love that are all part of being a father. If you're like most men, the experience—despite the ups and downs—has been overwhelmingly positive, and you wouldn't trade it for anything. In fact, being a dad has become such an integral part of your life that you probably can't imagine *not* being one.

But one day, completely out of the blue, you'll look at your child and realize that the intense love you felt just the day before has been replaced by a numb, hollow feeling. And the delight you took in raising her and being part of her life has been supplanted by complete and utter ambivalence. You're feeling overburdened, underappreciated, and you can hardly remember the last time you had a conversation with someone who knows more than forty words. You feel like chucking this whole dad thing and starting a new life somewhere else, as far away from your kids as you can get.

Most of the time these feelings of ambivalence last only a few minutes or a few hours. Sometimes they go on for days or even weeks. But no matter how long they last, one thing is pretty much guaranteed: the instant after the ambivalence starts you'll get hit by feelings of guilt, guilt for having had the ambivalence in the first place. And it'll stick around long after the ambivalence is gone. After all, goes the internal monologue, if I'm not a completely committed father 100 percent of the time, I must not be cut out for the job at all.

Most mothers are quite familiar with this little ambivalence/guilt pattern. But because they are generally more willing to discuss their worries and concerns with other mothers, they learn rather quickly that it's perfectly normal. They still feel bad about it or maybe even scared, but at least they know they're not alone.

Men, on the other hand, don't learn this lesson. If we have a few other fathers with whom we can talk things over, we're incredibly lucky. But it's still pretty unlikely that we'll actually talk to them about *this*. It's already hard enough to ask for advice about diaper changing, discipline, or nutrition. But having ambivalent feelings is a serious weakness, perhaps a character flaw (or at least it sure seems like one). And we're certainly not going to expose any weaknesses or character flaws to another man who would just laugh anyway.

Hopefully just reading this section has been enough to convince you—at least a little—that your changing feelings toward your children are completely normal. If you're still worried, though, or if you need more reassurance, force yourself to spend a few minutes talking to someone about what you're feeling— a close friend, your clergyman, you therapist, even your partner (it's going to be harder to talk to her, but at least she'll know exactly what you're talking about). And remember this: you're going to have these feelings dozens of times throughout the course of your fatherhood. So you'd better start getting used to dealing with them now.

"How do you expect me to parent if you won't child?"

You and Your Baby

Identifying Your Parenting Style

So you've been a dad for almost two years, and you've probably noticed that the way you parent is quite a bit different from the way your parents parented. You may also do things much differently than your friends and perhaps even your partner. Sure, everyone has a unique parenting style. But according to Diana Baumrind, a sociologist at the University of California at Berkeley, almost all of them fall into three basic categories: authoritarian, authoritative, and permissive. The chart on pages 86–89 describes these three styles.

Discipline Ideas

- ♦ **Be firm.** Set reasonable limits, explain them, and enforce them.
- ♦ **Be consistent.** Your child will learn to adapt to inconsistencies between you and your partner; if you allow jumping on the bed but she doesn't, for example, the child will do it when he's with you and won't when he's with your partner (see pages 53–55 for more on dealing with disagreements). But if you allow jumping one day and prohibit it the next, you'll only

confuse your child and undermine your attempts to get him to listen when you ask him to do something.

♦ **Compromise.** Kids can't always tell the difference between big and little issues. So give in on a few small things once in a while (an extra piece of birthday cake at the end of a long day might avoid a tantrum). That will give the child a feeling of control and will make it easier for him to go along with the program on the bigger issues (holding hands while crossing the street, for example).

♦ **Be assertive and specific.** "Stop throwing your food now" is much better than "Cut that out!"

♦ **Give choices.** Kathryn Kvols, author of *Redirecting Children's Behavior*, suggests that if your child is, for example, yanking all the books off a shelf in the living room, you say, "Would you like to stop knocking the books off the shelf or would you like to go to your room?" If he ignores you, gently but firmly lead the child to his room and tell him he can come back into the living room when he's ready to listen to you.

♦ **Cut down on the warnings.** If the child knows the rules (at this age, all you have to do is ask), impose the promised consequences immediately. If you make a habit of giving six preliminary warnings and three "last" warnings before doing anything, your child will learn to start responding only the eighth or ninth time you ask.

♦ **Link consequences directly to the problem behavior.** And don't forget to explain—clearly and simply—what you're doing and why: "I'm taking away your hammer because you hit me," or "I asked you not to take that egg out of the fridge and you didn't listen to me. Now you'll have to help me clean it up."

♦ **No banking.** If you're imposing punishments or consequences, do it immediately. You can't punish a child at the end of the day for something (or a bunch of things) he did earlier—he won't associate the undesirable action with its consequence.

♦ **Keep it short.** Once the punishment is over (and whatever it is, it shouldn't last any more than a minute per year of age), get back to your life. There's no need to review, summarize, or make sure the child got the point.

♦ **Stay calm.** Screaming, ranting, or raving can easily cross the line into verbal abuse, which can do long-term damage to your child's self-esteem.

♦ **Get down to your child's level.** When you're talking to your child— especially to criticize—kneel or sit. You'll still be big enough for him to have no doubt who the boss is.

♦ **Don't lecture.** Instead, ask questions to engage the child in a discussion

PARENTING STYLE The parents . . .	AUTHORITARIAN (THE BOSS) ♦ Are frequently uncompromising, dictatorial, strict, and repressive. ♦ Attempt to shape, control, and evaluate the behavior and attitudes of the child in accordance with some kind of absolute (often theologically motivated) standard.
The child . . .	♦ Must obey.
The power . . .	♦ Is with the parent.
Life at home can be . . .	♦ Tense ♦ Rigid ♦ Oppressive
Discipline tools	♦ Parents value obedience as a virtue and favor punitive, forceful measures to curb self-will at points when the child's actions or beliefs conflict with what parents think is correct conduct. ♦ yelling ♦ commanding ♦ ordering ♦ rewarding ♦ punishing ♦ bribing ♦ threatening

AUTHORITATIVE (THE GUIDE, THE LEADER)	PERMISSIVE (THE SERVANT, THE BYSTANDER)
◆ Are approachable, reasonable, and flexible. ◆ Attempt "to direct the child's activities but in a rational, issue-oriented manner," says Baumrind. ◆ Don't regard themselves as infallible or divinely inspired.	◆ Are often passive, weak, inconsistent, and yielding. ◆ Consult with the child too much about policy decisions and give too many explanations for family rules. ◆ Don't ask the child to clean or take on many household responsibilities. ◆ Allow the child to regulate his own activities as much as possible.
◆ Is encouraged to think and to be a participant in the family.	◆ Is subtly encouraged to control others. ◆ Is left to follow his own wants and instincts.
◆ Is shared between parent and child.	◆ Is firmly in the hands of the child.
◆ Relaxed ◆ Orderly ◆ Consistent	◆ Chaotic ◆ Uncontrollable ◆ Wild
◆ Parents exert firm control at points of parent-child divergence but do not hem the child in with restrictions. ◆ Parents use reason as well as power to achieve objectives. ◆ requests ◆ incentives ◆ consequences ◆ negotiation ◆ conflict resolution ◆ family councils	◆ Parents try not to exercise control and don't encourage the child to obey externally defined standards. ◆ Parents are tolerant and accepting toward child's impulses, using as little punishment as possible ◆ pleading ◆ waiting and wishing ◆ giving up and doing nothing

(continued on page 88)

(continued from page 87)

PARENTING STYLE	AUTHORITARIAN (THE BOSS)
The effect on the child	♦ Associated with low levels of independence and social responsibility as well as lower cognitive competence.
	♦ Negatively associated with good grades.
	♦ Child learns to obey out of fear of punishment.
	♦ Child learns to subvert and manipulate underhandedly.
	♦ Child is so used to being controlled that he doesn't learn to develop self-control, and as a result can often be unruly and uncooperative when parents aren't present.
The parent-child relationship	♦ Cold, rigid, and based on fear.
	♦ Verbal interchange between parent and child is discouraged. Instead, children are taught to blindly accept the parents' word on the way things ought to be.

of the problematic behavior: "Is smoking cigars okay for kids or not?" "Do you like it when someone pushes you down in the park?"

♦ **Criticize the behavior, not the child.** Even such seemingly innocuous comments as, "I've told you a thousand times . . ." or "Every single time you . . ." gives the child the message that he's doomed to disappoint you no matter what he does.

♦ **Reinforce positive behavior.** We spend too much time criticizing negatives and not enough time complimenting the positives. Heartfelt comments, like "I'm so proud of you when I see you cleaning up your toys," go a long way.

♦ **Play games.** "Let's see who can put the most toys away" and "I bet I can put

AUTHORITATIVE (THE GUIDE, THE LEADER)	PERMISSIVE (THE SERVANT, THE BYSTANDER)
♦ Positively associated with independent, purposive, dominant behavior.	♦ Associated with lack of impulse control and social responsibility, as well as low levels of independence and self-reliance.
♦ Positively associated with good grades.	♦ Negatively associated with good grades.
♦ Child develops self-discipline.	♦ Lower social and cognitive com- petence.
♦ Child is able to focus on the needs of the group.	♦ Child becomes self-centered and demanding.
	♦ Child doesn't learn the importance of consideration of others or of the needs of the group.
	♦ Child develops little self-control.
♦ Close, respectful, and marked by sharing and communication.	♦ Distant and often marked by resentment and manipulation.
♦ Parents encourage "verbal give and take, and share with the child the reasoning behind the policy."	♦ Parents make few demands for mature behavior and without limits the child can feel unloved and uncared for.
♦ Encourages the child's independence and individuality.	
♦ Recognizes the rights of both parents and children.	

my shoes on before you can" are favorites. But be sure *not* to put away more toys or to put your shoes on first—kids under five have a tough time losing.

♦ **Avoid tantrums.** See pages 68–73 for some tips.

♦ **No spanking.** See pages 92–93.

♦ **No shaking.** It may seem like a less violent way of expressing your frustra- tions than spanking, but it really isn't. Shaking your baby can make his little brain rattle around inside his skull, possibly resulting in brain damage.

♦ **No bribes.** It's tempting to pay a child off to get him to do or not do some- thing. But the risk—and it's a big one—is that he will demand some kind of payment before complying with just about anything.

♦ **Be a grown-up.** Biting your child or pulling his hair to demonstrate that biting or hitting is wrong or doesn't feel good will backfire. Guaranteed.

♦ **Offer cheese with that whine.** Tell your child that you simply don't respond to whining and that you won't give him what he wants until he asks in a nice way—and stick with it.

♦ **Set a good example.** If your child sees you and your partner arguing without violence, he'll learn to do the same. If he sees you flouting authority by running red lights, he'll do the same.

Discipline and Temperament

Naturally, not every approach to discipline will work equally well with every child. And one of the best ways to improve your chances of finding the right approach for your child is to take his temperament into consideration. Here are some of Jim Cameron's temperament-specific discipline tips:

♦ Energetic, slow-adapting kids need to have some areas in which they can practice their assertiveness. They need limits that are clear and consistent but reasonable and flexible (you may have to state the rule a few times, but he'll come around eventually). Too many limits will result in battles of will; too few will result in your being afraid of him all the time. It's especially tough for these kids to follow instructions in the evening, so keep them calm by reading or watching a video instead of wrestling.

♦ Slow-adapting kids are likely to protest just about everything you ask for, and it's awfully easy to interpret their foot-dragging as rebellion or as an attack on your authority. If you respond immediately with anger, your child will come to anticipate your anger and will resist even more. So instead, give several firm warnings, starting well in advance. Parents of slow-adapting kids sometimes just give in out of frustration or lash out with severe punishments, feel guilty, and become overly permissive again. "For slow-adapting children, loss of control over their own world [getting sent to their rooms] is the most effective punishment there is," says Cameron.

♦ Moderate-activity, moderate-frustration-tolerance kids have lots of tantrums. They want something, you don't give it to them, and they're off. . . . Their goal, of course, is to get you to give in. Don't. (See pages 68–73 for more on handling and preventing tantrums.)

♦ Moderate-activity, fast-adapting kids need to know exactly what the rules are and where the lines are drawn. Too many limits and they'll be frustrated by the lack of freedom. Too few and they'll run wild.

♦ Irregular, withdrawing kids are, not surprisingly, tough, and your expecta-

"Sure I'm bad. I'm a prisoner of my genes!"

tions are the key. Expecting your child to stay in his room at night is fine, but expecting him to stay in his bed or to go to sleep right away is a waste of time. The key here is to make repeated and firm requests for compliance. And try not to take your child's initial "deafness" as a personal affront.

Sexism and Punishment

It's all too easy to fall into the trap of treating boys and girls differently. And the way parents discipline their children is no exception. For example, boys are far more likely to be spanked, whereas girls are more likely to be sent to their rooms.

At the same time, parents—especially fathers—of girls are sometimes "overly involved with their daughters in ways that excessively protect them from experiences of failure, provide excessive direction, and generally inhibit their autonomy," says fatherhood researcher John Snarey.

You can take a major step toward reducing sexism by trying really, really hard to treat boys and girls the same way. This *doesn't* mean spanking your daughter or inhibiting your son's autonomy. In fact, you should do just the opposite—send your son to his room and give your daughter more freedom.

Spanking

A recent survey by *Child* magazine found that 37 percent of parents discipline their toddlers several times a day, and 27 percent discipline their child in public several times a week. It's not all that surprising, then, that 39 percent of parents spank their kids "often or sometimes" and 20 percent slap their kids' hands often or sometimes.

The big question, of course, is, "Does spanking do any good?" If you want to attract the child's attention in a hurry, the answer is yes. But if you're interested in any long-term positive effect, the answer is a resounding no. In fact, there's plenty of evidence that the long-term effect of spanking children is quite negative. (It's worth noting here that of the people polled in the *Child* magazine survey, only 4 percent felt that spanking was an effective way to get kids to be good.)

Basically, researchers confirm just what you might expect: spanking children does little more than teach them to resort to violence and aggression to solve their problems—not exactly the message most parents want to get across to their kids.

I still remember very clearly a scene that took place a few years ago at a bus stop not far from my house. A rather agitated woman was trying to keep her two kids—about five and seven years old—from fighting: "How many

Family Matters

The Old College Try

We all know it's going to cost a ton of money to send a child to college (realistic projections often exceed $200,000 for four years at a good school). But too many of us look at all those zeros and panic, thinking we're going to have to write a check to pay for the whole thing. My wife and I bought our house for about that amount (and in California, where $200,000 doesn't buy much) and never thought for a second of paying for the whole thing in cash.

So how *do* you finance your kid's education? Traditionally, parents have opened savings accounts in their children's names as a way of putting money aside for the child's education. However, according to financial author and counselor Eric Tyson, this is "usually a financial mistake of major proportions in the short- and long-term." The solution? Start socking away money—*into your own retirement account.* Sound a little counterintuitive? Well, here's a wonderful analogy Tyson uses to explain:

times," she said, smacking the older child, "do I have to [smack] tell you [smack] not to hit [smack] your brother [smack]?" Any guesses about where that little boy learned to hit his brother?

Author Doug Spangler suggests that fathers who spank their children are sending some very specific messages:

♦ It's okay to hit another person.
♦ It's okay to hit another person who is smaller than you.
♦ It's okay to hit someone you love.
♦ It's okay to hit someone when you feel angry and frustrated.
♦ Physical aggression is normal and acceptable under any circumstances.
♦ Daddy can't control himself or his temper.
♦ Fathers are to be feared.
♦ Children must always be quiet around their fathers.

Research also shows that children who get spanked are more likely to suffer from poor self-esteem and depression, and have a greater chance of accepting lower-paying jobs as adults. While this may not be a direct cause-and-effect relationship, there is clearly some correlation between being spanked and poor self-esteem.

If you were paying attention to the flight attendant before taking off on your last airplane trip, you'll remember that if those oxygen masks drop from the ceiling, you're supposed to put *yours* on first, *then* your child's, right? The idea is that if *you* can't breathe, you certainly won't be able to help anyone else. Tyson makes the same basic point about money: take care of *your* finances first—especially your IRA, 401(k), Keogh, or company-sponsored retirement— and your whole family will be better off.

But that still doesn't clear up the problem of how feathering your own personal retirement account instead of starting a college fund in your child's name will help put her through college. Well, here's how it works:

♦ Money you invest in your retirement accounts is often at least partially tax-deductible and always grows tax-free until you start withdrawing it. The dollars you invest in an account in your child's name are after-tax dollars and any interest and dividends may be taxable as income or capital gains.
♦ At the present time, financial-aid departments usually count just about everything you own as an asset—except your retirement accounts. They assume

"I wish you'd try harder to like school, Jeremy.
It's costing Daddy a bundle"

that 35 percent of all the money held in your child's name will be available for educational purposes each year. Only about 6 percent of the money held in your name is considered available for education, and funds in your retirement accounts are not counted at all. Therefore, the less money you have in your child's name, the more financial aid you'll qualify for.

♦ Plenty of financial-aid options are available: student loans (usually available at below-market rates), grants, fellowships, work-study programs, and so forth.

♦ You can always borrow against the equity in your home.

♦ If you'll be over $59\frac{1}{2}$ by the time your child starts college, you may be able to withdraw money from your IRA or other retirement account without incurring any penalties.

Wills and Trusts

By this time, hopefully, you've got your life insurance situation under control.

If You're Planning to Pay 100 Percent of Your Child's College Expenses

Despite all this sound financial advice, you may still be intent on paying cash for college. If you've got the money—and the desire—to do so, immediately disregard the above advice and start socking money away into an account in your child's name (with you as custodian). That way, you'll be able to save at least a little on taxes: until she's fourteen, the first $1,400 or so of your child's interest and dividends will be taxed at the (presumably lower) child's rate; the rest gets taxed at your rate. After age fourteen, however, *all* her income gets taxed at the rate for a single adult.

If not, put this book down right now and call your insurance agent. And while you're waiting for him to call back, you might want to review the section on insurance in *TNF I*, pages 191–96.

Knowing that your partner and kids will be financially secure in the event of your death should make you breathe a little easier. But don't relax completely—there are a few other things you have to worry about. For example, if, God forbid, you and your partner are killed tomorrow, who's going to take care of your kids? Who's going to make sure they get the kind of education and upbringing you want them to have? And who's going to get all your stuff?

The answers to these and other horrible-but-important-to-consider questions

Doing It Yourself

Without ever having gone to law school or earned a degree in accounting, you can probably write a will or set up a living trust by yourself. There are quite a few excellent books and software packages on the market that can take you through the whole process. Several excellent ones are listed in the Resources guide (page 217).

But don't be fooled. No lawyer can throw together a will or a trust in five minutes, and neither can you. It will take hours and hours of serious work and education. So if you have a lot of money or a complicated financial situation, or if you just feel more comfortable having a professional take care of things for you, your local or state bar association can give you referrals for attorneys in your area who specialize in wills and trusts. You should also talk to a good tax or probate lawyer if you aren't absolutely sure whether you need a will or a living trust or some other instrument.

Wills

ADVANTAGES

♦ You can distribute your assets exactly as you want.
♦ There is an automatic limit on how long someone has to challenge the terms of your will (varies from state to state). According to some estimates, one in three wills is contested, so this limit could be a very good thing.
♦ Creditors must make claims within a certain amount of time (again, varies from state to state).
♦ The activities of your executors, guardians, and trustees are supervised by the court.

DISADVANTAGES

♦ Probate. This is the name for the process through which everything in a will must go before it is completely straightened out. Probate can easily last as long as eighteen months. And until it's over, your heirs won't have access to most of the assets of your estate.
♦ Court fees, attorneys' fees, executor fees, accounting fees, and so forth can eat up 3 to 7 percent (or more) of the estate.
♦ In most cases, probate files are public records. This means that anyone can go down to the courthouse and take a peek at your will.

are up to you. They're outlined in a will or a trust, or both. Unfortunately, about half of all parents with young children don't have either a will or a trust.

If you die *intestate* (meaning without a will, trust, or other document that tells how you want your assets distributed), the details will be handled according to the laws of your state. In most cases, this means that a judge will appoint a guardian for your estate and another one for your children. Chances are, neither of these guardians will be the one you would have chosen.

So which is better? A will? A trust? Actually, the answer may be both. As a new parent, you absolutely, positively need a will to designate a guardian for your child. You can also use a will to distribute your assets, but many experts feel that setting up a *revocable living trust* is a better alternative. However, because of the time and expense involved, many decline to take advantage of the living trust alternative.

Some of the advantages and disadvantages of wills and living trusts are listed above and on the facing page.

As Long as You're Thinking about Depressing Things . . .

♦ Consider a *durable power of attorney*. This document (which you'll need an

Living Trusts

ADVANTAGES

♦ The costs and time delays of probate are largely avoided. After
your death, your survivors should
have control over your assets
without involving the courts.

♦ The trust document is not public,
so no one can see it unless you
show it to them.

♦ Assets are distributed as you
wish—either directly to your
heirs upon your death or gradually over time.

♦ A living trust "not only allows
your continued total control over
your affairs during your lifetime,
but provides a continuity in
management and supervision in
the event of your incapacity,"
says attorney Harvey J. Platt.

DISADVANTAGES

♦ Trusts generally cost more and
take longer to set up than wills.
It will also probably cost you a
few dollars to transfer ownership
of your assets from you personally to the trust. However, all the
probate-related expenses that
wills require can come to about
the same amount as the cost of
setting up a trust.

♦ Improperly prepared, a living
trust can cause some serious
problems. If the IRS feels that
your trust was not properly
executed, your estate could
wind up in probate—the very
situation you were hoping
to avoid.

♦ Since all your assets are transferred during your lifetime from
your name into the name of
the trust, you are giving up
personal ownership in a lot of
what you own. This can be
tough psychologically.

♦ Trusts may not reduce your
tax liability.

attorney to help you prepare) gives someone you designate the power to
manage your affairs if you become incapacitated. You can include a health-
care directive, which covers such topics as whether or not you want to be
kept on life support if things ever come to that.

♦ Consider making some gifts. You and your partner can each transfer up to
$10,000 per year to each beneficiary tax free, thereby reducing the size of
your estate as well as the amount of estate taxes that your heirs will have to
come up with later. (Estate taxes, by the way, are usually due and payable
within nine months of death.)

24-27 MONTHS

Off to School

What's Going On with the Baby

Physically

♦ Your two-year-old seems to "think with his feet"—wandering around almost aimlessly, spending a few seconds engaged in some activity or other, then moving on to something else.

♦ He's quite comfortable with his body and its capabilities; he can run without falling down, walk up and down stairs by himself, jump off a low step, and rock or march in time to music.

♦ His hand-eye coordination is getting much better, and he's now able to make use of his blocks to build structures that are more complex than towers: houses, forts, horse corrals, long walls.

♦ Nevertheless, he still has some problems using one hand independently of the other. "If he holds out an injured finger for bandaging, he tends also to hold out his matching uninjured finger," write child development experts Louise Bates Ames and Frances Ilg.

♦ As recently as six months ago, your toddler could only focus on things pretty much right in front of his face. Now he's developing peripheral vision. He's also becoming aware of faraway objects such as planes, birds, and distant houses.

Intellectually

♦ At this stage of his development, he's not able to separate the *goal* of his actions from the *process* of achieving it. In other words, *how* he does something is just as important as *what* he does. For example, if he decides to make a painting, he's not just interested in being creative. He's equally interested in making a mess and exploring the feel of paint brush on paper. And if he clambers to the top of a climbing structure, it's as much because he likes climbing as to conquer Everest.

♦ Your child may be exhibiting what you may interpret as more aggressive behavior. But according to Ames and Ilg, many seemingly aggressive kids are not actually aggressive. "It's just that children want what they want and, if necessary, hit, push, struggle to get it."

♦ For at least the next year, your child's primary concern will be satisfying his own needs and wants. The fact that your back is killing you and you need a break is of no concern to him if he wants you to lift him into the air for the 327th time. And he's outraged that you're tired of reading him the same book over and over.

♦ His feelings of power over his surroundings are reinforced by his burgeoning language skills. "He behaves as if the words give him control over the situation . . . as if he controls his own exits and entrances by means of the magic utterance," writes Fraiberg. Now that he can say "bye-bye," he doesn't seem to mind quite as much when you leave him alone. And he's more cooperative about going to bed when he's the one telling you "night-night."

Verbally

♦ Until now, your child learned about his world *physically:* he had to touch, feel, or taste things before he could truly understand them. But from here on out, *language*—questions, answers, explanations—begins to take over as the toddler's primary means of acquiring information.

♦ Your toddler's passive vocabulary (the words he understands) now includes 200 to 500 words. His active vocabulary (the words he uses), however, consists of only 20 to 100 words.

♦ He's now using verbs ("I go to the store") and adjectives ("I'm a good boy"). His favorite word, though, is probably "again."

♦ Ames and Ilg have found that despite your toddler's quickly increasing knowledge of the language, he talks mainly to himself; second most to you and other familiar adults; and little if any to other children. Most of what comes out of his mouth is self-initiated (as opposed to being in response to something you've said).

♦ *Note:* Some two-year-olds speak in short, 3-to-5-word sentences. Others still speak one word at a time. Unless your child doesn't understand simple questions and requests, there's nothing to worry about.

Emotionally/Socially

♦ The first few months of the third year are usually happy ones for both toddler and parents. He's having fewer tantrums and is generally more cooperative than even a few months ago.

♦ Although he's still not playing *with* other kids very much, he's getting more content to play alongside them. "Several may gather around a sandbox, each scooping up his own sand," write Ames and Ilg. "They may all be doing more or less the same thing, and playing with more or less the same kind of material, and may all be in much the same place, but without much interaction."

♦ He already had a rather short attention span, but thanks (in part, at least) to his widening peripheral vision, he's even more distracted than before—after all, there are so many interesting new things crossing his field of view.

♦ After playing with their genitals for a while, boys and girls are now establishing a budding gender identity, identifying with (and becoming more attached to) the parent of the same sex.

♦ He may tell you in advance when his bowel movements are about to occur, indicating that he's finally ready to begin potty training (see pages 103–6 for more on this).

What You're Going Through

Pride—or Disappointment—in Your Child's Accomplishments

One of the best things about being a parent is that it gives you a chance to go back and do all the things you loved to do as a kid, all the things you missed out on, and all the things you did but want to do again. It's like having a second childhood.

The problem is, however, that some parents forget whose childhood it really is. Too many parents "expect their child to be their ambassador out in the world," writes the Work and Family Institute's Ellen Galinsky, believing that "what the child does reflects upon them."

Barbara and Philip Newman agree. "Parents may experience intense emotional reactions to their child's behavior," they write. "They can make you feel warm, joyful, and proud. They can make you feel furious, guilty, and disgusted. Because of the deep commitment and love most parents feel for children, their emotional reactions to a child's behavior can be especially intense. It's one thing if someone else's child is rude or selfish. But if your own child is rude or

"Do that thing you do, Billy, but this time do it the way I taught you."

selfish, intense feelings of anger, disgust, or embarrassment may be stimulated. You may feel pleased by the successes of a neighbor's child, but the success of your own child gives rise to the peculiar parental emotion called 'gloating.'"

In addition, too many parents expect their children to live out all their unfulfilled dreams and expectations and to do as well as, if not better than, the parents themselves. Part of the reason for this is a fear of failing, a fear that the parent hasn't done a good enough job, or that he hasn't adequately prepared the child to be a good citizen.

The bottom line is that you need to relax. Your child's failures are *not* a referendum on your parenting skills. Taking failure too personally (including your child's failure to act like you want her to) puts way too much pressure on the child. You had your turn. Now move over and let someone else have a clear shot at being a child.

As simple as it sounds, your child is not an extension of you. You occupy "overlapping but not identical futures," say the Newmans. "Your children serve to connect you to the past, but they also free you from the past."

Thinking about Sexism

A few months ago, we talked about how easy it is for parents to fall into the trap of treating boys and girls differently. Given that kids learn most of what

"Just keep saying to yourself 'I'm not a sexist, I'm not a sexist . . .'"

they know from adults, it shouldn't come as much of a surprise that this kind of gender-based double standard works just as well the other way. In other words, kids treat men and women differently.

"Children learn the different roles that males and females play with children before the age of three," writes researcher Beverly Fagot. "And once this difference has been learned, the children will react to adults outside the home on the basis of this learned differentiation." Fagot found that in preschool classrooms, kids "elicited many kinds of play behavior from the male teachers; but when children needed materials or needed some caretaking, they approached female teachers."

So what can you do? Basically, just be a good role model. If you are a full participant in your home, and you love, nurture, and care for your children, they—boys and girls alike—will come to realize that men can be parents too. Second, make sure your children get the message that men and women and boys and girls are not locked into any particular roles or futures because of their gender. Your children should be free to dream of becoming whatever they want to. This means that besides telling our daughters that they can grow up to be doctors, we need to tell our sons that they can grow up to be nurses (an idea my older daughter still has a problem with, even though the father of one of her best friends is, indeed, a nurse anesthetist).

So if your daughters (like mine) demanded Matchbox cars for their birthdays, tore the heads off their Barbie dolls, and refused to be in the same room with a tutu, let them alone. And if your son wants to play with dolls or wear your partner's nail polish or lipstick, let him alone. A friend who has a particularly gentle, sweet little boy once confided that she was worried about her son's lack of physical aggressiveness and was concerned that he might be gay.

Forcing your child into a particular type of behavior—either to conform with or buck gender stereotypes—can scar them for life.

You and Your Baby

Potty Training: The Real Thing

The following steps were adapted from some of those suggested by pediatrician T. Berry Brazelton. Each one takes about a week, but if your child falters or loses interest, don't push. Take a break and pick up where you left off in a few days.

1. Leave a potty seat on the floor in the bathroom. Tell the child the little one is for him, the big one is for grown-ups.
2. After a week or so, have the child sit on the potty seat in his clothes while

---

Toilet Training Success Boosters

♦ Don't flush in front of the child. While some kids may be fascinated, others may be terrified, believing that a part of them is being flushed away (see pages 40–47 for more on fears).

♦ Minimize or eliminate liquids within an hour of bedtime. This will increase the chances that your child will wake up dry—something that will boost her confidence.

♦ Be positive, but not too positive. Too much excitement about the contents of a diaper can give the baby the idea that what she's produced is somehow valuable—a twisted notion that may result in her wanting to keep it for herself (inside her body if necessary).

you sit on yours (clothed or otherwise). You might want to read a story to keep him there.

3. After another week, ask the child once a day if you can take his diapers off so he can sit on his special toilet. You sit on your toilet as well and tell him that you, mommy, grandpa, grandma, and everyone else he knows does this every day. My younger daughter loved this stage and would sit on her potty seat for a few minutes shouting "peeeeeeee" (but without actually peeing).

4. A week later, take off the child's dirty diaper and dump the contents into the toilet. Emphasize that just like there's a special place for everything else, the toilet is the special place for urine and BM, and that that's where grown-ups put theirs. *Do not flush in front of the child* (see page 103).

5. Let the baby run around naked during the day for ten to twenty minutes. Tell him he can go to the potty anytime he wants to.

6. Over the course of a few days, leave the baby's diapers off longer and longer. Remind him every half-hour or so to go to the bathroom. If he has an accident, don't make a big deal about it—it happens to everyone.

7. Don't worry about night training for a while—at least until the child is regularly dry after waking from his naps and occasionally dry in the morning.

BOYS AND GIRLS DO IT DIFFERENTLY . . . AND SO DO THEIR PARENTS

Ninety percent of girls are bowel trained by 2 years, 7 months, while 90 percent of boys aren't bowel trained until 3 years, 1 month—a difference of 6 months. Ninety percent of girls are bladder trained by 3 years, 6 months, while 90 percent of boys take until 4 years 10 months—a difference of 16 months.

Although boys lag behind in toilet training, there is no significant biological reason for the delay. Some experts believe that the real reason girls are "trained" sooner is that women have traditionally done the training and girls have an easier time imitating their mothers than boys do. In addition, boys may not want to imitate their mothers.

It's completely normal for boys this age to start developing a male gender identity and rebel against their mothers (the same way girls this age start developing a female gender identity and rebel against their fathers). So a little boy may balk at sitting down when urinating (it's no fun to sit when you can stand), and may resist mom's instructions on how to grasp his penis—after all, she doesn't even have one!

"I think he's downloading."

Besides being done with potty training earlier, girls also have a much shorter time between bowel and bladder training (11 months) than boys (21 months). This difference may be the result of girls' not being taught to differentiate between the two functions. (Girls can't see either their urination or defecation and wipe after both, while boys can see their urine—and are encouraged to aim it—and wipe only after moving their bowels.)

Men and women traditionally have very different ways of teaching toilet training:

As you can see, "The female mode is compatible with and enhancing to the formation of a female gender identity," writes Moisy Shopper, who's done an exhaustive study of toilet training (don't ask why). "The child is encouraged to be like mother; by seeing mother's eliminative functioning, they have an intimacy with each other's bodies that fosters the girl's gender *and* sexual identity." Using the female mode to train boys "in no way enhances the boy's potential for further body differentiation or supports the sexual differences between him and his mother," writes Shopper. "In fact, in many ways it is antithetical to the boy's maturation."

THE TRADITIONAL MALE MODEL	THE TRADITIONAL FEMALE MODEL
♦ Urinary control is taught as a stand-up procedure with emphasis on skill, mastery, and fun.	♦ Sitting down for all elimination, wiping.
♦ Wipe only after bowel movements.	♦ Wiping after both kinds.
♦ Active participation and modeling by the father and/or other males.	♦ Use of the mother herself on the toilet as a model for imitation.
♦ Encouragement to touch and control the penis so as to aim the urinary stream.	♦ Discouragement from touching self.
♦ Greater tolerance for absence of bathroom privacy.	♦ Greater need for bathroom privacy.
♦ Control, function, and naming of urine is sharply differentiated from control, function, and naming of feces (boys tend to talk about "making pee pee" as opposed to "pooping").	♦ Minimal distinction between bladder and bowel training in vocabulary, timing, or technique (girls tend to talk about "going to the bathroom").

FOR BOYS ONLY

Basically, the primary role in toilet training boys should be yours. This, of course, does not mean that your partner can't toilet train your son (except for providing a model for how to urinate standing up, there's no reason she can't) or that you can't toilet train your daughter. Plenty of women support their sons' budding masculinity and encourage them to urinate standing up, holding on to their own penises.

A small number of mothers, however, won't allow their sons any autonomy, Shopper finds. And they feel "that *they* must hold their sons' penises as they pee. This is a rotten idea because your son may begin to question whether his penis belongs to him or to his mother, and that's just how serious sexual problems develop later in life."

When boys have a male model, they are much less conflicted about becoming toilet trained since training no longer carries the connotations of gaining their mother's love, submitting to her, and becoming like her.

Reading

CREATING A READING ENVIRONMENT

Having books and other reading materials readily available to your child will help her make books part of her daily life. And one of the best ways to do this is to be sure there are plenty of books on shelves or in racks that she can reach without having to ask for help.

The goal here is to have your child view reading as something she can do whenever she wants, without fear of being punished. So give her free and open access to board books and any other inexpensive or easily replaceable books you won't mind getting torn up or stuck together with drool. Keep the books you had as a child (and any others that you want to keep in one piece) far, far away and take them down only for special occasions.

SOME ADVANCED READING CONCEPTS

By now you've probably gotten into a nice, regular routine with your child, reading together in a quiet place at times when you won't be interrupted.

"Surely there must be a video of this?"

As you're reading (or planning your reading), make a conscious effort to keep the experience as interesting as possible for both you and your child. Here are some things to keep in mind:

- **Tone.** It's better to read stories that are slightly too advanced for your child (and explain a word or concept now and then) than ones that are too easy.
- **Variety.** Children's book illustrators use a huge variety of techniques: line drawings, photos, watercolors, charcoal, paint, collages, woodcut, needle-point. Expose your child to as many approaches as possible and discuss what's unique about each of them.
- **Talk.** If your toddler interrupts the story to ask questions, follow her lead. You can interrupt the reading too. Questions like "How do you think he's feeling?" "Why did the bunny do that?" or "What's going to happen when she opens the closet door?" will help your child develop critical thinking skills and encourage her to be a more active participant.
- **Act out.** Instead of reading *Little Red Riding Hood* for the 639th time, assign roles.
- **Set an example.** Let her see you and your partner reading for pleasure.

Here are a few more books to check out from your local library or add to your collection:

Alfie Gets in First (and other Alfie books), Shirley Hughes, Bert Kitchen
Animals of the Night, Merry Banks
The Baby Blue Cat and the Smiley Worm Doll, Ainslie Pryor
Basket, Ella George Lyon
Bathwater's Hot (and others in the series), Shirley Hughes
Brown Bear, Brown Bear, What Do You See?, Bill Martin, Jr.
Carl, Alexandra Day
Changes, Changes (and others), Pat Hutchins
Corduroy (and others in the series), Don Freeman
Eat Up, Gemma, Sarah Hayes
The Elephant and the Bad Baby, Elfrida Vipont
Emma's Pet, David McPhail
First Words for Babies and Toddlers, Jane Salt
Follow Me (and many others), Nancy Tafuri
Freight Train, Donald Crews
General Store, Rachel Field
The Great Big Enormous Turnip, Alexei Tolstoy
In the Small, Small Pond, Denise Fleming
It Looked Like Spilt Milk, Charles Shaw

Kate's Car, Kay Chorao
Let's Make Rabbits, Leo Lionni
The Little Engine That Could, Watty Piper
Mary Wore a Red Dress and Henry Wore His Green Sneakers, Merle Peek
Millions of Cats, Wanda Gag
The Mitten, Jan Brett
Moon Game, Frank Asch
Moonlight (and many others), Jan Ormerod
Mr. Gumpy's Motor Car (and others in the series), John Burningham
Peter Spier's Little Cats (and many others in the series), Peter Spier
Polar Bear, Polar Bear, What Do You Hear?, Bill Martin, Jr.
Pretend You're a Cat, Jean Marzollo
Rosie's Walk, Pat Hutchins
The Runaway Bunny, Margaret Wise Brown
Sheep in a Shop, Nancy Shaw
Shopping Trip (and others), Helen Oxenbury
The Tale of Peter Rabbit (and many others), Beatrix Potter
Up a Tree, Ed Young
Umbrella, Taor Yashima
A Very Busy Spider (and others), Eric Carle
A Very Special House, Ruth Krauss
Watching Foxes, Jim Arnosky
We're Going on a Bear Hunt, Michael Rosen
Where's My Teddy?, Jez Alborough
Who Said Red?, Mary Serfozo
Yellow Ball, Molly Bang

ESPECIALLY FOR OLDER SIBLINGS

These books deal in a particularly sensitive way with the special concerns of kids who suddenly (and usually against their will) are displaced from the center of the universe by a baby sister or brother. For more, see pages 110–12.

101 Things to Do with a Baby, Jan Ormerod
Dogger, Shirley Hughes
A New Baby at Your House, Joanna Cole
Tales of Oliver Pig (and others in the series), Jean Van Leeuwen

CONCEPTS

Alphabatics, Suse MacDonald
Anno's Counting House (and others), Mitsumasa Anno

26 Letters and 99 Cents, Tana Hoban
Color Zoo, Lois Ehlert
Colors (and other concept books), Jan Pienkowski
Of Colors and Things (and other photography books), Tana Hoban
Duck, David Lloyd

FOLK TALES
Little Red Riding Hood, James Marshall
The Three Little Pigs, Joseph Jacobs

GOING TO SCHOOL/DAY CARE
Going to Day Care, Fred Rogers
My Nursery School, Harlow Rockwell

POETRY/RHYMES
Egg Thoughts and Other Frances Songs, Russel Hoban
The Land of Nod and Other Poems for Children, Robert L. Stevenson
The Owl and the Pussycat, Jan Brett
Whiskers and Rhymes, Arnold Lobel

Family Matters

Family Planning

For a lot of couples, the question about whether to have another child isn't really a question; it's a given. For others, though, it's more complicated. Quite often one spouse wants a second (or third) child, while the other isn't nearly as excited about the prospect—for a variety of reasons. Although I wanted a second child quite a bit, my memories of the incredibly long and painful labor my wife endured delivering our first baby made it almost impossible for me to consider putting her through another similar experience.

Besides the pain aspect of pregnancy and childbirth, there are plenty of other factors that may affect your decision (or at least how you vote when you and your partner get around to discussing the issue):

♦ Do you really like being a parent? Is it as much fun as you thought it would be? Is it more—or less—work than you thought? Generally speaking, a second child is less stressful than the first; you'll feel like an old hand when the second baby does things that made you panic with the first one. As a result, you'll probably enjoy the second child's childhood more than the first one's.

AGE DIFFERENCE BETWEEN CHILDREN: 9 to 18 months

ADVANTAGES

- Because they're close in age, there's a better chance the kids will be great playmates.
- Your first child will adjust to the change more easily than if he were older; he won't really know what's going on and won't feel quite as displaced.

DISADVANTAGES

- You may not like having two kids in diapers at the same time.
- Your older child is still really a baby. He has plenty of baby needs and is going to have a tough time waiting for you to meet them.
- "You can expect her to act very clingy at times, perhaps alternating with aggressive behavior towards you or others," says nurse practitioner Meg Zweiback.
- Because they're close in age, they may compete with each other more.

AGE DIFFERENCE BETWEEN CHILDREN: 18 to 36 months

ADVANTAGES

- This is the most common age difference in the country, so some of your friends will probably have kids similarly spaced.
- Your older child is now more capable of waiting a bit before having his needs satisfied.
- The older child is more articulate and can entertain himself for limited amounts of time.
- The older baby is mature enough to enjoy the new baby and also to enjoy time away from you without seeing it as a threat.

DISADVANTAGES

- The two kids are far enough apart to have very different schedules, activities, and interests. This means that if you're doing the driving you'll probably end up feeling like a taxi driver.
- The older child is more likely to see the younger one as an invader. As a result, there's going to be more friction between the two.

AGE DIFFERENCE BETWEEN CHILDREN: 36+ months

ADVANTAGES

- The older child is even more articulate, more able to satisfy his own needs, and less likely to try to hurt the new child.
- The older child can—and may very well want to—help out quite a bit.

DISADVANTAGES

- A child who has been an only child for so long may have a very difficult time sharing you and your partner with anyone else.

♦ Can you afford it? And if you can't, does it really make a difference? My parents, who were both starving grad students when I was born, claim that I spent my first two years sleeping in a dresser drawer.

♦ How are you and your partner going to divide the labor around the house? Are you both satisfied with the way things got handled the first time around? Two kids is going to be more than twice the work of one: each requires a certain amount of care and feeding, plus there's the additional job of keeping the two of them from killing each other.

♦ Do you have brothers or sisters, or were you an only child? How did you like growing up that way? Do you think your child would be better or worse off with a younger sibling?

♦ Do you think you'll be able to love the second baby as much as the first? This is one of the most common concerns of prospective second-time (and beyond) parents. The simple answer is that your capacity to love your children is infinite.

♦ The pregnancy is going to be different, especially for your partner. First, because the physical changes are familiar, she might not be as fascinated by what's going on inside her body. Second, many of the physical changes may happen sooner than they did the first time: she'll probably "show" sooner, she may gain more weight this time, and she may be more tired (being a parent is exhausting enough; trying to do it while you're pregnant is something altogether different).

♦ Try not to let the first baby's temperament influence your decision—it has *absolutely no* influence on how your next baby will turn out.

FILLING THE GAP

Once you make your decision to have another child, you will probably need to decide on how far apart to space them (see chart on page 111).

Looking for Preschools

During the first eighteen months of your child's life, he should be the focus of his caregiver's attention. "Without this confirmation of self-importance, the child may experience insecurity that, in turn, will encumber the emergence of creative behavior," says psychologist John Rosemond. But over the second eighteen months, your child's needs change, and he needs to be taught—gradually—that he isn't the center of the universe.

Most preschools begin taking kids at thirty-three months (two years, nine months). But in major metropolitan areas, good preschools fill up months, sometimes even years, before the start of the fall semester. So get your applications together now. (It may seem kind of absurd to have to *apply* to get into a preschool, but if Robert Fulgum is right, and you're really going to learn everything you'll ever need to know in kindergarten, maybe it's not so crazy after all.)

As with anything to do with education, preschools have lately become the subject of much controversy:

THE BAD	THE GOOD
• Full-time day care for babies is likely to damage their development, British parenting guru Penelope Leach has found.	• One study found that sixth graders who had entered a model full-time day-care program as toddlers posted higher math scores than their peers.
• Too much group day care can jeopardize infants' attachment to their parents, psychologist Robert Karen has determined.	• Kids who go to preschools tend to be more self-reliant and confident. But they're also more boisterous, competitive, or likely to fight, according to researcher John Bates.
	• There doesn't seem to be any evidence that day care for children *over* a year hurts their attachment to their parents.
	• Family problems such as stress and insufficient income are as much as twenty times more powerful than day-care problems.

Overall, the consensus is that three-mornings-a-week preschools are fine. The potential problems start when the discussion shifts to full-time day care: seven or eight hours a day, five (or more) days a week.

THE CHOICES

There are literally dozens of preschool opportunities in your community, most of which fall into one of the following categories:

◆ **Cooperative.** The parents help out a lot, volunteering in the classroom, organizing activities, creating the curriculum.

◆ **Orthodox.** The teachers are trained in a specific method or philosophy of educating young children. This may involve using certain equipment or teaching methods. Montessori is the most common.

Temperament and Preschool

TRAIT	SPECIAL CONSIDERATIONS
ENERGY LEVEL	
• High	• Your child will need lots of room to run around, plenty of indoor activities for rainy days, lots of ways to burn off excess energy. He will, however, need some moderately structured activities. Look for a program that has many kids his age or older: he'll admire their skills and want to emulate them. And make sure the teachers' energy level is at least as high as your child's.
• Low	• This child needs a quieter, smaller setting, and small groups.
• Moderate (especially those who are also a bit slow-to-warm)	• Your child will probably stick to the sidelines for a few days, watching and learning. He'll jump in after about a week. He likes more structure and predictability, and doesn't do well in large preschools, especially if there are a lot of more active kids his age—they can be frightening.
SENSORY THRESHOLD	
• Low	• Look for a fairly calm, subdued, relaxed environment. Lots of noise, colors, and activity can frighten your child.

◆ **Free-form.** The school may include the best (or the worst) of a variety of educational philosophies.

◆ **Academic.** Structured classes in traditional subjects (math, language). Many early childhood development experts think this may be too much too soon.

WHAT TO CONSIDER WHEN CONSIDERING PRESCHOOLS
Perhaps the most important factor is your child's temperament and how it meshes with what the school has to offer (see the chart above and on the facing page).

Another important factor is stability—particularly that of the children. "In child-care settings, the availability of a stable group of age-mates results in more complex, coordinated play," say Newman and Newman. "Children who

TRAIT	SPECIAL CONSIDERATIONS
ATTENTION SPAN	
• Short	• This child will need a constantly changing array of things to do and play with. Look for a staff that is large enough so that a teacher can spend extra time with your child to expose him to new things.
PREDICTABILITY	
• High	• This child will need a regular schedule, regular meal and nap times, and so forth.
• Low	• This child doesn't need much in the way of scheduling, but should have some anyway.
ADAPTABILITY	
• Slow	• Avoid schools with rigid schedules and highly structured activities. Also avoid unstructured schools. Look for teachers who will make a special effort to involve your child and introduce him to new materials slowly. Make sure you can stay with your child for a few minutes each morning (for at least the first week or so) to help ease his transition.
• Moderately slow-to-adapt, intense	• This child may occasionally bite or hit other children. This will fade as he becomes more articulate. He may be upset when you drop him off at school and just as upset when you come to pick him up.

have had many changes in their child-care arrangements are less likely to engage in complex social pretend play."

GENERAL GUIDELINES

Finding the right preschool will probably take a while, and you shouldn't give up until you've got exactly what you were looking for or have come as close as you possibly can. As a minimum, the day-care center you choose for your child should comply with your state's rules and regulations. But standards vary wildly from state to state, so licensing and accreditation are not necessarily the guarantees of quality that they ought to be. On the national level, however, the National Association for the Education of Young Children (NAEYC) accredits programs that meet their extremely high standards. They'll send you info on finding accredited providers in your area. Call (800) 424-2460 or write to NAEYC, 1509 16th Street NW, Washington, D.C. 20036-1426.

But accreditation isn't all there is. You should also keep the following general guidelines in mind (some of which were suggested by the NAEYC and the American Academy of Pediatrics):

RATIO

♦ The younger the kids allowed in the preschool, the lower the teacher-child ratio should be. In a typical preschool, kids' ages range from two and a half to five. Overall, there should be no more than seven kids to each adult caregiver, and the total size of the group (not including the teachers) shouldn't exceed twenty.

NUTRITION AND HEALTH

♦ No smoking on the premises.

♦ Proof of immunization required of each child.

♦ If the school provides meals and/or snacks, they should be varied, wholesome, and nutritious. Menus should be available in advance.

♦ Rest and nap times should be scheduled and each child should have a clean, individual place to sleep. There should also be special quiet activities for kids who don't nap.

♦ Teachers wear disposable gloves and wash hands with soap and water whenever changing diapers. They should also wash their hands after helping a child go to the bathroom and before touching food.

♦ Parents should be notified immediately of any accident or contagious illness, and there should be a clear policy for what to do (isolation, to start) with kids who get sick while at school.

♦ Teachers should give medication to children only with a parent's written permission.

♦ Emergency numbers should be clearly posted near a phone.

♦ At least one teacher (but all would be better) should have up-to-date first aid and CPR certifications.

GENERAL CLEANLINESS

♦ Hot running water, soap, and paper towels should be available—at kid level—and should be used after going to the bathroom and before all meals and snacks.

♦ The entire area—kitchen, tabletops, floors, sleep areas—should be clean. All garbage cans, diaper pails, and bathrooms should be cleaned thoroughly and regularly disinfected. So should toys that tend to end up in toddlers' mouths.

A Few Preschool Red Flags

As far as I'm concerned, any school that doesn't satisfy *all* the qualifications listed on these pages should be viewed with suspicion. Beyond that, though, here are a few things that should make you take a prospective preschool off your list completely and run the other way.

♦ Parents are not allowed to drop in unannounced. You need to call before visiting or coming to pick up your child.
♦ Your child is unhappy or scared after more than a few months.
♦ The staff seems to change every day.
♦ The staff ignores any of your concerns.
♦ You child reports being hit or mistreated, or you hear similar reports from other parents. Check this one out thoroughly, though. Kids have been known to fabricate stories.

SAFETY

♦ Outlets, heaters, and radiators are covered.
♦ Equipment is up-to-date and meets current safety codes.
♦ Cleaning fluids, medicines, and any other potentially dangerous substances are kept in places inaccessible to the children.
♦ There is an emergency plan, including regular fire drills. Fire extinguishers should be available as required.
♦ The school has a plan for dealing with violent children. While some hitting, pushing, and biting is pretty normal for kids this age, anything more serious (stabbing, hitting with large objects, or repeated, unprovoked attacks) are not.
♦ Children are not allowed to ride in any moving vehicle without a car seat.
♦ Children are not released to any adult whose name is not on a written list provided by you and your partner.
♦ Outdoor areas are safe from animal contamination (for example, the sandbox should be tightly covered).

PROGRAM

♦ To the extent possible, substitute teachers should be familiar to the kids.
♦ Children have daily opportunities to participate in a variety of active and quiet activities, including free play, art, music, and group and individual play.
♦ Children have adequate time to play outside every day, weather permitting. There should be plenty of space for active, physical play, such as climbing, running, and jumping.

♦ Indoor areas must be large enough to accommodate all the kids at one time. The area should be well organized so kids know where things go and what happens where. There should be a wide variety of age-appropriate toys, books, and materials. And there should be more than one of each toy so that the kids don't have to wait in long lines to play.

♦ Parents should be welcome at any time, without advance notice.

♦ Overall, the preschool should be a place you wish you could have gone to when you were a kid.

EASING THE TRANSITION

Several months before our older daughter's first day of preschool, my wife and I started trying to get her ready. The school principal had sent us a five-page handout on how tough this first big separation can be for kids, and my wife and I spent hours with our daughter reading books about other kids' first days, talking about who else would be at school, telling her about our own school experiences, and describing the fun things she would get to do. We bought her new clothes in her favorite colors and a Little Mermaid lunch box and reassured her over and over that we'd pick her up every day right after lunch and that, of course, we still loved her.

"Think of it as a brief interlude in, as opposed to a major disruption of, your life."

Even the school itself tried to help ease the transition. A few weeks before school started, one of the teachers came over to the house and spent hours playing with our daughter and getting to know her. She also brought along a Polaroid camera and left our daughter a snapshot of her with her new teacher. And on the morning of the fateful first day, we gave her honeycomb and cookies shaped like her favorite alphabet letters, to remind her that learning should be a sweet experience. By the time we got in the car for the drive to school on the first day, I felt pretty confident that we had prepared her both psychologically and emotionally for this milestone.

As soon as we got inside the building, I knew I was right. My daughter caught sight of a few of her friends and the teacher who had come to our house, and promptly disappeared, laughing and giggling. I shouted a good-bye (which she barely acknowledged), reminded her when I'd be back to pick her up, and walked out to the car.

Some kids won't even notice when you've gone on the first day of school. Others will freak out completely. Either way, here are some absolute musts (and must nots) for the first days:

♦ Prepare *yourself*. For more on this, see pages 177–79.
♦ No matter how well adjusted your child seems, never just drop her off on the first day. Go inside and get her settled.
♦ Never sneak out, even if she's deeply involved in some activity.
♦ Create a good-bye routine (kiss, do a quick drawing together, wave bye-bye through the window).
♦ Don't chastise your child for crying. Reassure her that you love her, that you'll be back.
♦ Don't be upset if your child comes home covered with dirt, paint, glue, sparkles, or even an occasional bruise. It means she's interacting with other people and having fun.

PASSING THE BUCK

Coincidentally, the same week that my older daughter was admitted to pre-school, a friend of mine was admitted to the University of San Francisco's medical school. My friend was griping about how much her tuition cost and was surprised when I wasn't more sympathetic. But when I told her that my daughter's preschool was more expensive than med school, she stopped.

Naturally, not all preschools cost as much as medical schools, but it's not going to be cheap. If you have the money, great. But most of us could use (or wouldn't turn down) a little financial assistance. And asking your employer to help out a little may be your best bet. Here are a few alternatives:

♦ Direct financial assistance. Your employer pays for all or part of your expenses at the preschool of your choice.

♦ Negotiated discounts. Your employer—maybe in conjunction with other local employers—can negotiate group rates or discounts with a nearby preschool.

♦ Employee salary reductions or set-asides. You can have your employer put up to $5,000 of your pretax salary into a Dependent Care Assistance Plan (DCAP). This will enable you to reduce your preschool expenses by paying for them with before-tax dollars instead of after-tax ones. Your employer will save money too, since he or she won't have to pay social security tax or unemployment insurance on your DCAP money. (If your employee benefits department requests a reference, it's Section 129 of the 1981 Economic Recovery Tax Act.)

Of course, asking your boss for help—or anyone else, for that matter—isn't easy. In fact, the reason employees most often give for *not* asking their bosses to get involved in employee day-care problems is fear of losing their jobs. This may explain why fewer than six thousand of the nation's six million employers offer some kind of child-care assistance to their employees.

Nevertheless, it's worth a try. The first thing to do is to remind him or her that some assistance programs won't cost the company a cent (see above). Then read your employer this quote from the Child Care Action Campaign (CCAC): "Studies have shown that working parents' anxiety about their child care arrangements erodes their productivity—and directly affects employers' profit lines."

If those approaches don't work, follow the CCAC's advice and:

♦ Talk to other employees. Do any of them have trouble finding or paying for a good preschool? How do their worries affect their productivity?

♦ Find out what other employers in your field are doing about preschool. Some prospective employees are making decisions on which companies to work for based on benefits, and if the competition offers a more family-friendly environment, your company will have to follow suit.

♦ If you're in a union, speak to your union rep. Have other employers bargained for family-friendly benefits? You may be able to include some in the next contract negotiation.

♦ Encourage other employees to let management know about child-care problems.

The Child Care Action Campaign produces a variety of pamphlets that can help you approach your employer with your preschool questions and suggestions. Contact them for a catalog at 330 Seventh Ave, 17th floor, New York, NY 10001, or by calling (212) 239-0138.

Time for a Financial Tune-up

What's Going On with the Baby

Physically

♦ You may have noticed that your child looks different lately—less like a baby and more like a little kid. Her head doesn't seem so out of proportion to the rest of her body, and she's lost most of her baby potbelly.

♦ She's getting much better at dressing herself and is especially interested in shoes (although she's still more than a year away from being able to lace them up). She can, however, manipulate Velcro fasteners.

♦ Your child's emotions are more frequently expressed physically than verbally. When happy, she may jump up and down with glee; when angry, she may throw something down.

Intellectually

♦ "Self-control is still dependent upon factors outside himself, namely the approval or disapproval of his parents," writes Selma Fraiberg. Your child's still a long way away from developing a conscience or a true ability to regulate her own negative impulses. But this is an important first step.

♦ Another by-product of her improving memory is her new ability to imitate you when you *aren't* there with her. This signals the beginning of her ability to engage in fantasy play.

♦ She continues to choose less physical and more intellectual ways of solving problems. She does a lot less by trial and error and a lot more by thinking things through. For example, rather than pull you over to the bookshelf and point to the book she wants you to get down, she may simply tell you to "bring me book."

♦ Your toddler's able to focus on incredibly tiny details—ones you probably would never notice. In the middle of the 400th read-through of *Goldilocks and the Three Bears,* my older daughter suddenly stopped me and pointed out that the artist had made an error: in a picture of the bears' breakfast table, both the daddy bear's porridge (which is supposedly too hot) and the mommy bear's porridge (supposedly too cold) were steaming. What an outrage.

♦ She's now able to distinguish a group of two objects from a group of more than two. She may not, however, have a word for the larger group.

♦ Although concepts such as "yesterday," "tomorrow," and "last week," are still beyond your toddler's grasp, she has a fairly good idea of what "pretty soon," and "in a minute" mean.

Verbally

♦ Your toddler is probably increasing her vocabulary by two to five words per day. She's so thrilled with the sound of her own voice that she'll repeat her new words over and over.

♦ She runs around naming every object she knows, and will accompany just about everything she does with a steady stream of chatter.

♦ She makes a lot of really cute (but extremely logical) grammatical errors ("I went to he's house," "Give the cup to she," are common). And she is still unclear on past and future tenses: "I go to store" can mean "I am going now," "I went," or "I will go."

♦ She still spends a lot of time talking to herself and would rather engage a grown-up in conversation than another child.

♦ Perhaps the most interesting language-related development is that at this age, according to Fraiberg, "language makes it possible for a child to incorporate his parents' verbal prohibitions, to make them part of himself." This isn't always 100 percent successful, though. You may find her sitting on the floor, eating sugar out of the box, and saying, "No, baby not eat sugar," between mouthfuls.

♦ In addition to "Whazzat?" your toddler now asks such questions as "Why?" and "Where is ____?" According to Ames and Ilg, your child will master more space words (in, out, up, down, in front of, behind, and so on) in the six-month period from two to two and a half than in any other six-month period of her life.

Emotionally/Socially

- Your toddler shows incredible pride in the things she's able to do, and actively seeks your approval. She will implore you a hundred times a day to "Look at me!!!" as she climbs up the stairs to the slide, fills up her bucket with sand, draws a straight line, or rides her trike.

- You might not be able to tell yet, but she's slowly becoming more interested in other kids. You'll realize it for yourself when, out of the blue, she starts making a strange noise or using a word she never had before—the same noise or word used a few days before by that two-year-old at the park, the one your child seemed to be ignoring completely.

- Another way she shows her interest in other kids is by physically exploring them. Unfortunately, this may entail some hitting, pushing, shoving, and hair-pulling. But remember, your child isn't intentionally being mean; she's still learning about the difference between animate and inanimate objects and is fascinated by cause and effect. As Ames and Ilg write, "A child may begin stroking another child's hair because he likes the way it looks, then may pull it to see how it feels."

- Marked by near-instant 180-degree mood swings and arbitrary mind changes, this can be an exceedingly demanding time for you and your child.

What You're Going Through

Taking a Long, Hard Look at . . . Yourself

I always feel proud when someone tells me how much my daughters look like me. And I feel tickled inside when my parents or other relatives tell me how much the girls act like I did as a kid. But I'm a little less enchanted when one of the girls spits out one of my "God damn its" when she can't tie her shoes.

When this kind of thing happens to you (and if it hasn't yet, it will very soon), you may suddenly find yourself imagining your child imitating some of your less savory and less cute behaviors. And you'll be horrified. "The honest and direct response of children to some 'bad habits' forces men to confront these behaviors and consider the consequences, not only for themselves but also for their children," says parenting educator Glen Palm. If, for example, you eat a lot of candy bars and potato chips, you may find yourself questioning the kind of example you're setting and quit.

Palm describes one of his clients, a smoker whose father had died of lung cancer. The man hadn't been able to bring himself to quit until his three-year-old began pretending he was smoking.

*"Well then, do what I meant to say,
not what I'm alleged to have done."*

Emotional Changes

One of the most commonly heard complaints about men is that we are out of touch with our emotions or that we suppress them. A few years ago I think I might have agreed with this contention. But since becoming a father, I strongly disagree. Fathers—especially those who are actively involved with their children—feel tremendous joy, anger, affection, fear, and anxiety. The problem is that men in our society don't have places where they can safely express their feelings. "Society expects them to be the strong ones," say Phil and Carolyn Cowan. "And they worry that talking about their doubts and fears would only upset their wives."

As a result, men learn to regulate their emotions. But please remember: regulating is not the same as suppressing. "The ability to control one's own impulses in the service of caring for one's children and emotionally supporting one's spouse would seem to be an important marker of maturity," write the Cowans. Nevertheless, don't forget that *you* provide a crucial model for how your child learns to express his own emotions—fear, anger, disappointment, sadness, happiness, and excitement.

Besides regulating their emotions, fathers undergo a variety of other changes in the way they experience and react to the world around them:

♦ **Empathy.** "The desire for emotional intimacy with their children and the obvious responsibility of men to understand their children motivate them to think about their child's feelings," says Glen Palm. Learning to see the world from another person's perspective (in this case, your child's), is what empathy is all about.

♦ **Expressiveness.** "Parents learn to assist their child in expressing and understanding emotions," say Barbara and Philip Newman. And they frequently "develop strategies for helping children manage their fears and doubts." Seeing how emotionally expressive children can be often allows men to accept and express their own feelings more readily. "As fathers teach their children how to say 'I love you' or 'I'm sad because that hurt my feelings,' the fathers too learn to be more honest and open with their own emotions," adds Palm.

♦ **Selflessness.** Another major marker of maturity is the ability to take pleasure in doing something for someone else—without any hope of repayment.

♦ **Sensitivity.** Try to equate your child's bruised and unhappy feelings with physical bruises. This is exactly the approach taken by one father interviewed by parent-child communication experts Adele Faber and Elaine Mazlish. "Somehow the image of a cut or laceration helped him realize that his son required as prompt and serious attention for his hurt feelings as he would for a hurt knee," they write.

♦ **Outrage.** I know that before I was a father, I had seen plenty of parents hit or even abuse their children, and I'm sure it bothered me. But not like it bothers me now (see pages 171–74 for more on this).

♦ **Expansion.** Before becoming fathers, men are generally limited in the ways they express affection: kissing, hugging, holding hands, and sex. But having children frequently allows men to expand their repertoire, say the Newmans. Kissing, hugging, and holding hands are still appropriate affectionate gestures, but so are tickling, rocking, tumbling, snuggling, and stroking. Overall, fathers in the Cowans' studies reported that "having a child brought them more in touch with their feelings, and helped them learn how to be more comfortable expressing their emotions."

♦ **Patience.** "Learning patience is a primary goal of fathers—[this includes] controlling feelings of anger, improving the ability to listen, and coping with some of the tediousness of everyday parenting," says Palm.

You and Your Baby

More Computer Stuff: Getting Ready

Before you let your child sit down at the computer, there are a few things you should do to prepare for the big event.

- Don't allow anyone (even you) to bring food anywhere near the computer. Don't even do it when you're alone—you'll leave a dish next to the keyboard one night, and your child will remind you about it every day for the next six months.
- Get a plastic keyboard protector. Even if you do follow the no-food rule, a plastic protector also acts as a handy anti-slobber device.
- No fighting, kicking, running, or roughhousing near the computer. One good smack could destroy a lot of valuable stuff.
- If you are planning to share a computer with your child, you'll want to back up everything on your system first. Once you've done that, be sure to keep your personal files in an area of the computer your child won't be able to access. If you think you might be raising a future hacker, password-protect

"And always remember I'm here for you, son,
at Dadman@connect.pop.net."

Picking Software

Basically, what you're looking for in a software package for your child are the following factors:

- ease of use (by the child)
- ease of installation (by you)
- age appropriateness
- ability to challenge the child
- degree to which the program is childproof
- the program's ability to educate
- the program's ability to entertain
- flexibility (can be used for kids of varying ages)

As you might expect, the ad copy on any box of software will tell you that besides satisfying all the above criteria, the program will also make you rich and your child smarter and more beautiful.

You could buy the program and test it out, but it's nearly impossible to return software these days. And unless you're a specialist in early childhood education, you probably won't be able to make a very informed decision about the program's appropriateness.

Fortunately, there are several reliable organizations that thoroughly test and evaluate children's software:

Children's Software Review, for ages 3–14, 6 issues for $24.00 /
   (313) 480-0040

High/Scope Buyer's Guide, ages 3–8, $19.95 plus shipping and
   handling / (313) 485-2000

your adult applications. The last thing you want is for your baby to start playing around with your tax returns.

- Put colored stickers on some of the more commonly used keys: Enter, Backspace, the letters of your child's first name, cursor keys. Use the stickers as a temporary crutch to help your child remember where they are. Do not start saying, "Push the red key"—your child's next computer probably won't have stickers on the keyboard.

A NOTE ABOUT HARDWARE

If you think you can get away with putting a child of the '90s in front of your old Apple II or your 8086, think again. Your child may actually need a newer system than *you* do, one that uses the most advanced graphics, sound, and animation capabilities. So if you have an old clunker lying around, donate it to your favorite charity and get a tax deduction while you still can.

ALL ABOUT SOFTWARE

All your hardware precautions and preparations will be entirely wasted if the software you're running is worthless.

According to researchers Susan Haugland and Daniel Shade, there are two basic types of software: nondevelopmental (also called "drill-and-practice"), which, according to Shade, is the "computer equivalent of flashcards and is not good for preschoolers"; and developmental (open-ended), which provides children with "the opportunity to explore an environment, make choices, and then find out the impact of these decisions."

Haugland recently tested four groups of children: the first used nondevelopmental software; the second used developmental; the third also used developmental, but supplemented it with additional activities; and the fourth group used no computers at all.

After eight months, the kids in the three computer groups all showed huge gains in self-esteem over the kids in the fourth group. Children who used the drill-and-practice software experienced an amazing 50-percent drop-off in their creativity—a drop not experienced either by the kids who used open-ended software or by those who had no computer exposure. "Clearly," write Haugland and Shade, nondevelopmental software may have a detrimental effect on children's creativity."

Kids who worked with the developmental (open-ended) software had "significant gains on measures of intelligence, nonverbal skills, structural knowledge, long-term memory, and complex manual dexterity."

Talk, Talk, Talk . . .

"The amount of live language directed to a child was perhaps the strongest single indicator of later intellectual and linguistic and social achievement," say Newman and Newman. Here's how to maximize the effect of what you say:

♦ **Explain.** Label everything you can, talk about what you're doing ("I'm taking your dirty diaper off, I'm wiping your butt, I'm putting a clean diaper on you") and where you're going.

♦ **Expand.** If your child says, "Truck drive," you say, "Yes, the truck is driving by." Or if he says, "Juice gone," say "That's right, the juice is gone because you spilled it on the floor."

♦ **Prompt.** When your child points to something he clearly doesn't know the word for, tell him what it is. If he tries to pronounce something but makes a "mistake" ("baba" for bottle), say something like, "Yes, you're right. That *is* a bottle."

♦ **Don't make corrections.** Instead of correcting grammar or pronunciation mistakes, repeat the word or idea in a new, grammatically correct sentence.

♦ **Watch for some interesting word associations.** A friend once told me that whenever she recited "Wee Willie Winkie" to her son, she'd make a knocking gesture in the air during the "rapping at the windows" part. One day she was talking to the baby about wrapping birthday presents and she was surprised when the baby smiled and made the very same knocking gesture (Get it? rap/wrap).

LISTENING SO YOUR CHILD WILL TALK

Generally speaking, there's not really a lot of sense in talking if no one's listening. And the only way your child will ever learn how to be a good listener is if you show him the way. Here's how to do it:

♦ **Pay attention.** When your child wants to talk, face him and look him in the eye. Turn off the TV or radio, don't answer the phone, and disregard any other distractions. You may not even need to speak; sometimes all your child wants is for you to look at him. "One of the most important skills good listeners have is the ability to put themselves in the shoes of others or empathize with the speaker by attempting to understand his or her thoughts and feelings," writes Lilian Katz, director of ERIC, the Clearinghouse on Elementary and Early Childhood Education.

♦ **Allow your child to have her feelings.** Don't tell a kid who says she's sleepy (or hungry or sick or sad or angry) that she's not.

♦ **Keep things moving.** Asking questions whose answer is yes or no is the quickest way to end a conversation. Instead, pick up on something your child said and ask a question that restates or uses some of the same words your child used. "When you use children's own phrasing or terms, you strengthen their confidence in their conversational and verbal skills and reassure them that their ideas are being listened to and valued," says Katz.

♦ **Don't interrupt.** If you're having a discussion with your child, listen respectfully to his ideas—from beginning to end—before jumping in. You want him to afford you the same courtesy, don't you?

♦ **Be patient.** No matter how verbal he may be, your toddler still has a limited vocabulary and there may be occasional delays between what he's thinking and what actually comes out of his mouth. Let him struggle for a few seconds before you start filling in the missing words.

- **Get your child involved.** Asking your child for his vote about the dinner menu or weekend plans (and taking his advice once in a while), or asking for his opinion of a movie you saw together or on how to rearrange the furniture shows him you respect him and that what he says is important.
- **Acknowledge your child's feelings.** According to Faber and Mazlish, short, simple phrases like "Oh, I see," and "Hmmm," are much better for stimulating your child to talk than jumping in with advice.
- **Give your child's feelings a name.** If your child tells you he wants to smash a friend's face in, telling him, "I can see that you're really angry" is far better than telling him that he shouldn't talk that way about his friends. "Parents don't usually give this kind of response," say Faber and Mazlish, "because they fear that by giving a name to the feeling, they'll make it worse. Just the opposite is true. The child who hears the words for what he is experiencing is deeply comforted. Someone has acknowledged his inner experience." Lilian Katz adds, "Restating or rephrasing what children have said is useful when they are experiencing powerful emotions that they may not be fully aware of. . . . Your wider vocabulary can help children express themselves as accurately and clearly as possible and give them a deeper understanding of words and inner thoughts." But watch out: children usually hate it when you repeat their exact words back to them ("Daddy, I hate Bobby!" "It sounds like you really hate Bobby." Duh.)
- **Help them fantasize.** Rather than give a logical, rational response to your child's irrational request ("No, we can't go to Grandma and Grandpa's house for dinner—they live in Paris and it's too far to go right now."), jump in and fantasize ("I wish I could just snap my fingers and take us there right away.").
- **Watch for nonverbal cues.** Your child's mood, tone of voice, and energy level may tell you more about what he's feeling than what he actually says. Encourage your child to talk about his feelings.
- **Don't ask why.** Kids don't always know why they feel a particular way (do you?). "It's easier to talk to a grown-up who accepts what you're feeling," say Faber and Mazlish, "rather than one who presses you for explanations."

TALKING SO YOUR CHILD WILL PAY ATTENTION TO YOU
Once you and your child are able to communicate with each other verbally, you'll find that a lot of what you say to him is, in one form or another, an attempt to gain his cooperation. Here's how to improve the chances that your child will (a) hear what you say, and (b) respond the way you want him to:
- **Describe what you see, not what you think.** Instead of "You always take off your socks in the living room and dump sand on the rug. Do you

have any idea how long it takes me to clean up after you every day?" try something like, "There's sand on the rug."

♦ **Give information.** Instead of "What on earth is the matter with you? I've told you seven hundred times to stop jumping on that couch!" try "Couches are not for jumping on."

♦ **Say it with a word.** Instead of "I've been telling you for the past hour and a half to put your crayons away, get your clothes off and get ready for bed," you'll probably have better luck with, "Pajamas!" This approach, by the way, works equally well with teenagers, who also don't like long-winded sermons.

♦ **Talk about *your* feelings.** Rather than criticize the child in a personal way ("You're really annoying me with your constant shouting and screaming, you're such a pain . . ."), keep the focus on you ("I get frustrated when you yell at me like that. I do much better when people speak to me in a nice way.").

♦ **Make specific—not general—requests.** "I want you to help me put your cars back in the box" is much better than "Clean up your stuff."

♦ **Be consistent.** Don't mumble "No" a few times and then forget about it. That only encourages your child to ignore you.

♦ **Give choices.** "Do you want an apple or an orange?" is far more likely to get a response than "What do you want to eat?" Offering choices in this way is just about guaranteed to reduce the number of adult-toddler power struggles.

♦ **Don't ask questions if you don't want answers.** "Can you help clean up your room, please?" only gives the child the (incorrect) impression that he has a choice.

♦ **Don't repeat yourself.** If he didn't listen the first six times, why would you think he'd listen the seventh?

♦ **Don't make idle threats.** Kids often take a threat as a challenge. Will you really carry through? If you don't, you've lost credibility. If you do, you might have to raise the ante every time you want your child to do something.

♦ **Admit your mistakes.** Your child will learn that it's okay to be wrong once in a while.

♦ **Keep your promises.** Your child may not have a very developed sense of time, but he'll never forget that trip to the zoo or that candy bar you promised in a weak moment. And if *you* do, you've lost a ton of credibility.

♦ **Whisper.** Kids hate to miss anything that might have anything to do with them. Speaking softly has been known to stop even the loudest child in his tracks.

♦ **Do your scolding in private.** Take your child into a separate room—it'll be less embarrassing for both of you. It will also reduce your child's instinctive need to try to save face by flouting your authority in public.

♦ **Praise effectively.** Statements like "Great job" can become so automatic that they lose their meaning. Try to be more specific: "Wow! Did you ride your trike all the way around the block?" Besides being more satisfying, this type of praise encourages conversation.

♦ **Make a big deal out of good behavior.** As we've discussed elsewhere, your child craves your attention—any way he can get it. And if the only time you pay attention to him is when he's misbehaving, he'll misbehave as often as he can, feeling that behaving well is a waste of time since no one seems to notice.

Family Matters

Even More About Nutrition

Just a few months ago you may have been worried that your baby was eating only one food for days at a time. Well, at least he was eating. But now he may seem to be giving up food altogether.

And in a way, that's true. For the first two years of life your baby was storing body fat, and his weight was increasing about 9 percent every month. But now that he doesn't need all that fat, he's slowed way down, gaining only about 1 percent a month.

The good news is that your child isn't starving to death. He may go a day or two without eating much, but then the next few days he'll put away more food

---

Dealing with Desserts

Nutritionist Susan Kayman suggests putting all the food you'd like your child to eat on the plate at the same time—including dessert. The theory is that when dessert is no longer forbidden (and therefore less desirable), the child won't be any more attracted to a brownie than to a carrot.

But remember: although you're giving your child some control over his food intake, *you* pick the what and when, the child picks the whether and how much. So brownies don't have to be an option at all.

Oh, and by the way. For those of you who remember the four food groups, don't think you can get away with classifying marshmallows in the white group and chocolate in the brown.

---

than you would have thought possible. During those odd moments when your toddler *does* eat, he'll probably limit himself to only two or three foods.

The solution? Give your toddler some control over what he eats and when, says Jane Hirschman, author of *Solving Your Child's Eating Problems.* As we discussed on pages 47–50, your child's diet will probably balance out over the

Food and Your Child's Temperament

Researcher Jim Cameron has found that your child's eating habits— like just about everything else in his life—are greatly influenced by his temperament:

♦ The slow-adapting kid may consider your efforts to feed him intrusive and may try to get out of his high chair as if it were a straitjacket. He often rejects new foods, not because they taste bad but because they taste *new.* And old foods prepared in new ways may be rejected on principle.

♦ The intense kid may seem to exist only on five or six foods. Don't bother introducing a new food when your toddler is really hungry— he's probably tired and not in the mood for new things. His first reaction to new foods will be one of suspicion, so if you really want him to try something new, wait until he's a little hungry and not too tired. The more intense your child, the more problems you'll have trying to get him to stick to a strict eating schedule. The more you insist, the more likely your efforts will result in a tantrum.

♦ The energetic kid wants to be in complete control of his meals. He may refuse to be fed by anyone but himself, and may not eat if he can't hold the food (or at least the utensil it's supposed to be on). It's impossible even to guess how much he'll eat or when. If he's tired, he won't eat much, but you might get him to try an old favorite. If he's well rested, he'll eat even less (he'll want to run around instead). Have lots of snacks available for quick refueling and don't waste your time trying to get him into a high chair.

♦ The irregular, slow-to-warm kid may be the toughest of all. You can expect him to sit at the dinner table for a while, but don't expect him actually to eat anything. Instead, he'll want to eat on his own schedule; again, have lots of healthy snacks around for his swings through the kitchen.

The Dream Diet

Just in case you were wondering what an ideal toddler diet would look like, here it is:

- ♦ 1 serving of vitamin A foods every day (apricots, cantaloupe, carrots, spinach, yams)
- ♦ 1 serving of vitamin C foods every day (oranges, grapefruit, tomatoes)
- ♦ 1 serving of high-fiber foods every day (apples, bananas, figs, plums, pears, berries, peas, potatoes, spinach)
- ♦ Cruciferous vegetables a few times a week (broccoli, cauliflower, brussels sprouts, cabbage)

The fact is that getting a toddler to eat anything that remotely resembles the ideal diet is going to be a struggle. But here are a few things you can do to improve your chances:

- ♦ **Serve only 100 percent juice.** Anything that has the word *drink* in its name is probably more sugar than juice.
- ♦ **Limit fast foods.** Lunch meats, hot dogs, and many other processed fast foods contain sodium nitrates, which the American Cancer Society believes may cause cancer in children.
- ♦ **Limit candy and other junk food.** Kids between two and three consume about 1,500 calories a day, and a candy bar has about 200 calories—a pretty big chunk of the day's intake.
- ♦ **Limit caffeine.** A single can of Coke has the same effect on a toddler as drinking four cups of coffee does on you.
- ♦ **Set a good example.** If you stop at a convenience store for a candy bar, brush your teeth and don't leave the wrappers lying around. If your child doesn't smell the chocolate on your breath, he'll certainly recognize the empty packaging and know he's been left out.
- ♦ **Take things out of their original packages.** What's often most attractive about certain foods is the box they come in. Transferring cereals and other sugary things into a large jar or plastic container can make them a lot less attractive.

course of a few weeks. More important, says Hirschman, feeding your child on demand (within reason, of course) helps him learn to recognize when he's genuinely hungry (as opposed to being bored, bribed, or craving something just because he can't have it) and when he's full (rather than just going on a binge because he doesn't know when he'll get another chance to eat the food).

Giving your child some control over his own food intake will make him braver and more willing to try new things. He'll also end up eating more. Hirschman's theory—and it's a sound one—is that eventually, if he's not pressured, your child will come around to eating whatever everyone else in the house is eating.

If you're really worried about your child's eating habits, check with your pediatrician. Early signs of malnutrition include uncharacteristic constant crankiness, frequent illness, listless behavior, and little or no weight gain over a long period of time.

MINIMIZING FOOD FIGHTS

♦ **Relax.** If your child doesn't want to try a new food, leave him alone. And does he really have to eat in a high chair? Just put him someplace where

"Relax. The important thing is that he drinks his milk, not how."

he can't make a huge mess (or at least where his mess will be fairly easy to clean up).

♦ **Spy.** When your child is at someone else's house—especially one in which there are older kids to imitate—find out what he ate. He may try something at a friend's that he wouldn't touch if you gave it to him.

♦ **Keep foods far away from each other on the plate.** Kids this age like to keep everything in its own special place (just another way to exercise control), and mixing two foods—even if they're both favorites—could end up causing a tantrum. In a similar vein, kids like to have certain quantities of things and may ask for more milk in their glass even though there's already plenty there.

♦ **Peel foods with peels (apples, pears, plums).** Some kids are looking for any excuse not to eat something, and a tough-to-chew peel is a perfect pretext.

♦ **Grow a garden.** Even kids who don't like vegetables may be willing to eat something they planted, watered, and picked.

♦ **Get the child involved.** Have him set the table, decide on pizza toppings, make shopping decisions.

♦ **Have fun.** Even liver can look more appetizing if you cut it into the shape of a friendly animal or familiar cartoon character.

♦ **Encourage snacking.** Your child is burning tons of calories. Make sure he gets plenty to eat throughout the day, and if he wants some apple slices or a piece of cheese between meals, let him.

Giving Yourself a Financial Tune-up

Whether you're rich or poor, when it comes to money there are only three kinds of people:

♦ Those who spend less than they bring in and save the difference.
♦ Those who spend exactly what they earn and have nothing left over.
♦ Those who spend more than they earn and get deeper and deeper in debt.

If you're in the first category, congratulations! According to some studies, less than 20 percent of baby boomers are saving enough for their retirement, and 25 percent of adults ages 35–54 haven't even started saving.

If you're in either of the other two categories (or if you're in the first and want to make your financial situation even better), you're going to have to get under your financial hood and do a little tinkering. It's a simple process, really, with only two steps:

♦ Reduce your expenses (and your debts)
♦ Increase your savings

*"I'd like to give you more, but I can't.
I'm restrained by an 'allowance cap.'"*

REDUCING EXPENSES AND GETTING OUT OF DEBT
ON THE WAY

Although starting a savings or investment plan sounds like a lot more fun than going on a financial diet, the truth is that you can't save money until you've got a good handle on your expenses. The first step is to take a hard look at your current spending. It may be a little scary, but trust me, it's important.

Gather together every money-related scrap of paper that's crossed your hands in the past four or five months. Categorize them by type of expense (housing, insurance, medical, food, and so forth). Using several months' worth of expenses will help you average variable expenses, such as gas and clothes, and include irregular expenses, such as auto repairs or major appliance purchases. Be sure to include the money—especially cash—you spend on lunch, dry cleaning, gifts, and the like.

Once you've got this done, go over each of the expense categories to see where you can do some cutting. Here are a few areas in which you can produce almost immediate, and often painless, returns:

♦ Food. Buy in bulk from Costco or other discount outlets, use coupons, and eat out less.

♦ Comparison shop. Prices vary widely on everything from refrigerators to long-distance carriers, so check three or four places before you buy anything. And don't forget to check out mail-order prices—they're often cheaper and tax-free (if you and the mail-order company are in different states).

♦ Buy a home instead of renting one (for more on this see pages 182–87).

♦ Make a sensible tax plan (for more on this see pages 144–45).

♦ Car pool. This can help you reduce many auto-related expenses, such as gas and oil, repairs, and insurance rates.

♦ Auto insurance. If your car is more than five years old, you can probably save some money by getting rid of your collision and comprehensive coverages. Check with your insurance agent.

♦ Health insurance. If you and your partner are both on employer-paid plans, your employer might be willing to refund some of the money they pay for you if you can prove that you're covered under your partner's plan. If you're self-employed and paying for your own plan, consider increasing your deductible or putting your child(ren) on a separate plan. Sometimes "family" coverage is much more than two separate policies—one for the adults, one for the kids.

♦ Use savings to pay off your debts. If you have $1,000 invested at 10 percent, you're earning $100 a year, which becomes $72 if you're in the 28 percent tax bracket. If you owe $1,000 on a 20 percent credit card, your interest payment is $200 a year, which, since you're using after-tax dollars, is really $278 if you're in the 28 percent tax bracket. Get the point? In this scenario, taking the money out of savings would save you more than $200 a year. That may not sound like a lot, but it's enough to pay for most of the clothes your child will go through in a year, or a good chunk of your annual health club membership, or a few sessions with your therapist. You'd have to earn roughly 30 percent (before taxes) on your investment to justify not using your savings to pay off your debt. And if some emergency comes up and you really, really need the money again, you can always get a cash advance on your credit card.

♦ Stop charging. Especially for things that lose their value, such as gas, clothing, cars, furniture, and meals out. If you can't afford to pay cash for these things, maybe you can't afford them at all. Making only the minimum payment pays off your balance in no less than three years. But if you keep buying stuff, you'll never get clean.

♦ If you still insist on charging, at least try to pay off your balance in full every month.

♦ Use a debit card instead. These cards look just like credit cards but take the money directly out of your checking account. Keeping that in mind might just scare you out of using the card altogether.

♦ Take charge of your credit cards. Get credit cards that charge low interest rates and no annual fees. A few years ago I called my own credit card

When Things Get Really, Really Out Of Control

Of course you want to pay what you owe. Just about everyone does. But sometimes, despite your best intentions, things just get to the point where they're no longer manageable. Fortunately, debtors' prisons went out with the nineteenth century. But that probably won't keep you from feeling helpless, humiliated, infuriated, frustrated, and, often, somehow less than a man. Men are supposed to know how to handle money, after all.

If you've gotten to this point and you're feeling completely overwhelmed by your debts and you're being hounded by creditors and collection agencies, you have three basic options.

♦ Keep on doing what you've been doing. But since that hasn't worked up to this point, why keep making yourself miserable?

♦ Get some professional help. A far more sensible approach. The Consumer Credit Counseling Service (CCCS) is a nonprofit group that helps people avoid bankruptcy and restructure their debts. They also have free workshops and seminars on debt management. You can find a local CCCS office at 800-388-2227. You might also want to contact your local chapter of Debtors' Anonymous; check your white pages.

♦ File for bankruptcy. Truly the option of last resort. Bankruptcy can essentially wipe out all debts from credit cards, auto loans, medical bills, utilities, and a few others. On the downside, though, it'll screw up your credit report for at least seven years. And even after you're done, you'll still owe any debts related to alimony and child support, taxes (in most cases), and student loans. Bankruptcy isn't for everyone. So if you're even considering it, get some sound advice first. *How to File for Bankruptcy* by attorneys Stephen Elias, Albin Renauer, and Robin Leonard is a good place to start.

company (which had been charging me $50 a year and 20 percent interest) and told them I'd take my business elsewhere if they didn't do something about their excessive rates. After working my way through several layers of "supervisors," I now pay no annual fee and about 8 percent interest.

♦ Take out a consolidation loan. Chances are that your bank or credit union offers loans at lower interest rates than those you're paying now. In many cases the lender may want you to cancel your credit cards (or at least turn the cards over to them). If you own your own home, consider taking out a home equity loan. The interest you pay on these loans may be tax deductible. Either way, you'll be able to pay off your bills faster and at far lower cost.

BOOSTING YOUR SAVINGS

Now that you've done everything you can to cut your expenses, you're ready for the fun stuff.

For most people, the first big question is, How much should I try to save? Well, the answer depends on your goals. Many experts feel that you should shoot for an income at retirement that's about 70 percent of your current income. If you're in your twenties and just starting to save, you'll be able to accomplish this goal if you sock away 4 to 6 percent of your take-home pay. If you're in your thirties, that goes up to 7 to 12 percent, and if you're in your forties, it's 15 percent or more.

MANKOFF

"Now, where was I?"
"Return on equity, Pop."

DRIP a Little Savings into This

If you're going the do-it-yourself route and you're thinking about investing in stocks, here's a way to save yourself some real money.

Hundreds of companies now offer current shareholders dividend reinvestment plans (DRIPs) that allow them to buy stock directly from the company without having to pay a broker. Some make this service available to new investors as well. These plans almost always allow investors to reinvest dividends without commission. Many allow for automatic electronic purchases direct from your checking account, and several dozen actually allow DRIP participants to buy stock at a below-market rate. Finally, most plans will also let you sell your stock at rates far under what even a discount broker would charge.

So how can you find out about DRIPs? The hard way is to contact individual companies directly to find out whether they offer such programs. A much easier way is to check out the Direct Stock Purchase Plan Clearinghouse. Their phone number and web address is in the Resources section at the end of this book.

Whatever your situation, the most important thing is to save as much as you can as regularly as you can. Here are some things to keep in mind as you're getting started.

♦ **Out of sight, out of mind.** This means trying to have money taken out of your paycheck automatically—that way you'll miss it less than if you had to write a check out every month, and you'll be more inclined to do it regularly. Most employers have direct deposit and most financial institutions are more than glad to help you set up regular electronic withdrawals to a savings account of some kind.

The Best Investment

After paying off your credit cards, one of the most important—and safest—investments you can make is in yourself. If you never finished high school or college or grad school, get it done now. Over the course of your life, the increased salary you'll command and your increased self-esteem, confidence, and general level of happiness will more than pay for the cost of the increased education.

Picking a Financial Planner

Since most states don't have laws regulating or accrediting financial planners (who may also call themselves "advisors," "consultants," or "managers"), just about anyone can set up shop to dole out financial advice and sell products.

Most financial planners are paid on a commission basis, meaning that there's always at least the possibility of a conflict of interest. (In other words, whether or not your investments do well, the financial planner is assured his commission.) Commissions typically range from as low as 4 percent on some mutual funds to the entire first year's premium on a cash value life insurance policy. Others are paid on a fee basis and typically charge from $50 to $250 per hour.

This doesn't mean, of course, that fee-based planners are inherently better than their commission-based colleagues (although many experts believe that you'll be happier, and possibly richer, with someone who charges a fee). Your goal is to find someone you like and who you believe will have your best interests at heart. Here are a few things you can do to help you weed out the losers:

♦ Get references from friends, business associates, and so forth. Alternatively, the Institute of Certified Financial Planners (800) 282-7526 will give you some local references, and the National Association of Personal Financial Advisors (800) 366-2732 makes referrals only of fee-based (as opposed to commission-based) planners.

♦ Select at least three potential candidates and set up initial consultations (which shouldn't cost you anything). Then conduct tough interviews. Here's what you want to know:

♦ **Regularity.** Make your savings plan a habit for life. Making investments of the same amount each month is called "dollar cost averaging" and has some great benefits: when prices are up, you're buying a smaller number of shares. When prices are down you're buying more. On average, then, you'll be fine. This strategy also keeps you from falling into the trap of buying high (just to get on the bandwagon) and selling low (when the bottom has fallen out of the market).

♦ **Avoid temptation.** Don't put your long-term-savings money in any kind of account that has check-writing privileges. Making your money hard to get may increase the chances of your having it for a while.

◊ Educational background. Not to be snobby here, but the more formal the education—especially in financial management—the better. Watch out for fancy initials: many planners prominently display the letters CFP (for Certified Financial Planner) after their names. Forbes magazine recently called the CFP credential "meaningless."

◊ Level of experience. Unless you've got money to burn, let your niece break in her MBA on someone else. Stick to experienced professionals with at least three years in the business.

◊ Profile of the typical client. What you're looking for is a planner who has experience working with people whose income level and family situation are similar to yours.

◊ Compensation. If fee-based, how is the fee calculated? If commission, what are the percentages on each product offered? Any hesitation to show you a commission schedule is a red flag.

◊ Get a sample financial plan. You want to see what you're going to be getting for your money. Be careful, though: fancy graphics, incomprehensible boilerplate language, and expensive leather binders are often used to distract you from the report's lack of substance.

◊ References. How long have customers been with the planner? Are they happy? Better off? Any complaints or weaknesses?

♦ Check your prospective planner's record with state and federal regulators. You can call the federal Securities and Exchange Commission (202) 272-7450 or your state's equivalent to check on disciplinary action and to see whether your candidates have ever been sued.

♦ **Reinvest any interest and dividends.** It's almost like free money, so why take it out? Leaving earnings in the account also helps your balance grow faster.

♦ **Make a good tax plan** (see pages 144–45 for more on this).

♦ **Get an ESOP.** No, it's not a fable, it's an Employee Stock Ownership Plan, and it's offered by more than 10,000 employers across the country. Basically, these plans allow employees to purchase stock in their company without paying commission. Sometimes you can make your purchases with pre-tax dollars, sometimes with after-tax dollars. Some employers let you buy at below-market prices, and some even contribute extra money to your account, which vests (becomes yours) over time, usually five to seven years.

The next big question is, So what do I do with all the money I'm going to be saving? Again, there's no magic formula. Whether you put your money in government bonds or short the pork belly futures market will depend on your individual and family goals and how you feel about risk.

Correctly analyzing these things is a process that's far too complicated to cover here in a way that would be at all helpful. So unless you're already sophisticated financially, get yourself some help. It is, of course, possible to do it yourself, and if you think you want to try, Eric Tyson's *Personal Finance for Dummies* will walk you through the whole process. If you want a more personal touch, you'll need to get yourself a financial planner (see pages 142–43).

A Couple of Things about Tax Planning

Before (or at least at the same time as) you make any real changes to any part of your financial picture, you should be sure to talk to someone knowledgeable about the tax consequences. Your financial planner may be able to offer some help, but a good accountant would be a lot better.

One of the most important things to keep in mind is the changes in tax rates on capital gains (increase in an asset's value). Starting in July 1997, for example, if you've owned an asset (including shares of stock and mutual funds) for more than eighteen months, any capital gains are taxed at 20 percent, down from 28 percent under the old laws. If your taxable income is under $41,200 (for a married couple), your rate may be as low as 10 percent.

So why am I telling you this? Because it may have an effect on the way you invest your money. Because the capital gains tax rate is so much lower than regular income tax rates, you're probably going to want to move your high-yielding assets into something that allows you to defer your income for at least eighteen months (your IRA or other tax-deferred accounts, for example). Keep any lower-earning investments in your taxable accounts (checking or money market, for example). Of course, before you start moving things around, check with your accountant.

Here are a few other critical ways to save on your taxes:

♦ Immediately start a 401(k) if you're eligible for one through your employer. These plans offer participants a series of great benefits. First, since your contributions are taken out of your paycheck before you pay taxes, you reduce your taxable income. Second, the balance of the account grows tax-free until you start making withdrawals—sometime after age 59½ or so.

Sometimes there's a third benefit: your employer may match at least a portion of your contribution, giving you some free money that will also grow tax-free. Remember, though, that 401(k)s are not savings accounts. If you make withdrawals before age 59½, you'll have to pay at least a 10 percent penalty to the Feds and a smaller percentage penalty to your state. And then you'll get hit with a bill for income tax on the full amount withdrawn. That could eat up 50 percent of what you've saved—not the kind of return you were hoping for.

♦ Start an IRA. Starting with the 1997 tax year you and your partner (if you're married) can each contribute $2,000 to an IRA—even if one of you doesn't work for pay (this is up from a total of $2,250 for single-earner couples under the old laws). Like a 401(k), your taxable income is reduced by the amount you contribute to your IRA and the earnings grow tax-free until you start withdrawing it.

♦ If you or your partner is eligible for a company-sponsored retirement plan, you won't be able to deduct your IRA contributions. But make the contributions anyway; the earnings are still tax-deferred.

♦ Consider selling your house. If you're married and filing jointly, the first $500,000 in gain from the sale of your principal residence is now exempt from tax. If you're not filing jointly, the exemption is only $250,000. Either way, you can do this every two years.

Notes:

Hey, Who's In Charge Here?

What's Going On with the Baby

Physically

- There's almost nothing your two-and-a-half-year-old can't do on his feet. He can walk short distances on tiptoe, broad jump with both feet, make sudden starts and stops while running, turn sharp corners on the move, and even step over obstacles.
- His arms and hands are coming along nicely too. He can now differentiate between the two sides of his body (in other words, when pointing with one finger, he doesn't extend the same finger on the other hand). He can also draw an ✕ on purpose and can consistently catch a large ball.

Intellectually

- Kids this age are still quite egotistical and have trouble controlling their impulses. Your toddler may have to pull the books out of the bookshelf 275 times before he's able to forgo his own pleasure in favor of parental approval.
- Symmetry, order, and patterns are especially important to your two-and-a-half-year-old. Half an apple (or a cookie with a bite taken out of it) is completely unacceptable. And if you forget to fasten your seatbelt before starting the car, you're likely to get a stern talking to.
- Band-Aids are your child's best friend, so you'd better stock up. Every single bump, scrape, or bruise—whether you can actually see it or not—can be "cured" instantly with a Band-Aid. "It's as if a leak in the container, the

body, is sealed up and his completeness as a personality is reestablished by this magic act," says Selma Fraiberg.

♦ Although he's just as physically active as before, he seems to be a bit more focused. Instead of doing things and going places for the simple pleasure of doing or going, he now has a specific goal in mind for each action.

Verbally

♦ Your toddler is not much of a conversationalist. He still initiates most verbal interactions but often doesn't respond when you speak to him.

♦ When you speak to him, he seems to understand just about everything you say. But he gets extremely frustrated if you don't understand what he's trying to say.

♦ He's the absolute master of the word *no*. And his negative reactions to you (or refusals to cooperate) are more likely to be verbal than physical.

♦ He talks, sings, and hums to himself while playing.

♦ He still hasn't mastered the concept of large chunks of time (yesterday, today, tomorrow), but he can express small pieces and sequences. "I get dressed now, *then* I have my cereal."

♦ Feeling pretty confident about his budding language skills, your toddler is now starting to play with language (in almost the same way as he plays with objects). He knows what words are "supposed" to sound like and laughs hysterically when you replace a few words of a familiar nursery rhyme with nonsense syllables. Soon he'll begin to imitate these language games and start giving silly-sounding names to objects he doesn't know.

Emotionally/Socially

♦ He's rebellious, defiant, negativistic, and exasperating; he doesn't know what he wants but he knows that he doesn't want to do most of the things you want him to do. Sound like a teenager? Could be, but it's also a description of the average child between the ages of two and three. Not surprisingly, psychologist Fitzhugh Dodson calls this period "first adolescence."

♦ He may drive you nuts with his seeming inability to make a decision and stick to it. If you're taking care of him, he'll demand his mother. If she is, he'll demand you. According to Ames and Ilg, the bottom line is that your two-and-a-half-year-old wants "*whatever* person is not available at the moment, and if everyone *is* available, his demand may change to 'Me do it myself.'"

♦ Being contrary and disobedient is an exhausting job for so young a child, and your toddler is likely to be tired a lot. Unfortunately, tiredness usually makes tantrums worse.

♦ For most toddlers, this is a fairly aggressive time, and violence is common. Fortunately, most aggressive behavior is still experimental and not intended to cause real harm. Ames and Ilg have found that it's "as if the child wonders what kind of response he will get. Thus, a child may hit, grab at, or push another child, then look closely to see what is going to happen."

What You're Going Through

Power Struggles

Here are perhaps the three most important words you will ever hear as a parent: *choose your battles.* Basically, this means that you should think carefully about whether it really matters that your child wants to wear one blue sock and one orange instead of a matched pair. As your child gets older, she becomes more independent. And the more independent she becomes, the more she tends to resist the limits you set. It's all part of growing up: your child needs to know how serious the rules are and how you'll react when they're violated.

I used to spend huge amounts of time arguing with my younger daughter, trying to get her to put her shoes on before getting in the car. I'd threaten, cajole, plead, and bribe, and gradually I'd wear her down and she'd put them on. But the moment she was strapped in her car seat and I was behind the wheel, she'd yank off her shoes and smirk at me in the rear-view mirror. Finally, I gave up, and we're both a lot happier. And for about six months my older daughter absolutely refused to sleep in her own bed. When my wife and I told her she couldn't sleep in ours, our daughter started sleeping on the floor, on the stairs, in the kitchen—anywhere but in her own bed. We argued with her for a while but eventually decided that since she was getting a good night's sleep, we'd leave her alone. A few days after we stopped complaining, our daughter retreated to her own bed.

A friend who lives in Chicago told me that his son suddenly began refusing to get into the family car unless he was stark naked. My friend and his wife made themselves and their son miserable for a few days before shrugging their shoulders and giving up. The three of them enjoyed several peaceful months, and when winter came their son rather sheepishly asked for some clothes.

Children, writes Ellen Galinsky, "have extremely accurate sensors and can tell when a parent is unsure of a limit and then will muster all of their force to dislodge it." Earlier we discussed the importance of setting firm, consistent limits for your child. But believe me, if you're prepared to go to the mat to enforce compliance with every request you make, you'll spend a lot of unnecessary time butting heads with your child. And you won't have the energy to enforce the rules that really matter, such as Don't go into the street unless you're holding hands with a grown-up.

The Mouth That Roars

In 1977 Art Linkletter wrote a book called *Kids Say the Darndest Things*. And boy, was he right. Every parent has dozens of stories about the shocking, embarrassing, horrifying, and hilarious things their innocent toddlers have said.

Has your child asked you (loudly, of course) whether that African-American woman in front of you is made of chocolate, or whether that obese man has eaten an elephant? He will.

I remember taking both my kids to a matinee a while back. The theater was crowded, so my older daughter had her own seat and the younger one, who had just turned two, sat on my lap. A few minutes into the movie, I felt something wet on my leg and instinctively put my hand on the baby's bottom to feel whether her diaper had leaked. Suddenly, at the top of her lungs, she screamed, "Get your hands out of my pants!" It was one of the more discomfiting (and funny) moments of my life.

"My dad says my mom is a Pagan because she serves
burnt offerings for dinner"

Fortunately, not everything your child says will make you want to disappear down the nearest hole. But in many ways the nonembarrassing statements and the ordinary "Why . . ." questions are harder to deal with than the embarrassing ones. They'll make you think about the world in a way you never have before, and jar you into realizing just how little thought most of us give to what's going on around us. How, for example, do you explain homelessness, sickness, natural disasters, and violent crime?

When faced with tough questions, the best thing to do, it seems to me, is turn them into learning experiences (even questions about people made of chocolate can lead to a discussion of what it means to have your feelings hurt).

One of the greatest sources of educational topics is the newspaper (it's got enough pictures to spark the child's interest and is a lot easier to censor than the television). Both my daughters "read" the paper with me in the mornings and ask me to explain the articles that accompany interesting photos. The coverage of Senator Bob Packwood's sexual harassment problems led to fascinating discussions about personal privacy and the times when it's okay or not okay to touch someone else.

Reading the newspaper with a child is also a great reminder of how much basic information adults just take for granted. Try explaining elections, natural disasters, or AIDS to your child and you'll see what I mean.

You and Your Baby

Early Readers
According to reading expert Jim Trelease, studies of children who learned to read early have identified four characteristics of their homes. The first two are fairly obvious and you're probably doing them already: the child is read to on a regular basis, and there is a wide variety of printed materials—books, magazines, newspapers, comics—available in the home at all times.

The remaining factors are somewhat less obvious but may be even easier to implement than the first two.

1. Paper and pencil are available to the child. Most kids get curious about written language by watching their parents write things.
2. People in the home stimulate the child's interest in reading and writing by answering questions, praising the child's efforts at reading and writing, taking the child to the library frequently, buying books, writing down stories that the child dictates, and displaying the child's creations in a prominent place in the home.

"I don't want to see The Lion King *again, I want to read a book."*

HOME LIBRARY UPDATE

Here are the latest additions to your child's ever-growing library:

Blueberries for Sal (and others), Robert McClosky

Bread and Jam for Frances, Russel Hoban

Carl Goes to Daycare (and others), Alexandra Day

The Cat in the Hat, Dr. Seuss

Curious George (and others), H. A. Rey

Frog and Toad Are Friends (and others), Arnold Lobel

The Gingerbread Man, Paul Galdone

Happy Birthday, Moon, Frank Asch

Harry the Dirty Dog (and others), Gene Zion, Margaret B. Graham

Madeline (and others), Ludwig Bemelmans

Mike Mulligan and His Steam Shovel (and others), Virginia Burton

The Snowman, Raymond Briggs

The Snowy Day, Ezra Jack Keats

The Story of Babar, Jean de Brunhoff

The Story of Ferdinand, Leaf Munro

Strega Nona (and others), Tommie de Paola

When I Am Old with You, Angela Johnson

Where the Wild Things Are, Maurice Sendak

To Watch or Not to Watch—Television, That Is

There's one (or two or three or four) in every home, but reading expert Jim Trelease believes that watching television may have a serious negative impact on children. Here's why:

♦ Television is essentially the opposite of reading. A good book will hold a child's attention. But television—even *Sesame Street*—is sliced up into such tiny, disjointed pieces that it teaches a short attention span.

♦ TV is a passive, antisocial, or at least solitary experience, especially for young children. Reading, however, which among small kids often happens with another person, usually includes conversation.

♦ TV deprives the child of the most important learning tool: questions. There's no one to ask and no one to answer.

♦ Most of the programming aimed at young children requires little or no thinking. Trelease cites a recent study in which a group of three- to five-year-olds were shown a "Scooby Doo" cartoon whose soundtrack had been replaced by one from a "Fangface" cartoon. Only 12.5 percent of the kids realized that the soundtrack didn't match the video.

♦ TV discourages thinking. It's nearly impossible to show a character thinking through a problem on TV, and commercials tend to give the message that there is no problem that can't be solved by artificial means—by buying something.

♦ TV discourages creative play.

♦ The messages kids get from TV are flawed. Most fathers are portrayed as

CONCEPTS
How Many Snails, Paul Giganti
If You Look Around You, Testa Fulvio
Numbers (and others), John J. Reiss
Trucks You Can Count On, Doug Magee

FOLK TALES
Goldilocks and the Three Bears, Jan Brett
Jack and the Beanstalk, Joseph Jacobs
Stone Soup, Marcia Brown
Teeny Tiny, Jill Bennett
The Three Billygoats Gruff, Marcia Brown

clueless, incompetent boobs, and beer commercial[s]
the way to be popular is to drink.

In addition, some researchers have speculated tha[t]
between television watching and obesity—probably b[ecause of the]
tendency to snack in front of the tube and not exercis[e]

There are, of course, exceptions to the above-mentioned drawbacks, and
you're probably not planning to toss your television out the window anytime
soon. So if you are going to let your child watch, at least try to keep the following guidelines in mind:

- **Preview and monitor quality.** Watch the things your kid wants to
  watch and assess whether you think it's good. There actually are some
  good-quality programs on the air (PBS's *Reading Rainbow* and *Mister
  Rogers' Neighborhood* are both excellent).
- **Watch together.** Little kids can't always tell the difference between
  reality and what's happening on the screen and may become frightened or
  confused. So use whatever you're watching as the topic for a discussion.
- **Set some basic rules.** For example, no watching during meals or in the
  middle of a family time. And don't just leave the TV on as background
  noise; turn it off when your show is done.
- **Don't use the television (or VCR) as a baby-sitter.** From experience
  I can tell you that this is an incredibly easy trap to fall into, and one your
  child may not be in any hurry to get out of.

POETRY
All Small, David McCord
Blackberry Ink, Eve Merrian
I'll Be You and You Be Me, Ruth Krauss
Where the Sidewalk Ends, Shel Silverstein

GOING TO SCHOOL/DAY CARE
Molly, Ruth Shaw Radlauer
School, Emily McCully

ESPECIALLY FOR OLDER SIBLINGS
Babies!, Dorothy Hinshaw Patent

r Max, Christopher G. Knight (photographer)
s Catalog, Janet Ahlberg, Allan Ahlberg
lius, the Baby of the World, Kevin Henkes
Let Me Tell You about My Baby, Roslyn Banish
The New Baby, Fred Rogers
Peter's Chair, Ezra Jack Keats
Shadow's Baby, Margery Cuyler
The Very Worst Monster, Pat Huchins
When You Were a Baby, Ann Jonas

Play: Getting Physical

One of the biggest myths about play is that extremely active play, especially roughhousing, teaches kids to be violent. The evidence, however, supports the exact opposite conclusion:

♦ Physical play is a model for socially acceptable assertion but not necessarily aggression, according to John Snarey, who has spent several decades studying fathers' impact on their children. "Children who roughhouse with their fathers, for instance, usually quickly learn that biting, kicking, and other forms of physical violence are not acceptable."

♦ "Paternal engagement and physical play as well as maternal verbal interchange are generally positively associated with desirable attributes such as helpfulness, leadership, involvement, and clear communication skills," writes psychologist Ross Parke, "and negatively associated with undesirable attributes such as being apprehensive, being unable to get along with others, and an unwillingness to share."

♦ Physical play builds children's—especially girls'— confidence, assertiveness, and academic achievement. Several studies of successful women have shown that almost all of them had fathers who engaged in a lot of physical play with them.

♦ As we've discussed before, fathers and mothers have a strong tendency to play differently with their boys and girls. And this serves to reinforce children's "socially acceptable" (that is, stereotyped) sex-typed behavior, especially for boys. So if you're interested in reducing the chances that your child will end up trapped in a set of gender-based behaviors, play with him or her actively and frequently.

♦ Parke and his colleagues have also found that for girls, high levels of physical play are associated with such desirable social attributes as positive emotional expressiveness and clarity of communication as well as originality, novelty, and creativity.

A Special Note to Fathers of Girls

Somewhere along the line, people got the idea that girls are delicate and that they shouldn't be played with as roughly as boys.

Well, according to fitness expert Bonnie Prudden, girls are actually hardier than boys. Although more boys are conceived, more girls are born. They survive childhood illness better than boys and ultimately live an average of seven years longer. And in tests of general fitness, girls out-perform boys every time.

The moral of the story? Treat your daughter like you'd treat your son (if you had one). She won't break. And, as the evidence I've cited in this chapter proves, she'll benefit enormously.

"Thanks dad, but I play catch on Monday, Wednesday, and Friday. Tuesday is my day to swing."

Sounds like throwing your kids around just about guarantees that they'll grow up confident, strong, and smart, doesn't it? Well, lots of physical play may increase the chances, but it's important not to force your children to play with you if they don't want to; it can do more harm than good. Research consistently shows that children whose fathers are overly "directive" (meaning they give too many commands) suffer: "Paternal directiveness . . . is associated with negative social attributes, such as being socially withdrawn, seldom being sought out by other children, being hesitant with other children, and being a spectator in social activities," says Parke.

Other Kinds of Fun

LARGE MOTOR SKILLS

♦ Taking a walk on a balance beam, along the curb, or even down a line on the sidewalk.
♦ Jumping over things (anything more than a few inches, though, will be too high for most kids this age).
♦ Throwing, kicking, rolling, and tossing balls of all sizes.
♦ Riding a trike.
♦ Spinning around 'til you drop.
♦ Pounding, pushing, pulling, and kicking.

SMALL MOTOR SKILLS

♦ Puzzles (fewer than twenty pieces is probably best).
♦ Clay or other molding substance.
♦ Finger paints.
♦ String and large beads.

THE BRAIN

♦ Matching games.
♦ Alphabet and number games (put colorful magnetic letters and numbers on the fridge and leave them low enough for the child to reach).
♦ Lots of dress-up clothes.
♦ Dolls of all kinds (including action figures).
♦ "Real" things (phones, computer keyboards).
♦ Sorting games (put all the pennies, or all the triangles, or all the cups together).
♦ Arranging games (big, bigger, biggest).
♦ Pattern games (small-big/small-big).
♦ Counting games (how many pencils are there?).

A FEW FUN THINGS FOR RAINY DAYS

♦ Pillow fights.
♦ A really, really messy art project.
♦ Cook something—kneading bread or pizza dough is especially good, as is roasting marshmallows on the stove (see pages 159–65 for more).
♦ Baby bowling (gentle tossing of the baby onto your bed).

- Other gymnastics (airplane rides: you're on your back, feet up in the air, baby's tummy on your feet, you and baby holding hands).
- Dancing to music.
- Hide and seek.
- A puppet show.

It's All in Their Heads

In the movie *Harvey*, Jimmy Stewart (in the lead role) had an imaginary friend (all right, a six-foot rabbit), and there's little doubt in our minds that he is more than just a bit nuts. But if your child has an imaginary playmate, there's nothing to worry about. In fact, as many as 65 percent of toddlers have imaginary friends.

According to Newman and Newman, imaginary companions serve several very important functions for toddlers:

- They take the place of other children when there are none around.
- They serve as a companion for pretend play.
- They serve as a confidant for children's private expression.

The existence of an imaginary companion may also help the child in his continuing struggle to draw a clear distinction between right and wrong. "Sometimes toddlers do things they know are wrong because they cannot stop themselves, and they find it difficult to accept responsibility for their misdeeds," writes Bruno Bettelheim. "They did not wish to be bad; they do not want to displease their parents; and the imaginary friend becomes a convenient scapegoat. Toddlers report that although they tried very hard to stop their friend, it went right ahead and did the 'bad' thing anyway. When children use an excuse of this kind, they are communicating that they understand the difference between right and wrong but are unwilling or unable to assume total responsibility for their misconduct."

While you should make every effort to go along with your child's claims about the existence of her imaginary buddy, don't let her imagination get the best of you:

- Don't let your child use the imaginary playmate to avoid dealing with the consequences of her actions.
- Don't use the imaginary companion to manipulate the real child (Maria cleaned up her room, so why don't you start cleaning yours?).
- Don't let the imaginary friend be your child's only friend.

♦ If it's not too cold, go outside, strip down to your underwear, and paint each other top-to-bottom with nontoxic, water-based paints.

♦ Otherwise, get bundled up and go for a long, wet, sloppy, muddy stomp in the rain.

♦ Get in the car and drive through puddles.

Group Activities

If you haven't already done so, it's a good idea to start getting your child involved in some regular group activities. Actually, it's a good idea for both of you: it'll give your child an opportunity to meet some new people and to practice her budding social skills. And while she's playing, you'll have a great opportunity to spend time with some adults who probably have many of the same questions and concerns you do.

If you're thinking about forming a regular play group, here are some things to consider:

♦ Find a place where you can easily keep an eye on the kids while you're talking to the grown-ups. A fenced park with benches can be great.

♦ Don't let the group get too large. Even if each adult keeps track of his or her own kids, any more than five or six is pushing it. And try to keep an even number so the little ones can pair off without excluding anyone.

♦ Meet regularly. As you well know, kids love routines.

♦ Bring some of your own toys. This should help reduce the amount of grabbing, shoving, and tears.

♦ Bring some food. Your child will probably prefer to eat someone else's, but some other kid will eat what you bring.

♦ Don't hover. Let the kids do what they want, as long as it's safe.

♦ Play with the other kids—but not too much. If the other little ones seem to be having too much fun with you, your child may get very jealous. Kids this age aren't too thrilled about sharing their daddies.

♦ Don't push togetherness. Kids may not want to play with each other all the time. They need plenty of time to play alone, too.

♦ Have a backup plan in case you get rained out of your regular place. Places like Chuck E. Cheese and Discovery Zone are hot foul-weather destinations. If your backup meeting place is your house, be prepared for a bit more friction than usual. Having to share his house *and* his toys may be more than your child bargained for.

♦ Keep your sick kid at home. Although chances are that whatever he's got has already been passed around, the other parents will be nervous anyway.

Music

During the last half of your child's third year, her language skills make a sudden, often dramatic spurt forward. You'll see this development in two distinct yet connected ways:

First, you'll notice that her imitation skills have become quite sharp: she can now repeat nearly any word or two-word phrase. She can also now tell when she's imitating something correctly and when she's not. Second, now that she's got a good grasp of the sounds that make up her native language, she'll begin using them as toys, amusing herself, and you, by making up her own "words." Musically, a similar development is taking place. "Once they've acquired a simple vocabulary of tonal patterns and rhythms, they can start creating their own songs," says music educator Edwin Gordon.

After a while she'll combine all these skills, and by her third birthday she may be able to sing all the words of a short song ("Happy Birthday to you . . .") or entire phrases of longer, familiar songs ("Baa, baa, black sheep, have you any wool? Yes, sir. Yes, sir. Three bags full," for example; she won't be able to sing the whole song for another few months). She may also make deliberate changes to songs she already knows ("Baa, baa, *blue* sheep . . .")—just for the fun of it.

Your child's sense of rhythm has also been developing nicely. Notice that now when she moves in response to the music she hears she's moving in time with the music (as opposed to making the seemingly random movements you saw just a few months ago).

This is a great time to try various imitation games with your child. Sing a note, then wait for her to repeat it. If she does that pretty well, try two notes, then three (a lot of kids can't do three-note patterns until well after they turn three, so don't get your hopes up too high). Also try tapping out various rhythms and asking your child to repeat them.

Cooking with Kids

Although it seems like a lot of trouble, cooking with your toddler can be a wonderful experience for both of you. Your child, of course, gets to make a huge mess for you to clean up. But besides that, here are a few things that Mollie Katzen, cookbook writer extraordinaire, says that kids get out of cooking:

- Confidence, self-esteem, and a feeling of accomplishment.
- Early math skills—measuring, counting, time sequences.
- Small motor skills.
- A greater understanding of cause and effect.
- An appreciation of the importance of following directions.
- Practice working as a team.

"I wouldn't go into the kitchen. It's become an area of unrest."

You, of course, benefit in very different ways. First of all, you get to use your time more efficiently—having fun *and* cooking dinner (or part of it) for the whole family simultaneously. It's not unlike taking a college course that satisfies a science requirement and a humanities requirement at the same time. Second, there's a good chance that your child will eat some of the food she makes, thereby expanding her food repertoire beyond plain pasta and white rice with soy sauce.

No matter what you're making, your child can participate in at least some part of the preparation. How long your child will actually stay in the kitchen with you usually depends on how much of a mess you'll let her make and whether or not what she's making is worth licking off a spoon. If you're willing to cooperate, just about any three-year-old can:

- Stir (my kids love this).
- Tear up leaves for salad (they hate salad but they love destroying things, so this works out nicely).
- Kneading and rolling out dough (my kids' absolute favorite kitchen activity).
- Break eggs (actually, this may be their favorite).

♦ Measure ingredients and dump them into bowls (if this isn't the favorite, it's certainly a close second, or third).

♦ Sprinkle toppings (Hmmm . . . that's a lot of favorites).

Here are some fun, simple, quick recipes that you and your child can make together. In fact, she can probably handle most of the tasks by herself if you let her. But a few things before you get started:

♦ Read the "Cooking Safety" section on page 163 very carefully.

♦ Don't force. If she doesn't want to do a particular step, let her alone.

♦ Have fun. Yes, she'll get flour all over the floor (and the walls and her clothes). And yes, she'll get broken eggshells into the batter. If you're not in the mood to deal with these things, save your cooking adventure for another day.

FRENCH TOAST

What you'll need:

4 eggs

1 cup milk

1 teaspoon vanilla extract (optional)

Pinch of cinnamon

6 to 8 slices of bread (Stale is fine; moldy is not. If you want to make this even more fun, cut the bread into animal shapes, cars, or faces before you start.)

1 tablespoon butter

Syrup, jam, sour cream, or any other kind of topping

1. Combine eggs, milk, vanilla, and cinnamon in a bowl.
2. Stir (or whisk, if you have one) until mixed thoroughly.
3. Pour the mixture into a pie pan or any bowl or dish that's large enough to hold a slice of bread.
4. Drop a slice of bread in the mixture, let it sit for a few seconds, flip it over, and do the same on the other side.
5. Heat a skillet and add some of the butter.
6. When the butter melts, spread it around and add a slice or two of the batter-soaked bread (as many as can fit on the surface of the skillet without overlapping).
7. Cook until light brown on the bottom. Be careful about this—most kids will refuse to eat anything that's anywhere close to being burned.

8. Flip over and cook until light brown on the other side (or somewhat less, if you happened to have overcooked the first side). Repeat until all slices are cooked.

9. Serve with your kids' favorite topping.

QUESADILLAS

What you'll need:

Cooking spray or 1 tablespoon butter or margarine

Two 6-inch tortillas (Wheat are usually softer, but if your child is allergic to wheat, corn is fine.)

Nice-sized handful of your child's favorite cheese, grated

Several tablespoons of refried beans (optional)

Several tablespoons of steamed rice

Several tablespoons of cooked fresh or frozen vegetables (optional)

1. Put the cooking spray, butter, or margarine in a skillet and place over medium heat.

2. Drop a single tortilla on the skillet and sprinkle some of the grated cheese all over it.

3. If you think your child will eat them, add the refried beans, rice, and/or vegetables.

4. Cover the first tortilla with a second one.

5. Cook for 30 to 45 seconds or until the cheese has melted enough to keep the two tortillas stuck together.

6. Flip over and cook for another 30 to 45 seconds. If you can flip the tortilla sandwich in the skillet, your child and all her friends will consider you the absolute coolest guy in the neighborhood. If you can't, practice.

MILKSHAKES

What you'll need:

1 cup milk

Large piece of your child's favorite fruit

Several ice cubes

1 to 2 drops vanilla extract (optional)

1 to 2 teaspoons chocolate syrup (optional)

1. Put all the ingredients in a blender.

2. Cover and blend until smooth.

Cooking Safety

Cooking with kids can be a huge amount of fun. But because it involves dealing with knives and flames, there's also the potential for getting hurt. Following these safety rules should help you get through the process with a minimum of bloodshed.

♦ Wash your hands before you start. No explanation necessary, right?

♦ Work at your child's level—either at the kitchen table or, better yet, at your child's very own table. This reduces the chances that she'll slip off the stool she's been standing on or that she'll pull a heavy bowl off the counter and onto her head.

♦ Keep pot and pan handles pointed toward the back of the stove. Again, this reduces the chances that hot things will get pulled off the stovetop.

♦ Remind your child about being careful about hot things. Electric stove coils stay hot even after they're turned off and so do pots and pans. Repeat the reminder every ten minutes, as necessary.

♦ Opening ovens, closing them, putting things into them, and taking things out are adult-only jobs. Don't even think about letting a three-year-old try any of these jobs.

♦ Dress appropriately. Long sleeves can get dragged through batter or yanked into blenders. Short sleeves are better. Topless is better still, and the most fun.

PRETZELS
What you'll need:
1 package yeast
1½ cups warm water
1 tablespoon sugar
1 tablespoon salt
4 cups flour
1 egg, beaten

1. Preheat the oven to 425°F.
2. Mix the yeast, water, sugar, and salt until everything is completely dissolved.
3. Stir in the flour.
4. Knead into a soft dough.
5. Roll into long ropes about the thickness of your finger.

6. Shape into pretzel shapes, numbers, letters, or anything your child feels like making.
7. Brush the beaten egg on the shaped dough.
8. Bake for 12 to 15 minutes.
9. Take out and let cool before eating.

POPCORN BALLS

What you'll need:

10 to 12 cups popped popcorn

1 cup corn syrup, OR 1 10-ounce package of marshmallows

$1/4$ cup butter or margarine (only if you use the marshmallows instead of the syrup)

1 or 2 packages of gelatin, any flavor(s) you like

1. Half-fill several large bowls with the popcorn.
2. Put the corn syrup, or the marshmallows and margarine, in a pan and melt over low heat.
3. Add the gelatin. Stir until it's completely dissolved.
4. Remove the mixture from the heat and pour it over the popcorn. Stir quickly so that the popcorn gets covered evenly.
5. Shape the popcorn into baseball-sized balls.
6. Place the balls on a sheet of waxed paper and refrigerate until firm.

EVE'S CHOCOLATE LEAVES

What you'll need:

16-ounce package chocolate chips

New $1/4$-inch paintbrush

Cookie sheet covered with waxed paper

Some thick leaves with stems, gently washed and completely dry.
    (Check with your local garden shop to make absolutely sure
    they're not toxic; camellia and magnolia leaves are pretty widely
    available and are fine.)

1. Melt the chocolate chips over low to medium heat or in the top of a double boiler.
2. Paint the surface of the leaves with a thick coat of the melted chocolate.
3. Put the painted leaves on the waxed paper–covered cookie sheet.
4. When you've painted as many leaves as your child thinks is fun, put the cookie sheet into the refrigerator until the chocolate has hardened.

5. Hold the leaf chocolate-side down, and with your other hand *gently* pull up the stem and carefully remove the leaf from the chocolate.

6. Show your child the way the stem and vein pattern of the real leaf has been replicated in the chocolate.

Family Matters

Preparing the Older Sibling

BEFORE THE BIRTH

♦ Don't start too early. Wait until the child asks some questions about his mother's physical changes, about why you're moving furniture around, and so forth.

♦ Don't make too big a deal about how great it's going to be to become a big brother and don't try to force him to get excited about the prospect.

♦ Take the older child to the prenatal doctor visits. If he's interested, have him hold the Doppler to hear the baby's heartbeat; take him to see the ultrasound pictures. If he's not interested, leave him alone.

♦ Some hospitals offer older-sibling prep classes. In them kids learn: the basics of what their mothers are going to go through during the birth; the kinds of things they can and can't do with their new sibling; and that Dad and Mom still love them very much, even though they aren't going to be the center of the universe anymore.

♦ Expose him to other babies you know. If you don't know any, the nursery at the hospital should have plenty of extras. (Although with many hospitals tightening nursery security, it may be harder to visit babies that aren't your own.)

♦ If you're moving the older child out of a crib, moving to a new house, or making any other major changes, do it long before the baby arrives. Otherwise, the older child will think he's being moved out to make room for the new baby.

AFTER THE BIRTH

Handling your older children's reactions to their new baby brother or sister requires an extra touch of gentleness and sensitivity. Although kids are usually wildly excited (initially, at least) at their new status as big brother or big sister, when it hits them that the baby is going to be a permanent visitor, things change. Psychologist Henry Biller found that most kids show some negative reactions, "often involving an increase in disobedience, demandingness and other forms of regressive behavior."

For example, older children who are already toilet trained may start wetting themselves again (my older daughter did this). They may become clingy, start using "baby talk," or have crying jags for no reason at all. It's as if your older child is saying, "If all you wanted was a crying baby, why didn't you say so? I can cry."

These behavioral changes are perfectly normal and are really the result of the older child's feeling that the baby has stolen something that was exclusively hers: your love and affection.

Interestingly, Biller also found that "children who had a highly positive relationship with their father were much less likely to have severe and continuing adjustment problems after the birth of a new sibling."

Here are a few things you can do to ease the transition for your older kid:

♦ As soon as the new baby is born, call the older child and tell her first. Let *her* make the announcement that she is a big sister to the other members of the family.

♦ Have the older child come to the hospital right away (even if it's past her bedtime). Take a few pictures of her holding the baby.

♦ Don't expect your older child to love the baby instantly. It can take a long, long time. Really. A friend of mine told me that for years, every time he drove by the hospital the baby had been born in, his oldest son would ask, "So can we take her back yet?"

♦ Don't make a big fuss about the new baby in front of the older child—it will only make the older one feel left out, jealous, and resentful, advises pediatrician Barton White. It could also result in the older child's trying to hurt the baby. Have everyone who comes to visit the baby spend a few private minutes with the older child first.

♦ Don't blame yourself. Friction between your older and younger kids is normal. Saying, "If only I'd done . . . he'd love the baby" is a waste of time.

♦ Get some special gifts for the older child.

♦ Go through your photo albums, reminding the older child of what a wonderful baby she was.

♦ Encourage the older child to get involved. Let her help as much as possible with "her" baby—holding, feeding, diapering, clothing, singing or talking, and running errands around the house. And be sure to be extra appreciative.

♦ Teach the older child how to play with the baby. It might be fun to show the older child how to elicit reflex actions from the baby (see *TNF I*, pages 38–39).

But never leave the baby alone with your older child, not even for a second (unless, of course, your older one is over twelve). Your primary consideration is, of course, to keep the new baby alive and uninjured. And you'll need to remind the older child (dozens of times) that hurting the baby is simply not allowed. And make it clear that doing so will result in not being allowed to play with the baby for a while.

♦ Give the older child some space of her own that's completely off-limits to the baby.

♦ Allow her to have things she doesn't have to share at all. With toys that must be shared, be meticulous about giving each child equal time—set a timer with a loud beep.

♦ Give the older child plenty of opportunity to be out of the home regularly— sleepovers at friends' and grandparents', off with the baby-sitter, and so on. Otherwise, she'll feel in competition with the baby all day. Be careful, though, not to do too much of this—you don't want to give the child the impression that you're booting her out.

♦ Spend plenty of time alone with the older child doing special activities focused exclusively on her needs, showing her you still love her. Just saying so won't do the trick.

♦ Give the older child a few privileges—a later bedtime perhaps.

♦ Encourage the older child to express her emotions. Ask a lot of questions about how she feels. Keep the questions focused on her—not on the baby. She's probably tired of being asked how she likes being a big sister.

♦ Treat every vocal expression of pain or rage as positive, Biller recommends. You can't force a child to feel love if she doesn't feel it. And it's far better for her to *say* something hurtful than to express the idea physically. If she needs to burn off some hostility, make sure she gets plenty of exercise.

♦ Empathize. Vicky Lansky suggests expressing your own occasional annoyance with the baby's demands to your older child, but not so often that he or she gets the idea that the new sibling is a permanent nuisance. Express your joy, too. And talk about your own experience as an older child (if you were one).

♦ Look at the world from the older child's perspective. Imagine how it feels to your toddler when she sees her younger sister wearing a hand-me-down— even if she outgrew it long ago. To her it can seem like there's nothing left of her.

♦ For a child, the expression "it's not fair" really means "it's not the same." So get two of everything, and make sure the older child gets the first pick.

♦ Be prepared. When older children are forced not to hit younger siblings (life is tough, isn't it?), their aggression doesn't just disappear. It has to come out somewhere, and frequently it is reborn as a temper tantrum.

Those Pearly Whites

Although a few dentists think kids should have their first exam at about six months, almost all of them agree that you shouldn't wait any longer than three years before getting your child's teeth checked. By this time she should be brushing at least once a day and flossing (you'll have to help) daily.

Like most new things, the first trip to the dentist can be a scary experience. So start preparing your toddler several weeks in advance. Tell her you're going to a special doctor who is going to count her teeth and take some pictures of them. Have her practice opening her mouth with you, just to show her that there's nothing to fear.

If you have the time, take your child by the dentist's office to meet the staff a few days before the appointment so she can get familiar with the surroundings. Though you shouldn't ever lie to your child about what is going to happen at the dentist's office, make a special point to stay away from words that might frighten her, such as drill, needle, shot, and pain. And save all of your personal dental horror stories until she's a teenager.

LOOKING FOR MR. GOODBRUSH

Just as it's more appropriate to take your child to a pediatrician than to your internist, your child should have his teeth looked at by a pediatric dentist—someone who specializes in children—*not* the guy you've been going to for the past twenty years.

At my daughters' dentist, the waiting rooms are filled with toys and bowls of fruit. The furniture is all bright colors and kid-friendly patterns. In the examining room there are televisions mounted on the ceiling so the kids can watch videos while their teeth are being cleaned. And in the x-ray area, kids sit on a horse—complete with saddle and stirrups—instead of a regular chair. What I want to know is, where the hell were the pediatric dentists when I was a child?

Despite all the attempts to distract your child, she may still scream, squirm, and try to escape. Don't be embarrassed. Any good pediatric dentist and her staff see the same little show a hundred times a day.

Some dentists think it's a good idea to have parents in the examining room with their children; others think it's a rotten idea. Fortunately, you know your child better than anyone, so you know whether you need to hold her hand or do everyone a service by waiting in the car.

33-36

Learning to Let Go

What's Going On with the Baby

Physically

♦ If it wasn't already, it should be fairly clear by now whether your child is left- or right-handed.

♦ Her hand coordination is constantly improving. She tries to imitate your writing and can draw a pretty passable circle (or at least a swirl).

♦ She very neatly lays out her clothes for the next day the night before and has no trouble putting on her own pants, socks, T-shirt, and jacket. Buttons, snaps, and zippers may still give her some trouble.

Intellectually

♦ As she approaches her third birthday, your toddler will be quite comfortable with many short-term time concepts. She regularly uses "soon," "in a minute," and the endearing "this day" (instead of "today").

♦ She's also deepening her understanding of spatial relationships—she's mastered "in" and "out," but the more abstract "near" has eluded her until now.

♦ She's very concerned that every object has its own special place, and she may get quite upset if things aren't where they're supposed to be.

♦ She can now count up to three. (She may be able to say her numbers up to ten, but she doesn't really know what they mean.)

Verbally

♦ By her third birthday your child will understand the majority of the conversational language she'll use for the rest of her life. And about 80 percent of what she says can be understood, even by strangers.

- Boys' verbal skills and vocabularies are still lagging a bit behind girls'. Boys generally tell shorter stories whose main characters are usually themselves. Girls' stories are longer and their main characters are more likely to be adults.
- Your toddler is finally able to use tenses (although not always completely accurately). My mother fell down and tore a ligament in her knee, and we told my younger daughter about it the next day. For months afterward, she would look up and announce: "Grandma fell down boom and hurt her leg yesterday."
- Kids acquire most of their understanding of time words in the six months between ages two and a half and three.

Emotionally/Socially

- Like their teenage counterparts, "first adolescents" are incredible know-it-alls. But the veneer of confidence is pretty thin. "It helps to remember that the child is bossy not because he is sure, but actually because he is unsure," write Ames and Ilg. "The world still seems big and dangerous to him. If he can command even a small part of it (his parents), it helps him to feel secure." As your toddler's language skills improve, thus enabling her to gain some control over her impulses, the world will become (in her eyes) much less dangerous.
- Your "first adolescent" is still quite negative and contrary. But it's critical to keep in mind that her negativity is part of an important developmental stage. "The first step toward a positive self-identity and sense of selfhood is a negative self-identity, a negation of the values and desires of his parents," writes psychologist Fitzhugh Dodson. "A negative self-identity must precede positive self-identity."
- It's taken a while, but your toddler is finally beginning to interact regularly with her playmates. These interactions are not, however, as pleasant as we'd like them to be. "The dominant drive at this age," write Ames and Ilg, "tends to be the effort to try, either verbally or physically, to keep others away from their things."
- Although her sense of humor is getting more sophisticated, it's still the incongruous that gets the biggest laughs: try to put on her shoes or wear her pants on your head and you're likely to reduce your toddler to hysterical laughter. Other funny things: accidents (unless someone is injured), silly questions ("Where are your wings?"), and adults imitating baby talk.

What You're Going Through

Speaking Up

I was second in line to buy stamps at the post office when a young woman came into the lobby, dragging a three-year-old boy behind her. "Now just sit down over there and shut up," she snapped, pointing the boy to an empty seat on a nearby bench. But instead of sitting, the boy began to run around the lobby. And that's when his mother grabbed him. "I'm sick and tired of you," she said as she slapped his face, hard. "And you better quit that crying or I'll—" He didn't. She did, this time knocking him to the floor.

I was stunned. Whatever that little boy had done, it certainly didn't warrant the treatment he was getting. At first I wanted to say something to the woman, but I couldn't bring myself to do it. Then I looked around the post office, hoping

"Excuse me for sounding like a Jewish mother, but may I point out that your kid is getting wet."

that maybe someone else would say something. But everyone seemed to be concentrating on the return addresses on the envelopes they'd brought. The woman was still smacking her child when my turn came. I bought my stamps, exchanged helpless looks and shoulder shrugs with the clerk, and quickly left. I sat outside in my car for a while, furious—not only at that woman for hitting her child but also at myself and at everyone else in that post office. How could a bunch of adults have stood by silently?

Certainly, seeing an adult abuse a child is something that bothers just about everyone. But to parents concerned about the safety and welfare of our own children it's especially disturbing. Unfortunately, though, it happens all the time. And since we're likely to be spending time in places where there are other families around, we're likely to see more than our share.

WHY WE DON'T SPEAK UP

Most of us know what we'd do (or at least what we *think* we'd do) if someone tried to hurt our children. So why are we so hesitant to speak up when someone else's kids are being abused? Are we just uncaring and insensitive? "Not at all," says psychology professor Mark Barnett. "Historically, children have been regarded as personal property. And we still tend to believe that parents have the right to deal with them however they see fit."

Another reason we don't speak up when we see someone treating a child inappropriately is that most of us try to blend into our surroundings, hoping that someone else will take the lead. But when no one does, "We downplay our own reactions and convince ourselves that what we initially thought was abusive behavior really wasn't that bad after all," claims Dr. Ervin Staub. Staub refers to this extremely common phenomenon as "pluralistic ignorance."

But hesitating to "butt in" and taking one's cues from others are definitely not the only factors that keep us silent. Imagine this scenario: you're walking home alone at night, when you see a large man coming out the door of a house carrying a screaming child. He quickly stuffs her into the back seat and gets ready to drive away. He sees you staring suspiciously at him and glares back. Are you face to face with a violent kidnapper or just a frantic father taking a sick child to the hospital? If you play it safe and say nothing, you are probably experiencing one of the other feelings most likely to keep people from speaking up: fear of putting oneself in physical danger.

For better or for worse, passersby almost never have a *legal* obligation to do anything. (Doctors, dentists, teachers, social workers, and, in some states, the people who develop film at the local drugstore, however, are required to report suspected abuse to the proper authority.) But there are clearly times when all of us have a *moral* obligation to do something. Suzanne Barnard, a spokesperson for the Children's Division of the American Humane Society, suggests the following guidelines:

- If an adult is causing a child serious or life-threatening injury (hitting hard enough to leave a mark or actually drawing blood), do something.
- If a child has been abandoned or negligently left in a dangerous situation (locked in a car in hot weather with the windows closed), do something.
- If the child's actions make it reasonably clear that he or she is scared, or that the person doing the suspected abuse is a stranger to her, do something.

WHEN TO OPEN YOUR MOUTH

For some of us, confronting others is no problem. "I'd rather risk embarrassing myself to save a child," a friend of mine once told me, "than have to live with myself knowing that I could have done something but didn't." Of course, "confronting" doesn't have to mean "attacking." "If you can approach the parent in a non-judgmental way, there are things you can say that can help defuse the situation," says Barnard.

The National Committee for the Prevention of Child Abuse (NCPCA) endorses the following approach:

- Divert the *adult's* attention away from the child by sympathizing or by offering some praise for the child: "My child did the same thing just yesterday" or "He has the most beautiful eyes."
- Divert the *child's* attention by talking to her or pointing out something of interest.
- Say positive things—negative remarks or looks are likely to increase the parent's anger and could make matters worse.

For many of us, however, approaching a stranger—even to do something as simple as ask directions—is simply too embarrassing or daunting to do. So if you can't, don't feel guilty—you're not a wimp. You still can make an anonymous report to the appropriate authorities, who will check it out for you.

If you're in a store, contact the manager immediately and have him or her call the police (if the manager refuses, call the police yourself). If you're outside, try to get the adult's license plate number and then call 911. If you're concerned about a neighbor, call your county child protective services and give them the address.

THE FEAR OF MAKING A MISTAKE

But what should you do when the situation is not so clear-cut, or when you're seeing something that looks more like a flash of temper rather than a case of prolonged abuse? After all, as parents we've all come close to "losing it" on a particularly bad day. And what about that kid you know who's always covered with bruises?

Before calling the police, take a good, long look at the situation and make sure your suspicions are reasonable. As you well know, children are always having accidents and a few bruises and cuts are usually not an indication of abuse.

If you need help evaluating what you've seen, or if you want to know how to make a report in your area, call one of the following organizations and ask them how to get in touch with your county social services agency:

♦ CHILDHELP/IOF FORESTERS
National Child Abuse Hotline
1-800-4-A-CHILD or
1-800-2-A-CHILD (TDP) for the hearing impaired
♦ The American Humane Association
Children's Division
Denver, CO
(800) 227-4645

You and Your Baby

More on Sex Identity

A DIFFERENT KIND OF PLAYTIME

As you well know by now, the toddler years are the age of exploration, a time when your child explores her world and especially all the great things she can do with her body. The experts are essentially unanimous in saying that giving a child as much freedom as possible to explore her world is critical to the development of autonomy and self-confidence. And most parents are perfectly willing to let their children explore whatever they want to, until, that is, they start exploring their own genitals.

Genital self-exploration is a phase nearly all toddlers go through, and it is especially common right around the time they start making the transition from diapers to big-kid underwear. After all, when they were wearing their diapers all the time, their genitals were pretty hard to grab hold of. But now that they're accessible nearly all the time . . . (Reminds me a little of the old joke: Why do dogs lick their crotches? Because they can.)

Common or not, it's still a little discomfiting to watch a child play with his or her own genitals, and it's hard to resist pulling the child's hand away or shouting, "Stop that!" Maybe it's all those stories we heard about how masturbation causes blindness or hairy palms, or turns kids into perverts.

Whatever the reason, it's truly important that you resist the urge to step between your child and her genitals. Making a big deal out of it can give your child the message that that part of her body is dirty or that touching it is somehow wrong. For a little boy, "His penis is no more interesting than any other part of him," says Fitzhugh Dodson. "It is only when we react as though there is something bad or naughty about it that we teach him to become morbidly interested." The same obviously goes for little girls. The truth, of course, is that "our toddlers will only develop sex hangups if we teach them to," says Dodson.

At home, the best plan of action is neither to encourage nor to discourage genital exploration. In public places, however, gently redirect your child to another activity, telling her that private touching should be done in a private place, such as her own room in her own home. Here are a few more things you can do:

- Teach your child the correct names for human body parts—including penis, vagina, and rectum—just as you did for belly button, nose, and elbow.
- Explain physical differences between adults and children. Adults' pubic hair (and the hair on your chest, legs, back, and elsewhere) and adult-size genitals are of special concern to kids. The simple answer (one that's perfectly adequate for kids this age) is that as you get bigger, everything gets bigger and that when you get to be a grown-up you get hairier.
- Talk about touching. It's simply not okay for anyone (adult or child) to touch anyone else in his or her private area—except if the adult is a doctor or a parent bathing a child or changing her diaper. Bathroom privacy (closing the door, knocking) is also a good topic to bring up now.
- Stay away from intimate touching or sex in front of your child. But be warned: your child will walk in on you one day. And scrambling around trying to cover up may make your child think there's something wrong with your (and, by extension, her) body.

MODESTY VERSUS SHAME: WHY IT MAY BE TIME TO KEEP YOUR PANTS ON

At about the same time as your child develops an interest in her own body, she might become suddenly conscious of yours—and of the differences between yours and your partner's and between yours and hers (or his, if you've got a boy). This is most likely to come up if you have a habit of not wearing much clothing around the house.

Hyperactivity Alert

One of the most common—and least accurate—behavioral "diagnoses" these days is ADHD (attention deficit/hyperactivity disorder). While fewer than 5 percent of American children actually have ADHD, it is "diagnosed" far more frequently, often by people who have no business making a diagnosis of any kind. In my view, this overdiagnosis is a direct result of a combination of four factors:

♦ Teachers and day-care workers naturally prefer the kids who obey to those who don't. They also want children to be calmer—they're easier to care for that way.

♦ Research has shown that female teachers are less tolerant of physical activity than male teachers.

♦ Most day-care workers and preschool teachers are women.

♦ Since boys are perceived to be more active than girls, they are perceived to be "acting out," or hyperactive, seven to eight times more frequently than girls.

The natural consequence of this overdiagnosis is that it's becoming more and more common for kids to be drugged into submission. So if your baby-sitter, day-care provider, or preschool teacher tells you your child is hyperactive or suffers from ADHD, do not panic. Instead:

♦ Be skeptical. A lot of what is "diagnosed" as ADHD is nothing more than normal toddler behavior.

♦ Think about your child's temperament. Is he naturally active?

♦ If you're still worried, take your child to the pediatrician. Have him or her do an analysis of your child's diet—something that can have immediate impact on behavior.

♦ If your pediatrician suggests it, have your child tested by a qualified child psychiatrist.

♦ If the child psychiatrist suggests drugs, get a second opinion.

Generally speaking, there's nothing wrong with your child's seeing you or your partner naked. But how do you know when to be a little more modest around your child? The answer, of course, depends on many factors—your attitudes and comfort levels about nudity (do you think the human body is something to be proud of or something that should be kept completely private?), your child's awareness of the physical differences between you, and much more.

In my case, my daughters basically told me when to get dressed. I used to take baths with them, until one day, when the older one was about three, she decided to grab my penis in the bathtub—a pretty serious hint that I should either wear a swimsuit or she should bathe alone.

With my younger daughter the hint came a little earlier: one afternoon just after she'd turned two, she and I spent about half an hour talking about all the different kinds of tails animals have and why people don't have them at all. The next morning she strolled into the bathroom just as I was stepping out of the shower. We chatted for a second, but suddenly she gave me a stunned, betrayed look and pointed at my crotch. "Daddy has a tail," she announced. Clearly, she felt that I'd lied to her.

Just remember: your feelings about nudity (just like your feelings about everything else) rub off on your children. "In teaching and practicing modesty, we emphasize closeness, intimacy, and self-respect," writes child development expert Lilian Katz. "Shame, on the other hand, is generated by implying that curiosity about the body or nakedness is bad or by suggesting that feelings of sexual arousal experienced even by a young child (such as a young boy having an erection when he or someone else is naked) are in some way inappropriate or dirty. Scolding, teasing, or other strong reactions to curiosity, exploration, and exhibitionism (a child's deliberate act of running around naked) may make a young child feel guilty about early sexual feelings that are in fact quite natural and universal. It would help to respond to the child's feelings and curiosity by accepting and acknowledging them as understandable and at the same time by indicating that there's a time and place for everything."

More Adult Separation Problems

I don't think I'll ever forget the time I drove my older daughter a few blocks away from my house and abandoned her. Well, I didn't really abandon her, I just took her to preschool. But it was my first time, and somehow I felt I'd done something wrong.

When our first child was born, my wife and I both cut our work loads to three days a week so we could spend as much time as possible with her. And for the first two and a half years of her life, at least one of us was with her almost all the time. But as I sat in my car after dropping her off for her first day of preschool, I began to wonder what kind of parent I was, leaving her all alone with people I hardly knew. Would they read to her? Could anyone possibly teach her as well as my wife and I had? Who would encourage her? And who would love her? I was nearly overcome with a need to run back to the school, grab her, and take her home where she belonged.

After a few minutes of this sort of thinking, it became painfully clear that

"Soon you will be entering a phase son, in which you will no longer pay attention to anything I have to say. Please let me know when that changover occurs."

my wife and I had spent months preparing the wrong person for our daughter's first day of school.

Fighting the urge to go back to the school, I drove home and sat down in front of my computer. I tried to remind myself that up until then I had actually been looking forward to having my child in school, knowing I'd have a lot more time to write. But as I stared dumbly at the screen-saver, I kept thinking that maybe my priorities were in the wrong order. After all, what's more important, my getting to write a few articles or making sure my children get the best possible education? Eventually, though, I had to admit that school was clearly the best place for my daughter, especially a school taught by teachers all our friends agree are gifted.

What it really comes down to, I guess, is that I knew I was going to miss my daughter while she was at school. I'd miss the wonderful times we had—the rainy-day matinees and museums and the sunny-day outings, the hours spent cuddling on the couch reading the same book ten times in a row, or sitting at her table drawing. And most of all, I'd miss the long talks we had and the feeling of overflowing joy and pride I got from watching her learn new things and seeing how bright and articulate she'd become.

But missing her wasn't all there was. I was jealous, too. It just didn't seem fair that my daughter's teachers—people who hardly knew her—were going to be the beneficiaries of so much of her company. Oh sure, the two of us would still have plenty of afternoons together in the park, and we'd still make pizza dough, and soak each other with the hose while watering the garden, and hide under the covers in my bed, ready to scare my wife when she came home from work. But no matter how much time we'd spend together now, I knew it would never seem like enough because I'd always remember the time when I didn't have to share her with anyone.

She was still so small and helpless, but at the same time already off on her own. It really seemed like the end of an era.

I remembered then (and still do now) going into her room at night when she was a baby and marveling at her angelic, smiling face and her small, perfect body. It was always a struggle not to wake her up to play. Thinking about it now, I realize that I was jealous even of her dreams.

I guess I should have known what I was going to feel as I dropped her off on her first day of school. I remember going to pick her up at the park a few months before. I stood outside for a few minutes, watching her chat and play with her friends. She seemed so mature, so grown up, so independent. Until that moment, I'd felt that I knew her completely. I knew the characters she'd pretend to be, I knew what she liked and didn't like, and we told each other everything. But watching her interact with other people—sharing secrets I'd never hear—I realized that the process of separating from our parents doesn't begin by moving out of their house at seventeen or by joining the Marines. It really begins at three, in a park, digging tunnels in the sand with a friend.

Family Matters

Teaching the Kids about Money

For most parents, the thought of teaching our preschoolers about money is almost as scary as imagining having to teach them about sex. We know we're going to have to do it sometime, but we hope we can put it off for a while.

But think about it: there's really nothing in our lives that we use as frequently as money—from paying the rent and the electric bill to giving charity to a homeless family—and there's nothing that causes us so many problems. Money issues, for example, are a leading cause of divorce.

The point of this section, then, is to get you to start teaching your child about money—what it does and doesn't do—while she's still young. "If you don't know the real value of money, you can come to worship it too much," says Neale Godfrey, author of *A Penny Saved . . . : Teaching Your Children the Values and Life-Skills They Will Need in the Real World*. "Bad financial habits in childhood can lead to worse problems when you're grown up."

Your child probably knows a few more things about money than you think she does. For example, she knows in a general sort of way that one needs money to get things, and she knows (or thinks, anyway) that you always have some. Most kids absolutely refuse to accept "I don't have any money with me" as an excuse for not buying them whatever they want whenever they want it. "Why don't you just go get some out of one of those machines?" they say. If you're not careful about how you teach your children about money, says Godfrey, it can "take on a magical quality."

The best way to keep money from becoming too mysterious and alluring is to introduce the concept in a matter-of-fact way.

MAKING THE INTRODUCTION

♦ **Go to the store.** Stores provide a great opportunity to talk about lots of money-related things: how much things cost, how you know the prices, paying for things by check or credit card, the mechanics of making change. All these themes introduce the idea that things cost money.

♦ **Awareness.** Let your child look at the check in restaurants. Show him that the numbers on the check are (or should be) the same as the ones on the menu.

♦ **Identification.** Get four jars, label each with the name of a coin: penny, nickel, dime, quarter. Put a few of the appropriate coins in each jar. Then take a coin out of your pocket, tell the child what it is, and put it (or have him put it) in the correct jar.

♦ **Participation.** Let your child hand the money to the clerk and collect the change.

♦ **Counting games.** Have your child count out the forks and spoons when you're setting the table. Have him help you make recipes, scooping out the right number of spoonfuls of ingredients.

♦ **Equivalence games.** Using real coins, show your child that a nickel is the same as a stack of five pennies, that five nickels are the same as a quarter, or that two nickels are the same as a dime. Two dimes and a nickel for a quarter is too complex at this age.

♦ **Categorizing games.** As you're going up and down the aisles of the supermarket, have your child help you spot round things, red things, boxed

*"That's it, start saving your money now. You'll never see a dime
of Social Security."*

things, and so forth. Being able to organize items into groups is a critical
math and money-handling skill.

♦ **Comparisons.** Which products are a better bargain? If the store you're in
sells three oranges for a dollar, and the other store you go to has two oranges
for a dollar, which is a better deal? Why do you go to the other store at all?

♦ **Prioritizing.** Talk about which products your family needs and which
ones you want.

♦ **Be patient.** It will take years for all these ideas to sink in.

THE FAMILY PAYROLL

There are four things you can do with money: get it, spend it, save it, and
give it away. And since you need to do the first one before any of the others,
Godfrey suggests that parents put their kids on the family payroll by giving
them an allowance. (When the kids are older, you'll tie their allowance to the
performance of certain household chores. But for now, start with an uncon-
ditional allowance.)

Since they turned three, my wife and I have paid each of our daughters their
age in dollars—a veritable fortune to those us who had to make do on an
extremely sporadic fifty cents a week. But don't worry, it doesn't all go straight
into their pockets. Here's how it works:

You pay out the three dollars as ten quarters and ten nickels, and the first thing your child does is take 10 percent of her money (one nickel and one quarter) and put it into a jar marked "Charity." She gets to decide what to do with this money (either give it directly to a homeless person or combine it with some of your money and send it by check to a deserving organization).

She then divides the remaining coins into six neat piles—three with three quarters, three with three nickels. Next she takes a stack of each (ninety cents) and drops them into three different jars:

♦ The instant gratification jar. Bite your tongue. It's her money, so let her spend it however she wants—even if it's on candy. She'll learn awfully quickly that once it's gone, it's gone.

♦ The medium-term jar. This one gets saved up for a week or two and can then be cashed in for a larger toy or expense.

♦ The long-term jar. Basically, she'll never see this money again. Let it accumulate in the jar for a while, then take it (and your child) down to the bank and open up a savings account.

As wacky as this whole allowance scheme sounds, the opportunities for learning are amazing: counting, percentages, division, categorizing, the importance of helping others, the value of patience, the benefits of saving, and so much more.

To Rent or to Buy?

One of the most important choices you have to make as a parent is where you're going to live. If you're like most people, you'll base your decision on how close you are to friends and family; how far you are from your job; how good the schools and day-care centers are; the crime rate; the weather; and more. Once you've taken care of those important considerations, the next big question is whether to rent a home or an apartment or buy one.

Back in the 1980s, when homes were appreciating 10 to 15 percent or more a year, buying a house was the best option for just about everyone. But with inflation (and housing prices) stagnant, it's far from a slam-dunk kind of decision. There are clear advantages and disadvantages to both options.

If you already own a home, you're probably reasonably happy with your housing arrangements. But if you rent, you're probably feeling a little more unsettled. A recent survey by Fannie Mae (the Federal National Mortgage Association) found that 84 percent of renters feel that buying a home is better than renting. Nevertheless, most of them are still living in a rental. Here are the top five reasons why:

Renting

ADVANTAGES

- All you pay is rent (and utilities, unless they're included in the rent); no property taxes, no maintenance fees, no repair costs.
- If something needs repair or replacing, someone else will do it for you.
- You have nearly complete freedom to move almost anytime you want.

DISADVANTAGES

- You aren't building equity.
- You might have to deal with obnoxious neighbors on the other side of a thin wall or ceiling.
- You might have to deal with obnoxious landlords.
- Your rent will probably go up every year or two.
- You can be evicted.
- You don't have any real pride of ownership.

Homeownership

ADVANTAGES

- Pride of ownership: all that you survey is yours.
- You may be building equity.
- Real estate usually appreciates over time.
- There are some potentially large tax benefits: mortgage interest and property taxes are deductible, meaning that they reduce your taxable income and therefore the amount of taxes you pay.

DISADVANTAGES

- Sooner or later you're going to need to replace the roof or get some termite work done and it all comes out of your pocket.
- If the real estate market goes down you may actually lose money when you sell.
- Property taxes and homeowner's insurance costs usually rise every year.

- They can't find housing they can afford. Two-thirds of renters are in exactly this situation.
- They can't put together enough for a down payment.
- They can't find a house in the right neighborhood.
- They're bogged down by credit problems.
- They've received insufficient and/or confusing information about how to buy a house and obtain financing. In fact, only 45 percent of adults say they completely understand the home-buying process or are comfortable with it.

Doing the Numbers

One of the most important factors in the rent versus buy debate is the question of which option leaves you better off financially. Here's a worksheet that my accountant uses to help his clients work their way through this tough decision. It may help you do the same.

MONTHLY EXPENSES	RENT	BUY
Rent	_____	
Payment (principal and interest—you can get this info from a local title company)		_____
PMI (mortgage insurance charged by lenders if you make a down payment of less than 20 percent)		_____
Insurance (fire, liability, contents, etc.)	_____	_____
Utilities	_____	_____
Repairs and maintenance		_____
Major improvements	_____	_____
Total monthly expenses	_____	_____
Subtract the tax benefits of owning a home*		(_____)
Actual monthly expenses to rent vs. to buy	_____	_____

If the Buy figure above is lower than the Rent one, skip the rest of this worksheet and buy your house. In most cases, though, it isn't, and you've got one more small calculation to go.

The difference between monthly rental and buy expenses, × 12 _____

Cost of your new home _____ × the expected annual appreciation ___ % _____

If the appreciation line is greater than the one above, you're better off buying. If not, you're not.

———————————

*Tax benefits to owning a home
    monthly mortgage interest _____
    monthly property taxes _____
    other deductible expenses (if buying a home now allows you to itemize your deductions, you can deduct your state income taxes, charitable contributions, and several other expenses that you couldn't have taken before) _____
    total deductions _____
    your tax bracket (federal and state) ___ %
    total monthly savings (total deductions × tax bracket) _____

IF YOU'VE DECIDED TO BUY

Before you start running around all over town looking at open houses, there are a few things you need to do.

First, sit down and take a look at your finances. Start with a thorough review of your income and expenses for the past twelve months. How much can you afford to pay? Actually, what you think you can afford and what your lender

Dealing with Down Payment Woes

Down payments are a crucial part of every home purchase. And they're the source of an enormous amount of worry. Here are the two biggest reasons why you might be pulling your hair out:

1. The opportunity cost is too high. In other words, you're worried that you'll have to take your down payment money out of some kind of account that is currently earning you some money, and you're concerned about losing that income. But imagine this: If your $35,000 down payment (20 percent on a $175,000 house) was earning 10 percent a year, you'd bring in $3,500 each year (less after you've paid your taxes on it). But if your house appreciates by 4 percent a year—the national average—you're picking up $7,000 the first year and more every year after that.

2. You don't have enough to make a down payment. This is a bit tougher to overcome. But there are some possibilities:

   ♦ Try to save more. It's hard. Very hard. You might want to go back over some of the suggestions on pages 137–44.

   ♦ Shop around for a low down-payment loan. The Federal Housing Authority (FHA) has some programs that allow first-time buyers to put down as little as 3 percent. In addition, a number of national and local mortgage companies offer loans for 100 percent of the value of the property. Restrictions, as they say, apply, so check with a reputable mortgage broker.

   ♦ Get help from your family. As we discussed earlier (see page 97), each of your parents can give you $10,000 tax-free per year (for a total of $20,000, unless you have more than two parents). Besides helping you over the hump, this will reduce the size of their estate and, possibly, the amount of future estate taxes. If you do take money from your parents, though, be sure to get a letter from them explaining that what they've given you is a gift, not a loan.

thinks you can afford may well be two very different things. Generally speaking, lenders shoot for what they call a 28/36 debt ratio. This means that no more than 28 percent of your gross monthly income can go toward housing, and that your total monthly expenses combined (including housing) can't be more than 36 percent of your monthly income. Also, if your down payment will be less than 20 percent, the 28/36 ratio may drop to 25/33, a small but often significant difference.

Next, answer this question: How's your credit (and your partner's)? The best way to answer this question is to get yourself a copy of your credit report and look it over for yourself—before a potential lender has a chance to. Doing so will give you plenty of time to clear up any glaring errors or to come up with plausible excuses for why things aren't the way they should be. This may sound unnecessary, but it's amazingly easy to get your credit report screwed up and amazingly hard to get it unscrewed.

Many credit advisors suggest that as part of this process you cancel any credit cards or lines of credit that you no longer use. When calculating your debt ratios, many lenders take into consideration the available limits on your cards or lines of credit. So a card with a pristine $10,000 limit may look great to you, but to a lender it may be a potential liability and could end up reducing the size of the loan you can qualify for.

After you've gotten both of these steps out of the way, get a preapproval—not just prequalification—letter. This means that the lender has already checked your credit, verified your income, and nosed around in all your other financial affairs. They'll give you a letter saying exactly how much they'll actually lend you. (A prequalification letter, on the other hand, says only that based on your income, you *might* qualify for a loan in a particular amount—there's no guarantee that you'll actually get the loan, though.) If you qualify for a more expensive house than you're planning to buy, consider having the lender write your preapproval letter showing a smaller amount. This will keep your upper limit a secret when you get into a negotiation.

WHEN YOU SHOULDN'T BUY

Obviously, buying a home isn't for everyone. And here are three situations that should keep you out of the real estate market—even if you can afford it. Instead, figure out how much you'd be spending if you did buy and invest the difference between that and what you'll be spending on rent.

♦ You aren't planning to live in your new home for a minimum of five years. Commissions, transfer taxes, and other one-time fees will eat you alive if you don't give your house enough time to appreciate in value. This is especially true if you are in a job that requires you to move a lot. It isn't always easy to sell as quickly as you need to, and you might end up stuck with double house payments.

♦ You're in a very low income tax bracket. Many of the advantages of home ownership come in the form of tax deductions. So if you aren't paying much tax, you won't benefit nearly as much as someone in one of the higher brackets.

♦ If homes in the neighborhood you're thinking about buying into are either not appreciating or actually depreciating.

CONDOS AND CO-OPS

For those of us who want the benefits of homeownership without the hassles (the painting, the lawn mowing, the maintenance expenses), condos and co-ops may be the way to go. On the up side, the condo or co-op homeowners' association (or similar group) will handle all those things for you. But on the down side, they'll charge you quite a bit for it. Plus, you'll be assessed special fees for general expenses such as fixing the roof—even if you live five floors below it. In addition, condos and co-ops don't usually appreciate as fast as stand-alone homes.

More Communication Issues

As we've discussed throughout this book, you and your partner became parents at the same time but not in the same way. As a result, you and your partner have very different needs and expectations. Researcher Jay Belsky calls this phenomenon "His and Hers transitions."

YOU NEED YOUR PARTNER TO:

♦ Truly appreciate how hard it is to be an involved father today. She should also appreciate the commitment you've made to your family and the things you do for them—even if they aren't exactly what *she* wants.

♦ Understand that you and she will probably disagree on how you assess your level of support and involvement.

♦ Be patient. She needs to know that adults develop at different rates, just as children do. In many families the mother develops her skills faster, in others it's the father.

♦ Understand—and try to accommodate whenever possible—your desires for her attention and affection, your own space, time to see your friends, and a social life.

♦ Give you the freedom to do things your own way. "Many mothers, considering themselves the primary parent, have a difficult time watching their husbands parent differently from themselves, and take over to 'do it right,'" writes psychotherapist Jerrold Shapiro. "If you are an active father, you will have your own way of parenting. It is likely to be just as 'right' as a mother's way and quite different. You may have to listen to your partner's preferences and discuss your own. If you allow her to determine how children are to be fathered, your family may well end up with a second junior mother and no father." In my opinion, your partner has the right to determine exactly how the children are to be mothered. She has no right to determine how they are to be fathered.

♦ Support you in your efforts to be a good parent. "If fathers sense that their involvement is not only desired but also expected and endorsed by their wives, they'll be more involved. If not, they won't," writes psychotherapist Brad Sachs. Researcher Pamela Jordan agrees. "The mother plays a critical role," she writes. "She can bring her mate into the spotlight or keep him in the wings. The most promoting mothers . . . brought their mates into the experience by frequently and openly sharing their physical sensations and emotional responses. They actively encouraged their mates to share the experience of becoming and being a father."

♦ Know you love her and the baby even if you don't show it the way she wants you to. Men and women have very different ways of expressing love. And according to Shapiro, sometimes a wink, a smile, a pat on the shoulder or the butt is just as effective a way of saying I love you as actually saying the words.

YOUR PARTNER NEEDS YOU TO:

♦ Be a full participant in your home, not just "mother's little helper." This means taking responsibility for things without having to be asked (housework, meal planning, shopping) and assuming a major role in child care (including caregiving, arranging playdates, and doing clothes shopping).

♦ Understand that although she may occasionally neglect your emotional and physical needs in favor of the baby's, she doesn't mean to hurt you.

♦ Listen to her carefully when she wants to talk about her doubts and anxieties. It's "more important to have our needs heard than it is to have them met," says Brad Sachs. "Though the specific needs may not be met, the more general and overarching one—the need for support and connectedness—will be."

♦ Not make her feel guilty when she makes mistakes. She wasn't born knowing how to parent any more than you were.

♦ Support her in her efforts to regain her prebaby body.

- Support her in her efforts to reconcile work and family.
- Understand that she may be feeling tremendous guilt at not being able to live up to society's expectations of her (to be a good wife, mother, executive).
- Be sympathetic to her daytime loneliness and desire for adult company if she's a stay-at-home mom.

PUTTING IT TOGETHER

Belsky says that the main thing couples can do to transform their separate transitions into an "our" transition is to try to "reconcile the conflicting priorities of their individual transitions." In other words, learn to focus on the things you have in common rather than on your differences (although being aware of your differences is critical). "Couples who are able to focus their attention on what unites them and produces mutual joy usually end up at the end of the transition with a better, happier marriage," says Belsky.

DAD, THE VENTRILOQUIST

Here, according to Belsky, are the things that can make a couple's transition to parenthood easier:

♦ Surrender individual goals and needs and work together as a team.

♦ Resolve differences about divisions of labor and work in a mutually satisfactory manner.

♦ Handle stresses in a way that does not overstress one partner or the entire marriage.

♦ Fight constructively and maintain a pool of common interests despite diverging priorities.

♦ Realize that however good a marriage becomes postbaby, it will not be good in the same way as it was prebaby.

♦ Maintain the ability to communicate in a way that continues to nurture the marriage. "Most couples do not know" write the Cowans, "that some conflict and tension are inevitable in any intimate relationship. Nor do they realize that the key to a satisfying marriage is not whether a couple has challenging problems or whether they always resolve them, but *how they talk to each other* about them."

It's a tall order, but one that, if you're willing to put in the time and effort, will change for the better the lives of everyone around you.

What to Do If Communication Breaks Down

If you and your partner have tried everything to save your relationship—talking with each other, talking with a therapist, trial separations—divorce may be the only remaining option. This, of course, is a topic I'd rather not be writing about at all, but given that about half of all marriages in this country end in divorce, it's truly necessary to understand what to do if you find yourself contemplating yet another change in identity: from "father" to "single father." It's also necessary to understand the devastating way divorce affects everyone—you, your partner, and especially your children.

With any luck, you and your soon-to-be-ex will be able to remain civil enough to reach some kind of equitable agreement on child custody—without expensive lawyers and court costs. In fact, this is the case in about 80 percent of divorces nationwide. But whether your breakup is civil or acrimonious, there are a few things you should know before you make any major decisions:

♦ **Your defenses are down.** You're under stress; there are a thousand intense and scary feelings running through your head and a million details you have to take care of. You want to avoid more conflict. That's natural.

A Good Alternative to Litigation

There's no question that divorces can be expensive—especially if you and your wife can't communicate any other way than through your lawyers and in front of a judge. But if the two of you are getting along okay (not well enough to be married, just civil to each other), and you think you can continue to do so for a while, you might want to consider mediation. This means that the two of you would split the expense of hiring one person (instead of two) to help the two of you arrange custody and divide up your property. With mediation, the process usually costs less, takes a lot less time, and is much less psychologically damaging for everyone, including the kids, than a knock-down, drag-out court battle.

But a lot of men facing divorce tend to lose track of what's good for them and make decisions they end up regretting forever.

♦ **You need a strategy.** Make the right moves now and you can save yourself not only a lot of grief but a lot of money as well. And most important, you can minimize the damage the breakup of your marriage will have on your child(ren).

Some of what I suggest below may seem a little aggressive, but it really isn't. It's all about looking out for your own best interests instead of abandoning them. And far more important than that, it's about looking out for the best interests of your children. Please keep in mind that what you're going to read here is not an exhaustive treatment of the subject. And remember that every case is different and there are no easy solutions.

GET A LAWYER—NOW

The minute you suspect there's going to be a divorce, get yourself a lawyer. "Don't even consider representing yourself unless you have no possessions, no income, and no interest in the outcome of your case," says Timothy J. Horgan, author of *Winning Your Divorce*. Get the point? One recent study found that fathers who were awarded sole custody had been represented by lawyers 92 percent of the time, and those who won joint custody had lawyers 90 percent of the time. In contrast, among fathers who failed to win any type of custody, only 60 percent had hired lawyers.

And don't share a lawyer with your ex, either. "It's unrealistic to think that an attorney can simply shift from side to side and represent each of you with

> ### Gender Strategy
>
> Despite what you may have heard ("judges are more sympathetic to women lawyers" or "men are tougher"), the gender of your attorney probably won't affect your case in any way. But it is important to pay attention to his or her views on custodial fathers. Many lawyers of both genders believe that mothers should get custody of the children. Get the best person you can afford who shares your views and who you think will put the best interests of your child first.

equal vigor," writes Harriet Newman Cohen, co-author of *The Divorce Book for Men and Women.*

If a friend of yours was recently divorced (and ended up with what he wanted), get a reference. Or check with men's or fathers' rights groups. But beware: while support groups can be a valuable source of contacts and comfort, they also can be a hunting ground for unscrupulous lawyers who prey on men who are at their most vulnerable.

Two excellent (and safe) resources are the Children's Rights Council in Washington, D.C., (202) 547-6227; and Fathers' Rights & Equality Exchange, headquartered in San Jose, California (1-500-FOR-DADS). Both these organizations are nonprofit and have chapters in every state. Whatever you do, don't let recommendations substitute for face-to-face interviews with the top prospects. Although it may cost you a little up front, finding the right lawyer can make the difference between feeling helpless and being in control.

Hiring a lawyer does not mean that you're heading for the courtroom—if you're lucky, you'll never even meet a judge. Nor does hiring a lawyer mean that you're expecting a confrontation with your soon-to-be-ex. What it does mean, though, is that you're getting someone involved who, without any unpleasant emotional attachments, will protect your interests and make sure that your concerns are properly addressed. Most divorce lawyers have seen dozens of cases just like yours and know exactly what to look out for. Do you? And finally, your lawyer can also help you draft fair property settlements and custody arrangements that will hopefully avoid conflict in the future.

During the interview, ask a lot of questions and be completely honest about your situation—financial and emotional. If you aren't, you're just going to complicate your own case. Ask the attorney about the strengths and weaknesses of your case, and find out what approach he or she would take to getting you what you really want. Also, be sure to find out how well the attorney knows local judges and other divorce attorneys. Each judge has his or her own prejudices, and having a lawyer who can maneuver within the system may be critical to your case. And don't worry: any conversation you have while interviewing an attorney—even if you don't ultimately hire him or her—is completely confidential.

Here are a few ways to cut down on how much you'll be paying for your initial consultation:

♦ Before your first appointment, sit down and make a detailed list of all your assets and debts (including account numbers), real estate, full names and social security numbers of everyone in the family (kids, too), and your wife's and your birthdays, driver's license numbers, and dates of marriage and separation. Also bring along your tax returns for the last four or five years. You're going to need all this information soon anyway, and there's no point in paying someone $100 or $200 per hour to sift through your wallet, tax records, and other documents.

♦ Don't confuse your attorney's interest in your case with friendship. Sure, she'll interrupt her day to let you stop by and cry on her shoulder. She'll also charge you for it. And with many attorneys billing in quarters of an hour, that thirty-second plea for sympathy could set you back $50.

DON'T MOVE OUT

In the old days, men facing a divorce would move out of the house—it was considered quite the chivalrous thing to do. Today, however, moving out may be the dumbest thing you could possibly do. Depending on the state, "If you move out of your house, you're essentially abandoning any possibility of getting custody of (or even any sort of meaningful visitation with) your children," says Timothy Horgan. In some states, your wife's attorney may be able to argue that since you left your children with your wife, you aren't interested in having a relationship with them, and your custodial rights should be severely limited.

Unfortunately, the judge is likely to agree. Most divorce attorneys find that the courts are generally quite reluctant to make any changes to the status quo in custody cases. That means that the one who's living in the marital home has a great advantage.

If there's no other alternative to moving out—for example, the judge orders you to—keep these things in mind:

♦ Get a place as close as possible to your former home so you'll be able to see the kids every day.

♦ Explain the situation to the children yourself, stressing that it's not their fault. (You may want to check with a mental health professional about the best way to broach this topic.)

♦ Be alert to what your wife is saying about you to the children. If she's bad-mouthing you, you'll need to make doubly sure that the children understand what your leaving does—and doesn't—mean. One important warning: never respond to anything your ex is saying about you in front of the children. You never want to put your kids in the middle.

♦ Consider taking your valuables with you. "If you move out and leave your possessions behind, don't count on seeing them again," writes Harriet Newman Cohen. Alternatively, make a written inventory of every item of value you're leaving behind. A videotape would be even better.

A word of caution: try not to let your refusal to move out escalate into a huge confrontation between you and your wife (She: "Get out!" You: "Screw you!"). Your anger may later be used as the basis for your wife getting a court order to throw you out.

GET CONTROL OF YOUR FINANCES

In most states, assets and other property that have both your names on them (particularly things like checking accounts and money-market accounts) are assumed to be owned equally by you and your wife. But since it's tough to tell whose half is whose, there's nothing to stop your wife from completely cleaning out the entire checking account, leaving you penniless. Every divorce lawyer I've ever spoken with had literally dozens of stories about divorcing men who came home one day to houses that had been stripped bare and to checking accounts that were in much the same condition.

To protect yourself (and to make sure you've got enough to live on and to pay your attorney with) do the following immediately:

♦ Get *half* the money and any liquid assets you can put your hands on out of the joint accounts and into a separate account—in your name only. If you don't already know which accounts are liquid, have your accountant or your lawyer help you figure it out.

♦ But be sure to check with your lawyer before taking anything out of any joint accounts. In some states, doing so without the permission of your wife can get you in serious hot water. And beware: taking more than half can put you in the uncomfortable position of having to explain to a judge why you cut your wife off without enough money to live on.

♦ Switch your automatic payroll deposits and put any other new deposits into

Community Property

In some states (California, for example) everything acquired from the day you got married until the day you get separated is considered "community property." Even if you have a bank or stock account in your name alone, your wife is still entitled to half and vice versa. Just about the only exception to the community property rules is money or assets you or your wife owned *prior* to the marriage or inheritances left solely to either one of you even during the marriage. Things like a personal stereo and an inheritance might fit into this category. This is pretty complicated stuff, so if you live in one of the nine community-property states (Arizona, California, Idaho, Louisiana, Nevada, New Mexico, Texas, Washington, and Wisconsin), check with your lawyer.

your new account; any money that comes into the old, joint account may be lost forever.

♦ Get all your important financial records out of the house as soon as possible. Before doing this, however, make a complete copy of these records for your wife; she's entitled to one and making her (or her lawyer) ask for it later will cost you. Documents such as bank and credit card statements, tax returns, and life insurance policies can be stored in a safety deposit box or at your lawyer's office. And don't forget to change the account address, so future statements don't go to your wife.

♦ Keep an extremely accurate accounting of all deposits into and withdrawals from the new account—you don't want anyone accusing you of frittering away half the marital assets in Vegas.

Besides sharing ownership of all assets with your wife, you each also "own" half of all debts—mortgages, credit card balances, and so forth. So the next thing to do is close all your joint credit card accounts and credit lines, even the ones from department stores and gas stations. Do this in writing and mention the fact that you're getting a divorce—that usually speeds things up. Until you close these accounts, you'll be responsible for half of any debts your wife incurs until the divorce is final. Actually, according to the law, after the date of your legal separation you are responsible only for anything *you* charge (your partner is responsible only for what she charges). Unfortunately, most creditors don't really care about the law; all they want is their money, and they're perfectly willing to trash your credit rating if that's what it takes to get it.

KNOW THE DETAILS OF YOUR KIDS' LIVES

If you didn't want to be an active, involved father, you probably wouldn't be reading this book. So I'm assuming that at the very least you're going to want to get shared physical custody of your child(ren). If so, be aware that you've got at least two major obstacles to overcome:

♦ The strong societal assumption that women are biologically better parents than men.

♦ The old stereotype that fathers are less important to children than mothers.

Psychologist Richard Warshak, author of *The Custody Revolution,* calls these two ideas (which many men who don't know any better also buy into) the "motherhood mystique" and feels that they are responsible for the fact that mothers get primary physical custody more than 80 percent of the time.

So how do you overcome the motherhood mystique? Perhaps the best way is to demonstrate that you have exceptional parenting skills. And the best way to do that is to make sure you're up-to-date on everything that's going on in your kids' lives. The bottom line is that very few things can destroy your custody case more quickly than showing the judge that you lack knowledge about your child. Here are a few important things you should be doing (if you aren't doing them already):

♦ Get up early and make the kids' breakfast and lunch. Take them to day care.

♦ Get to know your children's day-care provider, doctors, playmates (and their parents)—and make sure they know you. They will be crucial ammunition if your wife's attorney tries to demonstrate what an uninvolved father you are.

♦ Get involved in arranging birthday parties, arranging play dates, and so on.

♦ No matter how long your work hours are, be sure to schedule some quality time with the kids *every day*—you've got to demonstrate a deep and continuing interest in, and commitment to, the kids.

Whatever you do, be predictable. "People who do custody evaluations (and who pass their recommendations on to the judges, who in turn usually rubber-stamp them) believe that schedule and stability are the two key ingredients for raising children," says attorney Tom Railsback. Maintain a written schedule of everything you do with your children, and keep receipts (with your signature on them) of doctor visits, clothing purchases, and so forth. And pay attention to the details: know their clothing sizes, favorite foods, and all the other telling details that can demonstrate that your role in your kids' upbringing is critical. Remember, whether or not your wife knows the answers to these questions is irrelevant. The judge will assume she does, but you'll have to prove you do.

The Language of Separation

Before agreeing to any kind of custody arrangement, it's critical that you understand the terms. The parent with *legal* custody is the one who is legally responsible for making decisions about anything that affects the health, education, and welfare of the children. Ideally you should have *joint* legal custody (this is already the law in several states). *Physical* custody simply refers to the child's primary residence. Again, you should seek nothing less than *joint* physical custody. But watch out: it's possible to have joint physical custody and still have the child's primary residence be at one or the other parent's home.

Finally, keep your wife completely up-to-date on anything pertinent that happens while you've got the kids: if you bought clothes, tell her; if your child was injured and you took him to the doctor, tell her. Besides being the right thing to do, keeping your wife informed shows that you're trying to keep open the lines of communication.

WATCH OUT FOR ALLEGATIONS OF ABUSE

One of the ugliest weapons being used these days is the accusation of child abuse. If you are accused, you will be presumed guilty—unless you can disprove the charges. And that's not easy. By the time you first hear that you're accused, your child has probably been seen by a therapist or a child protective services officer who sees it as his or her role to "validate" the accusation. And things move pretty quickly from there. The instant you're accused of having molested your child, all your contact with the child will be cut off until the question gets heard in court, and that could be anywhere from a few days to a few months later.

Assuming you're innocent (if you're not, please close this book immediately and turn yourself in), you'll probably feel like strangling your ex and her lawyer. Needless to say, this won't help. Most attorneys agree that aggressive behavior will just make the judge more suspicious and negatively inclined toward you. It's critical, then, to be as cooperative as possible.

And as hard as it might be for you, try to give your ex the benefit of the doubt—she may have seen something she genuinely thought was a symptom of abuse. Try to imagine how you'd behave if you'd seen something suspicious. And remember, your goal should be to get the truth out, not to get revenge.

An accusation of domestic violence may have nearly the same effect as an accusation of sex abuse: no access to your child until a judge rules on the charge. But keep in mind that, as strange as it sounds, men are the victims of domestic violence at least as often as women. The problem is that men rarely see their wives' shoves, slaps, or thrown dishes as violence. Now's the time to change your thinking. If your wife has been violent toward you or the kids, file charges immediately.

This does two things: it helps protect the kids from further abuse, and it helps protect you if she attempts to bring charges against you.

If you think your wife is the type who might use this kind of weapon, there are a few things you can do to protect yourself in advance:

♦ Don't let yourself get suckered into a fight, particularly on the phone. Your wife and her lawyer are just looking for evidence that you're violent and unstable. Don't answer questions like, "Why did you touch Sally down there?" Categorically deny her accusations, and end the conversation immediately.

♦ Tape your conversations with her. But before you turn on your recorder, check with your lawyer to make sure doing so is legal in your state. It's a tricky area of the law, so be careful.

♦ Stay squeaky clean during the entire divorce process: don't drink, don't drive too fast, don't even stiff a waitress on her tip. A sharp lawyer (employed by your wife) can make something as innocuous as a speeding ticket into just another example of what an irresponsible brute you are.

YOU MIGHT WANT TO KEEP A LOG

Again, because men are at a disadvantage when it comes to custody battles, it's important to keep detailed notes about everything that happens. Be sure to include:

♦ Details of visits with the kids.

♦ Conversations with your ex, especially if she's threatening or baiting you.

♦ Phone calls with your kids.

♦ Details about what the kids are up to when you're *not* with them. This will demonstrate not only that you are actively involved when you're with your kids but that you are concerned about them *all* the time. Be extremely careful, though, not to grill the kids about what they're doing with mom. This can put them in a very uncomfortable position.

A few warnings: first, do not show your log to anyone except your lawyer—not your friends, not your co-workers, and especially not anyone remotely connected with your wife. It's the kind of thing that could be twisted into yet another example of your controlling, obsessive nature. Second, take a lesson

There's No Such Thing as Winning Custody

In case you were thinking that you could "win" a custody battle, think again. The fact is that everyone loses, especially the kids. If your wife gets sole or primary custody, your relationship with your children will suffer greatly, and your children will bear the many negative consequences associated with long-term father absence (poorer academic performance, poorer social skills, increased chance of abusing drugs or alcohol or of getting in trouble with the law, and a greater likelihood of starting sexual experimentation early). But if you get sole or primary custody, your ex will miss out on having a relationship with the kids. And while this may sound like the perfect way to hurt her, keep in mind that the negative consequences of mother absence are just as significant as those of father absence. The bottom line is that the best parent is both parents.

from Bob Packwood: *everything*—good and bad—that's in your log may become part of the record. So if you've been having particularly nasty thoughts about your wife, keep them to yourself.

GET SOME COUNSELING

Regardless of how well (or badly) you and your ex get along, the simple truth is that the two of you will be coparenting your child until the day you die. For this reason, it is to everyone's advantage—especially the child's—that the two of you get to a point where you can communicate civilly and reasonably and that you do it as soon as possible.

One of the best ways to accomplish this is to go to joint counseling, which comes in two basic flavors: *predivorce* counseling and *coparent* counseling. As you could probably guess, predivorce counseling takes place in the early stages of the divorce process, most likely before any kind of custody or separation arrangements have been finalized. Predivorce counseling is designed to help you and your wife dissipate some of the anger and hostility between you, and to help you build a better base of communication. Then, hopefully, you'll be able to make mature, informed, and rational decisions and not get tripped up by your own vindictiveness. And the more mature and rational you are, the better off your kids will be.

Coparent counseling is similar to predivorce counseling, except that it happens *after* initial custody and separation arrangements are in place. You and your wife may find that your counselor's office is a safe, neutral place where you can have discussions about the kids.

WHAT TO DO IF YOU DON'T GET THE CUSTODY ARRANGEMENT YOU WANT

Although most states now have some kind of "gender-blind" legislation specifically barring judges from granting custodial preference based solely on gender, our family law system still favors women by a huge margin. As mentioned earlier, mothers are awarded sole custody over 80 percent of the time. Only 11 percent of men get sole custody of their children, and just 7 percent have joint custody. Women are presumed to be "fit" parents. Men have to prove it.

Worse yet, nearly 40 percent of noncustodial fathers have no legal access or custody rights at all. And the men who do have court-ordered access (as well as many of those who have joint legal custody) are traditionally limited to visits every other weekend, on alternate holidays, and for a couple of weeks in the summer.

The bottom line is that your chances of getting the kind of custody arrangement you really want are not great (they can, however, be greatly improved by following the suggestions on pages 000–00).

If you end up with limited access to your children, it's hard not to get depressed—the constant good-byes are going to be incredibly painful, and in some cases, seeing the kids may be a stinging reminder of the loss of your marriage. According to several studies, these two factors are among the major reasons divorced fathers taper off contact with their kids. So, as in most things, try to think of your kids before deciding you can't deal with seeing them. Seeing them may be painful to you, but not seeing you will be much more painful to them.

Right now the most important thing you can do is try to make the transition from one family to two as smooth as possible. And the place to start is by trying to keep communication with your ex as civil as possible. You may not have been terribly successful before, but it's more crucial now than ever: the children who suffer the least when their parents split up are those whose parents have the lowest levels of conflict (or at least those whose parents keep their conflicts to themselves). This doesn't mean that you and your ex have to be best friends or even that you have to speak to each other very often. What it does mean, however, is that you both have to agree to keep your eyes on what's really most important: your child(ren).

Do Some Reading with Your Kids . . .

There are plenty of good children's books that deal with divorce and how it affects kids. Here are a few you might want to take a look at:

Ballard, Robin. *Gracie.* New York: Greenwillow Books, 1993.

Brown, Laurence Krasny, and Marc Brown. *Dinosaurs Divorce: A Guide for Changing Families.* Boston: Atlantic Monthly Press, 1986.

Christiansen, C. B. *My Mother's House, My Father's House.* New York: Atheneum, 1989.

. . . AND FOR YOURSELF

Here are just three excellent books on divorce and custody issues that can help you remember the priorities: kids first, everything else last:

Adler, Robert. *Sharing the Children: How to Resolve Custody Problems and Get on with Your Life.* Bethesda, Md.: Adler and Adler, 1988.

Hickey, Elizabeth, and Elizabeth Dalton. *Healing Hearts: Helping Children and Adults Recover from Divorce.* Carson City, Nev.: Gold Leaf Press, 1994.

Oddenino, Michael L. *Putting Kids First: Walking Away From a Marriage Without Walking Over the Kids.* Salt Lake City, Utah: Family Connections, 1995.

Next to the the death of an immediate family member, getting a divorce is one of the most painful experiences you'll ever go through. And you certainly won't be alone; it will be hard on your ex and hard on your children as well. Rest assured, though, you *will* pull through. The breakup of a family is almost always a tragedy in the short term. But in the long term it sometimes turns out to be the best thing for everyone involved.

Selected Bibliography

Books

Adler, Robert. *Sharing the Children: How to Resolve Custody Problems and Get on with Your Life.* Bethesda, Md.: Adler and Adler, 1988.

Ames, Louise Bates, and Carol Chase Haber. *Your One-Year-Old: The Fun-Loving, Fussy 12- to 24-Month-Old.* New York: Delta, 1982.

Ames, Louise Bates, and Frances L. Ilg. *Your Two-Year-Old: Terrible or Tender.* New York: Delta, 1980.

Belsky, Jay, and John Kelly. *The Transition to Parenthood: How a First Child Changes a Marriage: Why Some Couples Grow Closer and Others Apart.* New York: Delacorte, 1994.

Berman, Phyllis W., and Frank A. Pedersen. *Men's Transitions to Parenthood: Longitudinal Studies of Early Family Experience.* Hillsdale, N.J.: Erlbaum, 1987.

Bettelheim, Bruno. *A Good Enough Parent: A Book on Child-Rearing.* New York: Vintage, 1987.

———. *The Uses of Enchantment: The Meaning and Importance of Fairy Tales.* New York: Knopf, 1976.

Biller, Henry B. *Fathers and Families: Paternal Factors in Child Development.* Westport, Conn.: Auburn House, 1993.

Biller, Henry B., and Robert J. Trotter. *The Father Factor: What You Need to Know to Make a Difference.* New York: Pocket Books, 1994.

Blakey, Nancy. *Lotions, Potions, and Slime: Mudpies and More!* Berkeley, Calif.: Tricycle Press, 1996.

———. *The Mudpies Activity Book: Recipes for Invention.* Berkeley, Calif.: Tricycle Press, 1989.

Bluestine, Eric. *The Ways Children Learn Music: An Introduction and Practical Guide to Music Learning Theory.* Chicago: GIA Publications, 1995.

Bornstein, M. H., ed. *Handbook of Parenting.* Hillsdale, N.J.: Erlbaum, 1995.

Brazelton, T. Berry, and Bertrand Cramer. *The Earliest Relationship: Parents, Infants, and the Drama of Early Attachment.* Reading, Mass.: Addison-Wesley, 1990.

Britton, James. *Language and Learning: The Importance of Speech in Children's Development.* New York: Penguin, 1970.

Bronstein, Phyllis, and Carolyn Pape Cowan, eds. *Fatherhood Today: Men's Changing Role in the Family.* New York: John Wiley & Sons, 1988.

Brott, Armin. *The New Father: A Dad's Guide to the First Year.* New York: Abbeville Press, 1997.

Brott, Armin, and Jennifer Ash. *The Expectant Father: Facts, Tips, and Advice for Dads-to-Be.* New York: Abbeville Press, 1995.

Butler, Dorothy. *Babies Need Books.* New York: Atheneum, 1980.

Canfield, Dr. Ken. *The Heart of a Father.* Chicago: Northfield, 1996.

Cantor, Ruth F., and Jeffrey A. Cantor. *Parents' Guide to Special Needs Schooling: Early Intervention Years.* Westport, Conn.: Auburn House, 1995.

Caplan, Frank, and Theresa Caplan. *The Second Twelve Months of Life.* New York: Bantam, 1977.

Cath, Stanley H., et al., eds. *Father and Child: Developmental and Clinical Perspectives.* Hillsdale, N.J.: Analytic Press, 1994.

———. *Fathers and Their Families.* Hillsdale, N.J.: Analytic Press, 1989.

Chen, Milton. *The Smart Parent's Guide to Kids' TV.* San Francisco: KQED Books, 1994.

Cohen, Harriet Newman, and Ralph Gardner, Jr. *The Divorce Book for Men and Women: The Step-by-Step Guide to Gaining Your Freedom Without Losing Everything Else.* New York: Avon, 1994.

Cowan, Carolyn Pape, and Philip A. Cowan. *When Partners Become Parents: The Big Life Change for Couples.* New York: HarperCollins, 1992.

Cowan, Philip A., et al. "Mothers, Fathers, Sons, and Daughters: Gender Differences in Family Formation and Parenting Style." In *Family, Self, and Society: Toward a New Agenda for Family Research.* Philip A. Cowan, Dorothy Field, and Donald A. Hansen, eds. Hillsdale, N.J.: Erlbaum, 1993.

Cullinan, Bernice E., and Lee Galda. *Literature and the Child,* 3d ed. Orlando, Fla.: Harcourt Brace, 1994.

Dacyczyn, Amy. *The Tightwad Gazette III.* New York: Villard, 1996.

Dodson, Fitzhugh. *How to Father.* New York: Signet, 1974.

Eisenberg, Arlene, et al. *What to Expect the Toddler Years.* New York: Workman, 1994.

Elias, Steven, Albin Renauer, and Robin Leonard. *How to File for Bankruptcy.* Berkeley, Calif.: Nolo Press, 1997.

Faber, Adele, and Elaine Mazlish. *How to Talk So Kids Will Listen and Listen So Kids Will Talk.* New York: Avon, 1982.

Flint Public Library. *Ring a Ring O'Roses: Finger Plays for Pre-School Children.* Flint, Mich.: Flint Public Library, n.d.

Fraiberg, Selma H. *The Magic Years: Understanding and Handling the Problems of Early Childhood.* New York: Scribner's, 1959.

Galinsky, Ellen. *Between Generations: The Six Stages of Parenthood.* New York: Times Books, 1981.

————. *The Preschool Years*. New York: Times Books, 1988.

Godfrey, Neale, and Tad Richards. *A Penny Saved . . . : Teaching Your Children the Values and Life-Skills They Will Need in the Real World*. New York: Simon & Schuster, 1996.

Gordon, Edwin E. *A Music Learning Theory for Newborn and Young Children*. Chicago: GIA Publications, 1990.

Gould, Jonathan W., and Robert E. Gunther. *Reinventing Fatherhood*. Blue Ridge Summit, Pa.: TAB Books, 1991.

Greene, Ellin. *Books, Babies, and Libraries: Serving Infants, Toddlers, Their Parents, and Caregivers*. Chicago: ALA Books, 1991.

Greenspan, Stanley, and Nancy Thorndike Greenspan. *First Feelings: Milestones in the Emotional Development of Your Baby and Child*. New York: Penguin, 1985.

Grossman, Elmer R. *Everyday Pediatrics for Parents: A Thoughtful Guide for Today's Families*. Berkeley, Calif.: Celestial Arts, 1996.

Hass, Aaron. *The Gift of Fatherhood: How Men's Lives are Transformed by Their Children*. New York: Fireside, 1994.

Hanson, Shirley M. H., and Frederick W. Bozett. *Dimensions of Fatherhood*. Beverly Hills, Calif.: Sage, 1985.

Heddle, Rebecca. *Science in the Kitchen*. London: Usborne Publishing, 1992.

Hickey, Elizabeth, and Elizabeth Dalton. *Healing Hearts: Helping Children and Adults Recover from Divorce*. Carson City, Nev.: Gold Leaf Press, 1994.

Horgan, Timothy J. *Winning Your Divorce: A Man's Survival Guide*. New York: Dutton, 1994.

Katzen, Mollie, and Ann Henderson. *Pretend Soup and Other Real Recipes: A Cookbook for Preschoolers and Up*. Berkeley, Calif.: Tricycle Press, 1994.

Kohl, MaryAnn F., and Jean Potter. *Cooking Art: Easy Edible Art for Young Children*. Beltsville, Md.: Gryphon House, 1997.

Kropp, Paul. *Raising a Reader: Make Your Child a Reader for Life*. New York: Doubleday, 1996.

Kutner, Lawrence. *Toddlers and Preschoolers*. New York: William Morrow, 1994.

Lamb, Michael E., ed. *The Role of the Father in Child Development*. New York: John Wiley, 1981.

Lehane, Stephen. *Help Your Baby Learn: 100 Piaget-Based Activities for the First Two Years of Life*. New York: Prentice-Hall, 1976.

Leonhardt, Mary. *99 Ways to Get Kids to Love Reading*. New York: Three Rivers Press, 1997.

McCoy, Bill. *Father's Day: Notes from a New Dad in the Real World*. New York: Times Books, 1995.

Minnesota Fathering Alliance. *Working with Fathers: Methods and Perspectives*. Stillwater, Minn.: nu ink unlimited, 1992.

Monroe, Paula Ann. *Left-Brain Finance for Right-Brain People: A Money Guide for the Creatively Inclined*. Naperville, Ill.: Sourcebooks, 1996.

Newman, Barbara M., and Philip R. Newman. *Development Through Life: A Psychosocial Approach*, 6th ed. Pacific Grove, Calif.: Brooks/Cole Publishing, 1994.

Oddenino, Michael L., and Jeff Carter. *Putting Kids First: Walking Away from a Marriage Without Walking over the Kids*. San Diego: Family Connections Publications, 1994.

Ostermann, Robert, et al. *Father and Child: Practical Advice for Today's Dad*. Stamford, Conn.: Longmeadow Press, 1991.

Pagnoni, Mario. *Computers and Small Fries: A Computer-Readiness Guide for Parents of Tots, Toddlers and Other Minors*. Wayne, N.J.: Avery Publishing, 1987.

Parke, Ross. *Fathers*, rev. ed. Cambridge, Mass.: Harvard University Press, 1996.

———. "Fathers and Families." In *Handbook of Parenting*. M. H. Bornstein, ed. Hillsdale, N.J.: Erlbaum, 1995.

Platt, Harvey J. *Your Living Trust and Estate Plan: How to Maximize Your Family's Assets and Protect Your Loved Ones*. New York: Allworth Press, 1995.

Polly, Jean Armour. *Internet Kids Yellow Pages*. New York: Osborne McGraw-Hill, 1996.

Pruett, Kyle D. "The Nurturing Male: A Longitudinal Study of Primary Nurturing Fathers." In *Fathers and Their Families*. Stanley H. Cath, et al., eds. Hillsdale, N.J.: Analytic Press, 1989.

Ross, John Munder. *What Men Want: Mothers, Fathers, and Manhood*. Cambridge, Mass.: Harvard University Press, 1994.

Sachs, Brad E. *Things Just Haven't Been the Same: Making the Transition from Marriage to Parenthood*. New York: William Morrow, 1992.

Schiff, Donald, and Steven Shelov, eds. *American Academy of Pediatrics Guide to Your Child's Symptoms: The Official, Complete Home Reference, Birth Through Adolescence*. New York: Villard, 1997.

Sears, William, and Martha Sears. *The Baby Book: Everything You Need to Know about Your Baby—From Birth to Age Two*. New York: Little Brown, 1993.

———. *The Discipline Book: Everything You Need to Know to Have a Better-Behaved Child—From Birth to Age Ten*. Boston: Little Brown, 1995.

Shopper, Moisy. "Toiletry Revisited: An Integration of Developing Concepts and the Father's Role in Toilet Training." In Stanley H. Cath, et al., eds. *Fathers and Their Families*. Hillsdale, N.J.: Analytic Press, 1989.

Silberg, Jackie. *300 Three-Minute Games: Quick and Easy Activities for 2–5 Year Olds*. Beltsville, Md.: Gryphon House, 1997.

Snarey, John. *How Fathers Care for the Next Generation: A Four-Decade Study*. Cambridge, Mass.: Harvard University Press, 1993.

Spangler, Doug. *Fatherhood: An Owner's Manual*. Richmond, Calif.: Fabus, 1994.

Spock, Benjamin, and Michael B. Rothenberg. *Dr. Spock's Baby and Child Care*. New York: Pocket Books, 1992.

Steinberg, David. *Fatherjournal*. Albion, Calif.: Times Change Press, 1977.

Sullivan, S. Adams. *The Father's Almanac*, 2d ed. New York: Doubleday, 1992.

Trelease, Jim. *The New Read-Aloud Handbook*. New York: Penguin, 1989.

Tyson, Eric. *Personal Finance for Dummies.* Foster City, Calif.: IDG Books, 1995.

Ulene, Art, and Steven Shelov. *Discovery Play: Loving and Learning with Your Baby.* Berkeley, Calif.: Ulysses Press, 1994.

Warshak, Richard. *The Custody Revolution: The Father Factor and the Motherhood Mystique.* New York: Poseidon, 1992.

White, Burton L. *The New First Three Years of Life.* New York: Prentice Hall, 1995.

Wright, June L., and Daniel D. Shade, eds. *Young Children: Active Learners in a Technological Age.* Washington, D.C.: National Association for the Education of Young Children, 1994.

Zweiback, Meg. *Keys to Preparing and Caring for Your Second Child.* New York: Barron's Educational, 1991.

Journals

Bailey, William J. "A Longitudinal study of Fathers' Involvement with Young Children: Infancy to Age 5 years." *Journal of Genetic Psychology* 155, no. 3 (1994): 331–39.

———. "Psychological Develpoment in Men: Generativity and Involvement with Young Children." *Psychological Reports* 71 (1992): 929–30.

Ball, Jessica, et al. "Who's Got the Power? Gender Differences in Partner's Perceptions of Influence During Marital Problem-Solving Discussions." Typescript, 1993.

Baumrind, Diana. "Current Patterns of Parental Authority." *Developmental Psychology Monograph* 4, part 1 (January 1971): 1–101.

Cohn, Deborah A., et al. "Mothers' and Fathers' Working Models of Childhood Attachment Relationships, Parenting Styles, and Child Behavior." Typescript, 1997.

———. "Working Models of Childhood Attachment and Couple Relationships." *Journal of Family Issues* 13 (December 1992): 432–49.

Cooney, Teresa M., et al. "Timing of Fatherhood: Is 'On-Time' Optional?" *Journal of Marriage and the Family* 55 (February 1993): 205–15.

Cowan, Philip A., et al. "Parents' Attachment Histories and Children's Externalizing and Internalizing Behavior: Exploring Family Systems Models of Linkage." *Journal of Consulting and Clinical Psychology.* In press.

Daly, Kerry. "Reshaping Fatherhood: Finding the Models." *Journal of Family Issues* 14 (December 1993): 510–30.

DeLuccie, Mary F. "Mothers as Gatekeepers: A Model of Maternal Mediators of Father Involvement." *Journal of Genetic Psychology* 156, no. 1 (1994): 115–31.

Deutsch, Francine M., et al. "Taking Credit: Couples' Reports of Contributions to Child Care." *Journal of Family Issues* 14 (September 1993): 421–37.

Dornbusch, Sanford M., et al. "The Relation of Parenting Style to Adolescent School Performance." *Child Development* 58 (1987): 1244–57.

Fagot, Beverly I. "Sex Differences in Toddlers' Behavior and Parental Reaction." *Developmental Psychology* 10, no. 4 (1974): 554–58.

————. "Teacher and Peer Reactions to Boys' and Girls' Play Styles." *Sex Roles* 11, no. 708 (1984): 691–702.

Fagot, Beverly, and Richard Hagan. "Aggression in Toddlers: Responses to the Assertive Acts of Boys and Girls." *Sex Roles* 12, nos. 3–4 (1985): 341–51.

————. "Observations of Parent Reactions to Sex-Stereotyped Behaviors: Age and Sex Effects." *Child Development* 62 (1991): 617–28.

Gordon, Betty Nye. "Maternal Perception of Child Temperament and Observed Mother-Child Interaction." *Child Psychiatry and Human Development* 13 (Spring 1983): 153–65.

Grimm-Thomas, Karen, and Maureen Perry-Jenkins. "All in a Day's Work: Job Experiences, Self-Esteem, and Fathering in Working-Class Families." *Family Relations* 43 (1994): 174–81.

Hall, Wendy A. "New Fatherhood: Myths and Realities." *Public Health Nursing* 11, no. 4 (1994): 219–28.

Haugland, Susan W. "The Effect of Computer Software on Preschool Children's Developmental Gains." *Journal of Computing in Childhood Education* 3, no. 1 (1992): 15–20.

Heath, D. Terri. "The Impact of Delayed Fatherhood on the Father-Child Relationship." *Journal of Genetic Psychology* 155, no. 4 (1994): 511–30.

Herb, Steven, and Sara Willoughby-Herb. "Books as Toys." *Topics in Early Childhood Special Education* 5, no. 3 (1985): 83–91.

Jewett, Don L., et al. "A Double-blind Study of Symptom Provocation to Determine Food Sensitivity." *New England Journal of Medicine* 323 (August 16, 1990): 429–33.

Jordan, Pamela L. "The Mother's Role in Promoting Fathering Behavior." *Health Care for Women International.* In press.

Katzev, Aphra R., et al. "Girls or Boys: Relationship of Child Gender to Marital Instability." *Journal of Marriage and the Family* 56 (February 1994): 89–100.

Lovestone, S., and R. Kumar. "Postnatal Psychiatric Illness: The Impact of Partners." *British Journal of Psychiatry* 163 (1993): 210–16.

McBride, B. A., and G. Mills. "A Comparison of Mother and Father Involvement with Their Preschool-Age Children." *Early Childhood Research Quarterly* 8 (1993): 457–77.

MacDonald, Kevin, and Ross D. Parke. "Bridging the Gap: Parent-Child Play Interaction and Peer Interactive Competence." *Child Development* 55 (1984): 1265–77.

————. "Parent-Child Physical Play: The Effects of Sex and Age of Children and Parents." *Sex Roles* 15, nos. 7–8 (1986): 367–78.

McKenry, Patrick C., et al. "Predictors of Single, Noncustodial Fathers' Physical Involvement with Their Children." *Journal of Genetic Psychology* 153, no. 3 (1992): 305–19.

Marsiglio, William. "Contemporary Scholarship on Fatherhood: Culture, Identity, and Conduct." *Journal of Family Issues* 14 (December 1993): 484–509.

Newman, Philip R., and Barbara Newman. "Parenthood and Adult Development." *Marriage and Family Review* 12, nos. 3–4 (1988): 313–37.

Nicolson, P. "A Brief Report of Women's Expectations of Men's Behaviour in the Transition to Parenthood: Contradictions and Conflicts for Counselling Psychology Practice." *Counselling Psychology Quarterly* 3, no. 4 (1990): 353–61.

Palm, G. "Involved Fatherhood: A Second Chance." *Journal of Men's Studies* 2 (1993): 139–54.

Pearson, Jane L., et al. "Adult Attachment and Adult Child–Older Parent Relationships." *American Journal of Orthopsychiatry* 63 (October 1993): 606–13.

Power, Thomas G., et al. "Compliance and Self-Assertion: Young Children's Responses to Mothers Versus Fathers." *Developmental Psychology* 30, no. 6 (1994): 980–89.

Pruett, Kyle D. "The Paternal Presence." *Families in Society* 74, no. 1 (1993): 46–50.

Reis, Myrna, and Dolores Gold. "Relationship of Paternal Availability to Problem Solving and Sex-Role Orientation in Young Boys." *Psychological Reports* 40 (1977): 823–29.

Rubenstein, Carin. "That's My Baby." *Parenting,* April 1990, pp. 87–90.

Samuels, Andrew. "The Good Enough Father of Whatever Sex." Typescript, n.d.

Sorce, James F., et al. "Maternal Emotional Signaling: Its Effect on the Visual Cliff Behavior of One-Year-Olds." *Developmental Psychology* 21, no. 1 (1985): 195–200.

Starrels, Marjorie E. "Gender Differences in Parent-Child Relationships." *Journal of Family Issues* 15 (March 1994): 148–65.

Stayton, Donelda, et al. "Infant Obedience and Maternal Behavior: The Origins of Socialization Reconsidered." *Child Development* 42 (1971): 1057–69.

Thornburg, Kathy R., et al. "Parent as a Teacher Inventory: Factor Analyses for Fathers, Mothers, and Teachers." *Educational and Psychological Measurement* 49 (1989): 689–95.

Whaley, Kimberlee K. "The Emergence of Social Play in Infancy: A Proposed Developmental Sequence of Infant-Adult Social Play." *Early Childhood Research Quarterly,* no. 5 (1990): 347–58.

Whitehurst, G. J., et al. "Accelerating Language Development Through Picture Book Reading." *Developmental Psychology* 24, no. 4 (1988): 552–59.

Resources

This list of resources is by no means a comprehensive guide. Rather, it is designed to offer some immediate answers to your questions and needs and to steer you in the right direction.

A special note about the Internet addresses listed here: If you don't have a computer or access to the Net, don't worry. Your public library probably does and you can still tap into these valuable resources there.

Advice, General

PARENTSPLACE.COM has one of the largest clearinghouses of parenting advice on the Net.

http://parentsplace.com/

Their bulletin boards are especially interesting. You can get answers from other parents on just about any aspect of parenting.

http://www.parentsplace.com/genobject.cgi/talking.html

FAMILY.COM has a bunch of columnists who dispense advice on just about every topic you can imagine. The site is run by Disney so expect more than a little advertising, but it's a great source of info and support.

http://www.family.com/

PARENTSOUP is run by the same people who own ParentsPlace.com. There's some overlap, but this is still another great source of valuable info.

http://www.parentsoup.com/

POSITIVEPARENTING.COM offers on-line parenting classes and links to other good parenting sites.

http://www.positiveparenting.com/

At-Home Dads

"AT-HOME DAD" NEWSLETTER has just about everything a stay-at-home dad could want to know. Each issue of the newsletter also includes the At-Home Dad Network, a listing of more than 300 dads across the country looking to connect their families through playgroups.

Peter Baylies, Publisher
61 Brightwood Ave.
North Andover, MA 01845
Tel.: (508) 685-7931
e-mail: athomedad@aol.com
http://www.parentsplace.com/readroom/athomedad/index.html

Bankruptcy

CONSUMER CREDIT COUNSELING SERVICE is a nonprofit group that helps people avoid bankruptcy and restructure their debts. To find a local CCCS office, call their toll-free number.

Tel.: (800) 388-2227

Elias, Stephen, Albin Renauer, and Robin Leonard. *How to File for Bankruptcy.* Berkeley, Calif.: Nolo Press, 1977. If you can't find it in your local bookstore, call the publisher (Tel.: [800] 992-6656).

College Savings

COLLEGE SAVINGS PLAN NETWORK
P.O. Box 11910
Lexington, KY 40578-1910
Tel.: (606) 244-8175
Fax: (606) 244-8053
http://www.collegesavings.org

Computers

COMPUTERTOTS
10132 Colvin Run Road
Great Falls, VA 22066
(800) 531-5053
http://www.computertots.com

Pagnoni, Mario. *Computers and Small Fries: A Computer-Readiness Guide for Parents of Tots, Toddlers and Other Minors.* Wayne, N.J.: Avery Publishing, 1987. Nearly ancient at this point, this book still covers the basics quite well.

Wright, June L., and Daniel D. Shade, eds. *Young Children: Active Learners in a Technological Age.* Washington, D.C.: National Association for the Education of Young Children, 1994.

Cooking and Other Messy Things

Blakey, Nancy. *Lotions, Potions, and Slime: Mudpies and More!* Berkeley, Calif.: Tricycle Press, 1996.

Heddle, Rebecca. *Science in the Kitchen.* London: Usborne Publishing, 1992.

Katzen, Mollie, and Ann Henderson. *Pretend Soup and Other Real Recipes: A Cookbook for Preschoolers and Up.* Berkeley, Calif.: Tricycle Press, 1994.

Kohl, MaryAnn F., and Jean Potter. *Cooking Art: Easy Edible Art for Young Children.* Beltsville, Md.: Gryphon House, 1997.

Credit Reporting Agencies

If you've been denied credit within the past sixty days you may be able to get a copy of your credit report for free. Otherwise, it'll cost you about $8.00. The big three credit gathering companies are:

Experian (formerly TRW)—Tel.: (800) 682-7654

Equifax—Tel.: (800) 685-1111

Trans Union—Tel.: (312) 408-1050

Divorce

AMERICAN FATHERS COALITION
2000 Pennsylvania Ave. N.W.
Suite 148
Washington, D.C. 20006
http://www.americanfathers.com

CHILDREN'S RIGHTS COUNCIL has a well-stocked catalog of resources, including great books on the subject for kids and their parents.
http://www.vix.com/crc/catalog.htm

FATHERS' RIGHTS & EQUALITY EXCHANGE
701 Welch Rd., #323
Palo Alto, CA 94304
Tel.: (415) 853-6877
e-mail: shedevil@vix.com (Anne Mitchell)

SINGLE AND CUSTODIAL FATHERS NETWORK
http://www.single-fathers.org/

Adler, Robert. *Sharing the Children: How to Resolve Custody Problems and Get on with Your Life.* Bethesda, Md.: Adler and Adler, 1988.

Cohen, Harriet Newman, and Ralph Gardner, Jr. *The Divorce Book for Men and Women: The Step-by-Step Guide to Gaining Your Freedom Without Losing Everything Else.* New York: Avon, 1994.

Leving, Jeffery M. *Fathers' Rights: Hard-Hitting and Fair Advice for Every Father Involved in a Custody Dispute.* New York: Basic Books, 1997.

Oddenino, Michael L., and Jeff Carter. *Putting Kids First: Walking Away from a Marriage Without Walking over the Kids.* San Diego: Family Connections Publications, 1994.

Financial Planning

DIRECT STOCK PURCHASE PLAN CLEARINGHOUSE

Tel.: (800) 774-4177

http://servo.golden-tech.com/clearing/

DRIP INVESTOR

http://www.dripinvestor.com/

Monroe, Paula Ann. *Left-Brain Finance for Right-Brain People: A Money Guide for the Creatively Inclined.* Naperville, Ill.: Sourcebooks, 1996.

Tyson, Eric. *Personal Finance for Dummies.* Foster City, Calif.: IDG Books, 1995.

Fun Stuff

CREATIVE CREATIONS has a constantly changing list of twenty fun things to do with kids of all ages.

http://www.waidsoft.com/funkids.html

Ellen Davis has a web site listing a bunch of fun activities.

http://ucunix.san.uc.edu/~edavis/kids-list/crafts/easy-and-fun.html

Blakey, Nancy. *The Mudpies Activity Book: Recipes for Invention.* Berkeley, Calif.: Tricycle Press, 1989.

Silberg, Jackie. *300 Three-Minute Games: Quick and Easy Activities for 2–5 Year Olds.* Beltsville, Md.: Gryphon House, 1997.

General Fatherhood

THE FATHERHOOD PROJECT is a national research and educational project examining the future of fatherhood and ways to support men's involvement in child-rearing.

c/o Families and Work Institute

330 Seventh Ave

New York, NY 10001

Tel.: (212) 465-2044

FATHERNET provides information on the importance of fathers and fathering and how fathers can be good parents and parent educators. It includes research, policy, and opinion documents to inform users about the factors that support and hinder men's involvement in the lives of children.

12 McNeal Hall

1985 Buford Avenue

St. Paul, MN 55108

Tel.: (612) 626-1212

http://www.cyfc.umn.edu/Fathernet/index.html

FATHER'S RESOURCE CENTER offers parenting classes, support groups, and workshops geared toward helping fathers become more capable and involved parents so that fathers, mothers, children, and, subsequently, all society will benefit.
430 Oak Grove Street, Suite B3
Minneapolis, MN 55403
Tel.: (612) 874-1509
Fax: (612) 874-1014
e-mail: frc@visi.com
http://www.slowlane.com/frc/

FATHERS HOTLINE can refer you to local and state father-friendly organizations.
Tel.: (512) 472-DADS (3237)
e-mail: dads@fathers.org
http://www.menhotline.org

FATHERWORK is a new home page designed to encourage good fathering. The folks at FatherWork view fathering not so much as a social role men play, but as the work they do each day to care for the next generation.
http://fatherwork.byu.edu

NATIONAL CENTER FOR FATHERING (NCF) offers resources designed to help men become more aware of their own fathering style and then work toward improving their skills. Call for a free issue of NCF's quarterly magazine, *Today's Father.*
10200 West 75th Street, #267
Shawnee Mission, KS 66204-2223
Tel.: (800) 593-DADS (3237)
e-mail: ncf@aol.com
http://www.fathers.com

NATIONAL CENTER ON FATHERS & FAMILIES is a great source of research and data on fathers, father involvement, and the like.
c/o University of Pennsylvania
3700 Walnut Street, Box 58
Philadelphia, PA 19104-6216
Tel.: (215) 898-5000

NATIONAL FATHERHOOD INITIATIVE conducts public awareness campaigns promoting responsible fatherhood, organizes conferences and community fatherhood forums, provides resource material to organizations seeking to establish support programs for fathers, publishes a quarterly newsletter, and disseminates informational material to men seeking to become more effective fathers.
600 Eden Road, Building E
Lancaster, PA 17601
Tel.: (800) 790-DADS (3237)
http://www.register.com/father/

General Parenting

ERIC CLEARINGHOUSE provides more information on parenting than you could
ever possibly go through.
   Tel.: (800) 583-4135 or (217) 333-1386
   e-mail: ericeece@ux1.cso.uiuc.edu
   http://ericps.ed.uiuc.edu/ericeece.html

NATIONAL COUNCIL ON FAMILY RELATIONS
   Minneapolis, MN
   Tel.: (612) 781-9331

"SMART FAMILIES" is a great newsletter published by Family University.
   P.O. Box 500050
   San Diego, CA 92150-0050
   Tel.: (619) 487-7099
   Fax: (619) 487-7356
   e-mail: FamilyU@aol.com

Health Concerns

KIDS HEALTH offers accurate, up-to-date information on issues ranging from child
behavior and development to nutrition, general health, surgery, and immunizations.
   http://kidshealth.org/

NATIONAL ORGANIZATION FOR RARE DISORDERS
   P.O. Box 8923
   New Fairfield, CT 06812-1783
   Tel.: (800) 999-6673

NORTHWEST COALITION FOR ALTERNATIVES TO PESTICIDES (NCAP)
publishes the *Journal of Pesticide Reform* as well as informational packets "Children
and Pesticides" and "Planning for Non-chemical School Ground Maintenance."
   P.O. Box 1393
   Eugene, Oregon 97440
   Tel.: (503) 344-5044
   Fax: (503) 344-6923
   e-mail: ncap@igc.apc.org

WEB DOCTOR will answer your specific questions on line.
   http://www.parentsplace.com/readroom/health.html

Grossman, Elmer R. *Everyday Pediatrics for Parents: A Thoughtful Guide for Today's
   Families.* Berkeley, Calif.: Celestial Arts, 1996.

Schiff, Donald, and Steven Shelov, eds. *American Academy of Pediatrics Guide to Your
   Child's Symptoms: The Official, Complete Home Reference, Birth Through
   Adolescence.* New York: Villard, 1997.

Music

CENTER FOR MUSIC AND YOUNG CHILDREN produces tapes for children that adults enjoy as well. They also offer parent-child music classes.

66 Whitherspoon
Princeton, NJ 08542
Tel.: (800) 728-CYMC (2962)

Bluestine, Eric. *The Ways Children Learn Music: An Introduction and Practical Guide to Music Learning Theory.* Chicago: GIA Publications, 1995.

Gordon, Edwin E. *A Music Learning Theory for Newborn and Young Children.* Chicago: GIA Publications, 1990.

On-line Conferences, Mailing Lists, and Newsletters

FATHER-L is an e-mail conference dedicated to discussing the importance of fathers in kids' lives. Send an e-mail to listserv@vm1.spcs.umn.edu and write "subscribe father-l" in the body of the message. Send a message to father-l@tc.umn.edu if you need more info.

PARENTING-L is a great way to get fifty quick, informative answers to just about any nonemergency question you might have. To subscribe, send e-mail to listserv@postoffice.cso.usuc.edu with "subscribe parenting-l" in the subject line.

THE PARENTS' LETTER, published by a pediatrician, is filled with good, basic information on such topics as health maintenance, immunizations, illness, behavior, and parenting skills. To subscribe, send an e-mail to majordomo@pobox.com with a blank subject line and write "subscribe letter" in the body of the message.

OTHER PARENTING LISTS:
kids-newborn (0-2/3 months)
kids-infant (3 months-1 year)

To subscribe to one or more of the above, send an e-mail to listserv@vm.ege.edu.tr using the following format (substituting your own name for mine, of course):

sub kids-newborn Armin Brott
sub kids-infant Armin Brott

Reading and Other Media

CHILDREN'S LITERATURE provides reviews of the latest kids' books, videos, and computer games.

7513 Shadywood Road
Bethesda, MD 20817-9823
Tel.: (800) 469-2070 or (301) 469-2070 (yes, it's the same number)
Fax: (301) 469-2071

Chen, Milton. *The Smart Parent's Guide to Kids' TV.* San Francisco: KQED Books, 1994.

Kropp, Paul. *Raising a Reader: Make Your Child a Reader for Life.* New York: Doubleday, 1996.

Leonhardt, Mary. *99 Ways to Get Kids to Love Reading.* New York: Three Rivers Press, 1997.

Trelease, Jim. *The New Read-Aloud Handbook.* New York: Penguin, 1989.

Temperament
TEMPERAMENT TALK
1100 K Avenue
La Grande, OR 97850
Tel.: (541) 962-8836
Fax: (541) 963-3572

Travel
FAMILY WORLD HOMEPAGE offers calendars (broken down into four regions) that include information on all sorts of fun places for families to visit in different parts of the country.
http://family.com

Wills and Trusts
Platt, Harvey J. *Your Living Trust and Estate Plan: How to Maximize Your Family's Assets and Protect Your Loved Ones.* New York: Allworth Press, 1995.

For many more interesting web sites, check out Jean Armour Polly's *Internet Kids Yellow Pages* (Osborne McGraw-Hill, 1996). Despite the title, it's a wonderful source of resources for parents, too.

If you have any comments or suggestions about the topics discussed in this book, you can send them to
Armin Brott
P.O. Box 2458
Berkeley, CA 94702
e-mail: armin@pacbell.net

Index

A

abuse, 125; allegations of, in divorce proceedings, 197–98; speaking up about, 171–74
activity level, 75, 78, 90, 114, 133
adaptability level, 32, 69, 74, 78, 90, 115, 133
ADHD (attention deficit/ hyperactivity disorder), 176
aggressive behavior, 99, 148
allowances, 181–82
ambivalence/guilt pattern, 82–83
Ames, Louise Bates, 98, 99, 100, 122, 147, 148, 170
anger, 125; at partner, 55; tantrums and, 68, 72; toddler's expression of, 36–37, 121
animals, 34; fear of, 40, 44–45, 46; imitations of, 15
animate vs. inanimate objects, 58, 81, 123
approach/withdrawal level, 74, 78, 90–91
art activities, 27–30
attachment, 17, 23, 32
attention span, 36, 100; preschools and, 115; reading and, 26, 66
audiation, 64
authoritarian parenting style, 84, 86–89

authoritative parenting style, 84, 86–89
auto insurance, 138
Azzara, Christopher, 64

B

babies: family planning and, 110–12; preparing older sibling for, 165–68
bad habits: of parents, 123
balance: toddler's sense of, 35
balanced meals, 47–48
Band-Aids, 146–47
bankruptcy, 139
Barnard, Suzanne, 173
Barnett, Mark, 172
Bates, John, 113
bath: fear of, 40, 42
bathroom privacy, 175
Baumrind, Diana, 84
bedtime, 99
Belsky, Jay, 50, 187–90
Bettelheim, Bruno, 61, 63–64, 67, 157
Biller, Henry, 165–66, 167
block building, 56
body: genital self- exploration and, 174–75; of parents, toddler's inter- est in, 175–77; taking pleasure in, 63
books, 107; turning pages of, 14, 15, 56. See also reading
bowel movements, 100

Brazelton, T. Berry, 68, 103–4
breath holding: in tantrums, 70–71
bribes, 89
Britton, James, 57

C

caffeine, 134
Cameron, Jim, 70–71, 90–91, 133
candy, 134
capital gains tax, 144
Caplan, Frank, 14, 37
car pooling, 138
catching, 35, 146
cause and effect, 22, 25, 123
Center for Human Develop- ment, 73, 78–79
chairs: high, 133, 135–36; for toddlers, 63
charging, 138–39. See also credit cards
Child, 92
Child Care Action Campaign (CCAC), 120
child custody, 190, 192, 193, 196–201; abuse allegations and, 197–98; books on, 201; keeping log and, 198–99; and knowing details of kids' lives, 196–97; terminol- ogy for, 197; unhappiness with arrangements, 200; "winning," 199

Children's Rights Council, 192

Children's Software Review, 127

choices, 72, 85, 131

climbing, 14, 80

Cohen, Harriet Newman, 192, 194

college education: paying for, 92–94, 95

Comfy Keyboard, 25

communication skills: fighting and, 53–55, 190; listening, 125, 129–30, 188; of new parents, 50–55; pretend play and, 63–64; (re)learning to talk and, 51–53; talking to toddlers, 128–29, 130–32. *See also* verbal development

community property, 195

comparison shopping, 138

compromise, 85

computer readiness, 24–25, 126–28

condos, 187

consistency, 84–85, 131, 148–49

consolidation loans, 140

Consumer Credit Counseling Service (CCCS), 139

containers: emptying and filling, 14, 22

contrariness, 57, 81, 147, 170

cooking with toddlers, 62, 156, 159–65; Eve's Chocolate Leaves, 164–65; French Toast, 161–62; Milkshakes, 162; Popcorn Balls, 164; Pretzels, 163–64; Quesadillas, 162; safety and, 163

co-ops, 187

coparent counseling, 199–200

correcting errors, 129

counseling, 53; in divorce, 199–200

counting, 169, 180

Cowan, Phil and Carolyn, 20, 52, 82, 124, 125, 190

creativity, 128, 152; art activities and, 27–30

credit: buying home and, 186

credit cards, 139–40, 186; divorce and, 195

criticism, 85, 88

D

dark: fear of, 40, 44

dating your partner, 40, 51

Davis, Clara, 47–48

day care, 113, 196. *See also* preschools

debit cards, 139

debt: bankruptcy and, 139; getting out of, 137–40

decision making, 147

dental care, 168

dentists: fear of, 45

Dependent Care Assistance Plans (DCAPs), 120

desserts, 133

details: focusing on, 122

discipline, 20, 84–93; parenting style and, 86–87; sexism and, 91; spanking and, 92–93; tantrums and, 68; temperament and, 90–91

disobedience, 81, 147, 166

distractibility level, 77, 79

dividend reinvestment plans (DRIPs), 141

divorce, 69, 179, 190–201; books on, 201; child custody and, 190, 192, 193, 196–201; counseling and, 199–200; financial issues in, 194–95; lawyers in, 191–93; mediated vs. litigated, 191; moving out of house and, 193–94

doctors: fear of, 45, 46

Dodson, Fitzhugh, 15, 147, 170, 175

domestic violence, 197–98

doorknob turning, 14

down payments, 183, 185

drawing, 14, 28, 30, 80, 146, 169

dressing, 56, 80, 121, 169

durable power of attorney, 97

E

eating, 16, 56. *See also* nutrition

education: college, paying for, 92–94, 95; increasing your own level of, 141. *See also* preschools

educational activities, 62

egotism, 57, 99, 146

embarassment at toddler's behavior, 100–101, 149–50

emotional sensitivity level, 76, 78

emotional/social development, 63–64, 128–29; at 12–15 months, 15–16; at 15–18 months, 36–37; at 18–21 months, 58; at 21–24 months, 81–82; at 24–27 months, 100; at 27–30 months, 123; at 30–33 months, 147–48; at 33–36 months, 170

emotions: father's changes in, 124–25; giving name to, 130; parents' expression of, 52, 131; toddler's expression of, 82, 121, 129, 130, 167

empathy, 125, 129

Employee Stock Ownership Plans (ESOPs), 143–44

energy level. *See* activity level

equipment-buying tips, 63

erections, 58

estate taxes, 97

Eve's Chocolate Leaves, 164–65

expansion: father's sense of, 125

expenses: reducing, 137–40

explaining, 128

expressiveness: father's increase in, 125

F

Faber, Adele, 125, 130
Fagot, Beverly, 102
failure: responding to, 101
family payroll, 181–82
family planning, 110–12
Fannie Mae, 182
fantasizing, 121, 130
fast foods, 134
fathers: additional education
  for, 141; ambivalence/
  guilt pattern in, 82–83;
  bad habits of, imitated
  by child, 123; disciplining by, 20, 68, 84–93;
  emotional changes in,
  124–25; fearful of being
  rejected by baby, 58–59;
  identity shift in, 82;
  intense reactions of, to
  child's behavior, 100–
  101, 149–50; involved,
  benefits of, 10, 39; limitations recognized by, 20;
  money issues and (see
  money matters); parent-
  ing's impact on thought
  processes of, 59–61; parenting style of, 84, 86–89;
  partner's relationship with
  (see partner, relationship
  with); physical exhaustion
  of, 16–17, 50; in power
  struggles with toddler,
  148–49; self-care for,
  17; separation issues for,
  17–20, 177–79; speaking
  up about abuse, 171–74;
  toddler's resemblance
  to, 123
Fathers' Rights & Equality
  Exchange, 192
fears, 16, 40–47, 81–82; of
  parent being rejected by
  baby, 58–59; parents'
  facial expressions and,
  41–46; parents' verbal
  reactions to, 46; and playing through scary situations, 46; trying to
  discover cause of, 41
feelings. See emotions

fighting with partner,
  53–55, 190
finances. See money matters
financial planners, 142–43
flap books, 26
food: reducing expense of,
  138. See also cooking with
  toddlers; nutrition
food allergies, 47, 49
401(k) plans, 93, 144–45
Fraiberg, Selma, 41, 57, 99,
  121, 122, 147
French Toast, 161–62
frustration, 32, 68, 69

G

Galinsky, Ellen, 17, 100,
  148
gender differences: play
  and, 154, 155; punish-
  ment and, 91; sexism and,
  91, 101–3; in toilet training, 104–6; toys and, 24,
  64–65; in verbal development, 170
gender identity, 100; toilet
  training and, 104, 105
genitals, 58, 100; adult,
  toddler's interest in,
  175–77; self-exploration
  of, 174–75
gifts: estate planning and,
  97
Gjerdingen, Dwenda K., 38
gloating, 101
Godfrey, Neale, 180, 181
Gordon, Edwin, 64, 65, 159
grammatical errors, 122,
  129
Greenspan, Stanley, 18
group activities, 158
Grunow, Richard, 64
guardians, 96–97

H

haircuts: fear of, 42–43,
  46–47
hair washing: fear of, 40, 42
handedness, 169
hand-eye coordination, 25,
  56, 98, 169
Hass, Aaron, 37, 38, 39

Haugland, Susan, 128
health insurance, 138
high chairs, 133, 135–36
High/Scope Buyer's Guide,
  127
Hirschman, Jane, 133–35
home: moving out of, when
  facing divorce, 193–94
home equity loans, 140
homeownership, 182–87;
  condos and co-ops, 187;
  down payment and, 183,
  185; inadvisable situa-
  tions for, 186–87; mortgages and, 185–86, 195;
  renting vs., 182–84; tax
  considerations and, 145
Horgan, Timothy J., 191,
  193
humming, 36, 63, 147
humor, 36, 37, 170
hyperactivity, 176

I

idle threats, 131
Ilg, Frances, 98, 99, 100,
  122, 147, 148, 170
imaginary companions,
  157
imagination, 36
imitation. See mimicking
impulse control, 146, 170
independence vs. depen-
  dence, 15–16, 32–33, 36,
  81; parents' separation
  issues and, 17–20; separation anxiety and, 16,
  30–32, 40
intellectual development,
  63–64, 128–29; at 12–15
  months, 14–15; at 15–18
  months, 35–36; at 18–
  21 months, 57; at 21–24
  months, 80–81; at 24–27
  months, 98–99; at 27–
  30 months, 121–22; at
  30–33 months, 146–47;
  at 33–36 months, 169
intensity level, 75, 78, 133
interrupting, 129
involving child in family
  life, 130

IRAs (individual retirement accounts), 93, 145
irrational requests, 130

J

Jordan, Pamela, 188
juice, 134
jumping, 80, 98, 146, 156
junk food, 134

K

Karen, Robert, 113
Katz, Lilian, 54, 55, 129, 130, 177
Katzen, Mollie, 159
Kayman, Susan, 132
kicking, 35, 56, 80, 156
Kutner, Lawrence, 9
Kvols, Kathryn, 85

L

language learning: passive vs. active, 15. *See also* verbal development
Lansky, Vicky, 167
lawyers: in divorce, 191–93
Leach, Penelope, 32, 113
life insurance, 94–95
limitations: recognizing, 20
limits: resisted by toddlers, 81, 148; setting, 20, 90
Linkletter, Art, 149
listening, 125, 129–30, 188
living trusts, 94–97

M

malnutrition, 135
matching games, 62, 156
Mazlish, Elaine, 125, 130
mediation: in divorce, 191
memory, 15, 121
Milkshakes, 162
mimicking, 15, 36, 64, 81, 121, 159; of parents' less savory behaviors, 123
mind changes, 123, 147
minibasketball hoops, 63
mistakes: admitting, 131
modesty, 175–77
money matters, 136–45; allowances, 181–82; bankruptcy, 139; boosting

savings, 140–44; college financing, 92–94, 95; in divorce, 194–95; financial planners, 142–43; home-ownership, 182–87; life insurance, 94–95; pre-school financing, 119–21; reducing expenses and getting out of debt, 137–40; tax planning, 144–45; teaching children about, 179–82; wills and trusts, 94–97
monsters: fear of, 43
mood, 75, 78, 123
mortgages, 185–86, 195
mothers: ambivalence/guilt pattern in, 83. *See also* parenting; partner, relationship with
Muñoz-Furlong, Ann, 49
music, 64, 65, 159

N

naming objects, 81, 122, 147
naps, 16
National Association for the Education of Young Children (NAEYC), 115–16
nature walks, 62
negativism, 57, 81, 147, 170
Newman, Barbara and Philip, 30, 59–61, 100–101, 125, 128
newspaper reading, 150
nightmares, 36
"No," 57, 147
noises: fear of, 40
nonverbal cues, 130
nudity, 175–77
numbers, 169
nursery rhymes, 81
nutrition, 47–50, 132–36; balanced meals and, 47–48; desserts and, 132; food allergies and, 47, 49; and ideal toddler diet, 134; and minimizing food fights, 135–36; at preschools, 116; tempera-ment and, 133

O

obesity, 153
object permanence, 31, 57
Oobleck, 62
ownership of objects, 57, 81

P

Palm, Glen, 123, 125
parenting: partners' differ-ences in, 187–88; styles of, 84, 86–89; thought processes affected by, 59–61
Parke, Ross, 154, 156
partner, relationship with, 10, 187–201; anger and, 55; communication skills and, 50–55, 190; dating and, 40, 51; divorce and, 69, 179, 190–201; father's needs in, 187–88; fighting and, 53–55, 190; focusing on common concerns in, 189–90; mother's needs in, 188–89; sex and, 37–40, 50, 51, 175
passing out: in tantrums, 70–71
patience, 125, 129, 187
peers: playing with, 58, 61, 100, 170; toddler's inter-est in, 123
penis, 58, 174–75; toilet training and, 104, 106
peripheral vision, 98, 100
permissive parenting style, 84, 86–89
persistence level, 77, 79
physical development: at 12–15 months, 14; at 15–18 months, 35; at 18–21 months, 56; at 21–24 months, 80; at 24–27 months, 98; at 27–30 months, 121; at 30–33 months, 146; at 33–36 months, 169
physical exhaustion: of parents, 16–17, 50
physical play, 14, 23, 154–56
Platt, Harvey J., 96

play, 21–24, 37, 61–65, 154–58; alone, 61–63; fantasy, 121; fun educational activities and, 62; fun things for rainy days, 156–58; gender differences and, 154, 155; group activities and, 158; with peers, 58, 61, 100, 170; physical, 14, 23, 154–56; pretend, 63–65; scary situations and, 46
play groups, 158
playthings: to avoid for 12–21 months, 23–24. *See also* toys
poetry, 26, 68, 110, 153
Popcorn Balls, 164
power struggles, 148–49
praise, 72, 132
predivorce counseling, 199
preschools, 112–20; adult separation problems and, 177–79; categories of, 113–14; easing transition to, 118–19; looking for, 112–13; paying for, 119–20; red flags for, 117; selection criteria for, 115–18; temperament and, 114–15
pretend play, 63–65
Pretzels, 163–64
pride: of parents, 100–101
problem solving, 81, 121–22
promises, 131
prompting, 128–29
pronouns, 58, 81
pronunciation errors, 129
Prudden, Bonnie, 155
punishment, 85; sexism and, 91; spanking, 92–93. *See also* discipline
puzzles, 56, 80, 156

Q
Quesadillas, 162
question asking: by parents, 32, 72, 129, 131; by toddlers, 150, 152

R
Radin, Norma, 10
Railsback, Tom, 196
rainy days: fun things for, 156–58
reading, 25–27, 37, 58, 66–68, 107–10, 150–54; advanced concepts for, 107–8; attention span and, 26, 66; books dealing with divorce, 201; creating environment for, 107; dealing with boredom in, 66; newspaper, 150; for older siblings, 109–10; poetry, 26, 68, 110, 153; suggested books for, 27, 67–68, 108–10, 151–54
regressive behavior, 166
regularity level, 76, 78, 90–91, 115, 133
reinforcing positive behavior, 88
rejection: fathers' fears of, 58–59
renting vs. buying, 182–84
repeating yourself, 131
restating or rephrasing what child says, 129, 130
retirement accounts, 92–94, 144–45
rhythm: sense of, 65, 159
rituals and routines, 31, 36, 40
Rosemond, John, 112
roughhousing, 154–56
running, 56, 80, 98, 146

S
Sachs, Brad, 54, 55, 188
safety issues, 33–34, 46, 117, 163
savings, 138, 140–44
scary stories: fear of, 44
scolding, 131–32
Sears, William, 34
security objects, 47
self-centeredness, 57, 99, 146
self-control, 121
self-esteem, 20, 93, 128

self-identity, 170
selflessness, 125
sensitivity, 125
sensory awareness level, 77, 79, 114
separation, 69. *See also* divorce
separation anxiety, 16, 30–32, 40
separation issues: for parents, 17–20, 177–79
sex with partner, 37–40, 50; in front of child, 175; scheduling, 51
sexism, 101–3; punishment and, 91
Shade, Daniel, 128
shaking toddler, 89
shame, 177
shape discrimination, 15
Shapiro, Jerrold, 188
Shopper, Moisy, 105, 106
silence, 64
singing, 36, 63, 65, 147, 159
sitters, 31
size discrimination, 15
sleep, 16; fear of, 44
smoking, 123
snacking, 136, 153
Snarey, John, 10, 91, 154
social development. *See* emotional/social development
software for children, 25, 127, 128
Sorce, James, 41–45
sorting skills, 21, 22
spacing between children, 111
Spangler, Doug, 93
spanking, 92–93
spatial concepts, 80, 122, 169
spontaneity, 50
stair climbing, 98
Staub, Ervin, 172
stranger anxiety, 16, 40
success: responding to, 101
support groups: divorce and, 192
swear words, 15
swimming pools, 33–34

T

tables: for toddlers, 63
talking to toddlers, 128–29, 130–32
tantrums, 37, 58, 68–73, 81, 100, 147; breath holding/passing out in, 70–71; causes of, 68–69; preventing, 71–73; in public, 72; temperament and, 69, 72, 90; what not to do about, 71; what to do about, 69–70
taxes: capital gains, 144; college financing and, 93, 95; estate and, 97; home-ownership and, 187
tax planning, 144–45
television, 152–53
temperament, 73–79, 112; discipline and, 90–91; eating habits and, 133; preschools and, 114–15; separation anxiety and, 32; tantrums and, 69, 72, 90
temper tantrums. *See* tantrums
tenses, 122, 170

Terry, Ann, 26
threats: idle, 131. *See also* warnings
throwing, 14, 35, 56, 80, 156
time concepts, 15, 57, 80, 122, 147, 169, 170
tiredness: of parents, 16–17, 50; of toddlers, 147
toilet training, 58, 100, 103–6; of boys vs. girls, 104–6; new baby and, 166; success boosters for, 103
tool use, 15, 23, 36
toys, 21–22; gender stereo-types and, 24, 64–65. *See also* play
Trelease, Jim, 150, 152
trusts, 94–97
Tyson, Eric, 92–94, 144

V

vacuum cleaners: fear of, 42
vagina, 58, 174–75
verbal development, 64, 68, 128–30; at 12–15 months, 15; at 15–18 months, 36; at 18–21 months, 57–58; at 21–24 months, 81; at 24–27 months, 99; at 27–30 months, 122; at 30–33 months, 147; at 33–36 months, 169–70

W

walking, 14, 35, 45–46, 56, 98, 146, 156
warnings, 46, 73, 85
Warshak, Richard, 196
Whaley, Kim, 21, 61, 63
whining, 90
whispering, 131
"Why" questions, 130, 150
wills, 94–97
Winnicott, D. W., 63
withdrawal level. *See* approach/withdrawal level
word associations, 129
work, 69, 189; preschool or day-care financing and, 119–20

Z

Zweiback, Meg, 111

CARTOON CREDITS

Frank Cotham © 1998 from The Cartoon Bank. All rights reserved: p. 60; Leo Cullum © 1998 from The Cartoon Bank. All rights reserved: p. 66; Liza Donnelly © 1998 from The Cartoon Bank. All rights reserved: pp. 151, 155; Joseph Farris © 1998 from The Cartoon Bank. All rights reserved: pp. 102, 135, 137; Edward Frascino © 1998 from The Cartoon Bank. All rights reserved: p. 94; Mort Gerberg © 1998 from The Cartoon Bank. All rights reserved: pp. 48, 73, 171; William Haefeli © 1998 from The Cartoon Bank. All rights reserved: p. 181; William Hamilton © 1998 from The Cartoon Bank. All rights reserved: p. 84; John Jonik © 1998 from The Cartoon Bank. All rights reserved: p. 62; Mary Lawton © 1998 from The Cartoon Bank. All rights reserved: p. 105; Arnie Levin © 1998 from The Cartoon Bank. All rights reserved: p. 29; Robert Mankoff © 1998 from The Cartoon Bank. All rights reserved: p. 140; Peter Mueller © 1998 from The Cartoon Bank. All rights reserved: p. 69; J. P. Rini © 1998 from The Cartoon Bank. All rights reserved: pp. 124, 149, 160; Peter Steiner © 1998 from The Cartoon Bank. All rights reserved: pp. 2, 54, 189 ; Mick Stevens © 1998 from The Cartoon Bank. All rights reserved: pp. 91, 126; Bob Zahn © 1998 from The Cartoon Bank. All rights reserved: pp. 8, 34, 53, 107; Jack Ziegler © 1998 from The Cartoon Bank. All rights reserved: pp. 19, 23, 101, 118, 178.

About the Author

Armin Brott, author of *The Expectant Father: Facts, Tips, and Advice for Dads-to Be* and *The New Father: A Dad's Guide to the First Year* and a contributing writer to *BabyTalk* magazine, has written on fatherhood for the *New York Times Magazine, Newsweek,* the *Washington Post, American Baby* magazine, *Parenting* magazine, and many other periodicals. His weekly radio show on parenting is carried by one of the largest radio stations in the San Francisco Bay area. He and his family live in Berkeley, California.